To ... [handwritten inscription]

DR. Charlie :)

[signature]

NOV 17 2020

SCOT FREE
By Charlie Mackenzie
Copyright © 2017 Charlie Mackenzie

Edited by Catherine Tô
Cover photography by Prabu Mahan
Cover design by Jacob Bloemberg

Youth Publishing House

CONTENT

FOREWORD

It was back in the mid '80s when I first set eyes on Charlie Mackenzie. He was sitting in the packed balcony at Bridge Street Pentecostal church in Leeds. He had already taken his first tentative steps in following Jesus, and when I met him, I looked into the face of a soft-spoken Scotsman. In the coming weeks and months, those features seemed to grow gentler and kindler, reflecting the revolutionary change of heart going on just below the surface. As assistant pastor at the church, I had a front seat at Charlie's transformation.

Eventually, Charlie left us to study at Bible college, and I knew something of his early years in pastoral ministry, but somewhere along the way I lost touch with him. Still, I never forgot him and the remarkable miracle we witnessed in his conversion to Christ.

And then one Monday morning, a couple of years ago, I had an email from Charlie Mackenzie – now a school principal in Vietnam! Over the past two years, many emails have passed between us. I have learned much of the details of the "missing years", and you will read them and no doubt be enthralled by them as you turn the pages of this book. It's a story about God's grace and goodness in a human life.

Charlie writes with a lightness of touch that makes for easy reading. His eloquence in speech translates to the written page. What you find here is non-fiction. Some of it surely belongs to the category of "You couldn't make it up." God is the great Author; He writes amazing life stories. He is the main character of the book you have in your hands, and He is still working on Charlie's tale. I can't wait to read what comes next!

Stephen Thompson
Pastor, The King's Church, Boston Spa

INTRODUCTION

This book is all about people. It's about being friendly, real, no matter who you meet, and treating everyone with kindness, respect and dignity. As you read this book you will meet many people who have left an indelible print on my mind and heart and hopefully, I have left a mark on them. But above all, it's about how we communicate with each other.

I heard a lovely story of a couple who visited a small town in northern England and they recalled to a friend many weeks afterwards, that at around 1pm every day the whole town was filled with a fragrant aroma of flowers. They discovered from their friend that in the center of that town was a perfume factory and at 1pm daily, the factory workers went home for lunch, and as they did so, they brought a beautiful fragrance with them. That's what this book is all about. Bringing the fragrance of God to everyone through the life of one of his workers.

Charlie Mackenzie
2017 Hanoi

CHAPTER 1

The night air seethed with an arctic-like chill. A nauseating mixture of stale vomit, urine, tobacco and the whiff of rotten food assaulted my nostrils. Dressed in my stylish clothes, I walked into the dimly lit communal cell. Inside lay a dozen men who stared at me with hostility and aggression. As I entered, they sized me up. They sat on their hard benches, too wound up to sleep; their tense bodies itching for a fight.

But I had no fight left within me. Only hours earlier I had been revelling with my subordinates, enjoying my windfall of cash from a mixture of hard work and dishonest gain. Now I was joining a cell full of criminals.

The clanking keys of the warden locking up behind me signalled I was stuck there. Moving inconspicuously, I climbed into an unoccupied rubber mattress on the floor.

My name brand clothes were now dirty and beer stained. My ribs were sore from the blows I'd taken from the police officer's baton strikes. My wrist chaffed from the handcuffs. I was still reeling from the fact I'd ended up here. I'd gone from managing my lucrative business, and having the world at my feet, to being locked up. The euphoria I felt from gliding from one high paying gig to the next, while constantly looking over my shoulder, turned to hopelessness.

I wanted to believe I wasn't one of the criminals. That I didn't belong there. But no matter how well I dressed, how successful I was, how many VIP lists I was on, it didn't change who I was. An outsider. A law-breaker. The scum of society. Like these men. Maybe I was not so different from them. Maybe this was *exactly* where I belonged. Maybe this was exactly what I *deserved*.

I tried my best to sleep, but not too deeply, not trusting any of my cellmates.

As I drifted to sleep in my hung over state, a series of memories came to mind. Being chased by knife wielding clients. Narrow getaways in the van. Cleaning fresh blood splatter off the walls for a mobster. Invitation-only parties at exclusive nightclubs.

It was so cold, I curled up to keep warm, and for the briefest moment, I was transported to my childhood in Inverness. I held onto this one bright memory before it flittered away. I focused upon the warmth of the sun. The smell of freshly cut grass. The sensation of my father picking up my half-asleep, curled up young body while I snuggled close to him, his faded overalls stained with tractor fuel. I remembered Mum's warm and comforting apron which I buried my face after being bullied at school. She'd stretch her arms around me and hold me tight. All of this was my "Dionach" – my safe place; my sanctuary; my refuge.

For now, I couldn't be further from "Dionach". I couldn't bear to let my parents see how far I'd fallen. There seemed to be nowhere else I could turn. Not to my fair-weather friends who were enamored by the high life, like me. Not to my slippery workers whom I had to watch constantly.

I wondered how I, the son of gentle Highlander parents, had gotten here and how long my sentence would be for. As my mind wandered, I began to reflect back on the very start.

CHAPTER 2

In the small dismal tenement apartment on Kingsmills Road, Inverness, I was always trying to evade the twins who bullied me, and my cat who *hated* me. The "bad pins" (I couldn't say the word "twins" yet) were older than me by four years and made my two-year-old life miserable. When these neighborhood kids were not pulling my hair or stealing my cat, they'd call me names. The looks on their faces told me those words were "not nice". I'd run away to "Dionach" when things become too hard or painful. I don't know where I first heard this name but it is the Gaelic name for safety or refuge. For me, Dionach was an old wooden box at the end of our overgrown garden. I'd crouch inside it and feel a strange sense of security and peace flow over my tiny body and soul.

I would stay there all afternoon if the weather was good, falling asleep blissfully inside, while the bad pins searched unsuccessfully for me. Dad would come home from his work on the railway yard and ask where his "Wee Charlie" was. Mum would tilt her head in the direction of the garden and say knowingly, "He's away to Dionach for the day." Dad would walk over to my "refuge", stand and smile at the sight of my little body below, before lifting me up and carrying me inside. I would snuggle into his overalls. The stale smell of his tractor diesel-stained clothes became another indicator that I was safe and secure.

When I was three, Dad's work at the railway yard dried up and we moved south to the bustling Stirlingshire industrial town of Falkirk, in the *unfriendly* Lowlands of Scotland. Dad took a job driving a tractor at a local sawmill. Within a month, he was able to sell our Kingsmills apartment and buy a two-roomed tenement flat opposite an ironworks, situated 100 yards from a small gospel hall.

This new hostile frontier was like moving from heaven to hell. The Highlands may have had the "bad pins", but manners, hospitality and kindness were generally in abundant supply. By comparison, Falkirk despised outsiders. Falkirk's motto was, 'Touch ane touch a'' which translated as "Pick a fight with one of us and we will all fight you".

For a time, I was sheltered from the small town prejudices. I found joy in the days spent at home with my mother drawing, singing and dancing, and walking down the canal bank to meet Dad. We'd wait outside the sawmill gate for up to an hour for Dad to return, driving a trailer full of tree logs into the yard. After spotting us, Dad would peck Mum on the cheek and would whisk me up onto his big blue tractor and let me pretend that I was driving it.

On weekends, Dad worked the earth. He hired an allotment of land for a cheap rate, dug and irrigated it and planted vegetables. I loved kneeling beside him in the late afternoon, smelling the warm moist earth and the linseed oil that Dad used to clean his hand tools. He painstakingly removed unwanted weeds and in their place, planted seeds that would grow to become carrots, turnips and my favorite – potatoes! He would tell me in his soft Highland accent, "You've got green fingers, laddie, you'll make a great gardener one day." I'd hug him and say no one in the world would ever be better than my dad.

Dad let me have my own herb garden. He made a three by two foot wooden box from discarded timber and connected a framed pane of glass on top. This instantly turned the unpredictable Scottish climate into a Mediterranean summer. I grew basil, thyme, mint and my favorite, the Trachelospermum jasminoides or jasmine. My mother used to say it was the most fragrant in my garden. Months later when my jasmine outgrew the glass box by 18 inches, she cut some clippings and put it under her pillow to "help her sleep fragrantly".

Those times with Mum and Dad were precious, but in the harsh new environment of Falkirk, I soon encountered bullies who were far worse than the "bad pins" would ever be.

When I was five, a nine-year-old local, Susan Wright, used to slap, bite and scratch me whenever I was sent on an errand to buy a loaf of bred or a pint of milk. She'd snarl, "Give me your money," before yelling threats and curses. Next came the thrashings until I cried and dropped the money. I was so afraid of her, I'd lie to my parents about dogs and wild cats attacking me and big boys from across the canal running away with the money. Susan had big brothers so it was useless even trying to stand up to her.

This continued for a soul-destroying year, until Harvest Thanksgiving in September 1963. Mum bought me a new shirt and trousers for the occasion and while I was waiting for Dad to take me to church, I was allowed to play downstairs on the communal green. I wasn't outside more than a few minutes before she pounced. Susan slapped me across the face hard before ripping my shirt. While I was on the ground crying she stole the pennies I'd saved for the church collection plate. I stayed there until she left before rehearsing what I'd say to my parents. "A big dog, a wild cat, a rooster…" Instead, I rushed into the flat and into the arms of Mum who was wiping her hands on her apron after washing the dishes. "SSSSSSSusan Wrrrrright," I stammered, bawling into her damp clothes and feeling her tight embrace around my tiny quivering frame. Dad entered the room and lifted me up.

"We are going to put an end to this," he said.

Dad took my hand and walked me onto the green outside. Susan was waiting with her brothers and a crowd of troublemaking adults from the tenement, all hoping for some free entertainment at my expense. My dad crouched down and whispered reassuringly to me.

"Today, this little witch is going to lose her spell over you Charlie. I am here, go do what you have to do."

I looked up, my eyes pleading him to take me home, but he patted me on the back and looked into the crowd in front of us. With her brothers and half the tenement population behind her, all telling her to finish off the Highland intruders, Susan Wright walked within a few feet of Dad and I. She cursed out loud, screaming what she was about to do to me.

I looked up at my dad who whispered, "Now Charlie."

At this, Susan came running towards me, fingers outstretched like claws, swinging her arms like a demented banshee. Suddenly I felt a courage that was not mine. I grabbed her head and pushed it down to her knees and simply held it there. Susan shrieked and tried to kick, scratch, bite and punch, but my hold was firm. Eventually I heard a sound that I never ever thought I would hear… sobbing.

My dad stepped forward and said gently, "You can let her go now my boy, she will never hurt you again."

Quivering from adrenalin, I released her from my grip. She ran home, roaring in pain.

Her brothers stepped forward menacingly and rolled up their sleeves for a fight. Keeping his eyes fixed on them, my dad, who was no more than five-foot-six, slowly picked up a fallen, leafless branch from a nearby rowan tree. Sweeping the entire crowd with his defiant gaze, he held out the stick and stepped forward, speaking calmly in his lilting Highland accent.

"If anyone of you, men or boys touches even a hair on my son's head, so help me God, I will gladly put you in an early grave."

Dad placed his arm in front of my chest. Side by side, we both walked slowly backwards and up the stone stairway to our flat, where he hugged me and wiped my tears.

"Let's get ready for church," he said. My heart swelled with pride for him that day. Dad became my all-time hero and would remain so until he died in 2001. Meanwhile, the stunned crowd downstairs dispersed and Susan Wright never bothered me again.

If I thought Susan Wright was bad, a whole school of them was far worse. The kids at elementary school singled me out almost immediately because of my prominent Highland lilt. I wasn't given a regular place on the school football team because they couldn't trust someone from "outside their community" to be able to play! The only time (out of pure desperation) that I was invited to play was in an important league match three years later.

After I scored the winning goal, I was asked to play the following week. I refused. "You didn't want me at the beginning of the football season, you are not having me halfway through it," I thought.

The sensation of never really being welcomed onto the team stayed with me. I didn't know it at the time, but the experience gave me a deep-rooted empathy for outsiders and underdogs and strengthened my resolve to make others feel accepted. I'd use any means at my disposal to reach out to those on the fringes. I'd later invite poor, football-crazy kids who couldn't afford club memberships to form teams, and throw myself into training them.

***

My school, Langlees Primary, was opposite the main aluminium works, which was a major employer for many townsfolk. The school dished out preferential treatment liberally to supervisors' children and others from the plant. Every Christmas, there was an elaborate party at the plant and I was about the only kid in school who was never invited.

The National Robert Burns Poetry Recital Competition lit a fire inside me. My school was a part of it, and all the students were invited to recite the Burns poem, *Up in the Morning Early*, which went like this...

Cauld blaws the wind frae east to west,
The drift is driving sairly;
Sae loud and shill's I hear the blast
I'm sure it's winter fairly.

Chorus

Up in the morning's no for me,
Up in the morning early;
When a' the hills are covered wi' snaw,
I'm sure it's winter fairly.

I immersed myself in the poem, rehearsing daily before school and at night before bed. Within a week I had it nailed! When I recited it in front of my parents, they shook their heads and said, "No Charlie, there's no passion there, tell it like you mean it, say it like a Highlander." Dad showed me how to emphasize certain words like Caaaaauuullld, (Cold) and Blaaaaws, (Blows) and to pretend I was shivering when speaking about the wind. I felt stupid doing it but hey, they were my parents and I loved them.

The next day I was called up at school to recite in front of three teachers on the "Poetry Panel" and year four. My turn came after two girls who'd recited perfectly. Their voices were monotone and lifeless but nonetheless, they didn't get a word wrong. My heart sunk. I took a deep breath and launched out with all the exaggerated drama of a village play.

"Caaaauuuuld Blaaaaawws the Wiiind, Frae Eaaaassst tae Weeest," I said, shivering and wrapping an imaginary coat around myself. The students went into hysterics! Rolling around slapping each others' backs and howling out loud while pointing at me. I suddenly felt foolish and stammered over my lines, "The drrrrift was, I mean as, no, that's not right, I mean IS, driving sairly…"

"That's fine Charles, we'll let you know," the panel leader said, without looking up. I left, head down. The two girls who had recited before me giggled as I vacated the hall.

My mum was waiting at the school gate. "How did you get on?" she asked excitedly. "Not great," I mumbled as we walked home.
The next day at assembly, the headmistress, Miss Fordyce, decided she'd read out the names of the five finalists. All the usual suspects were there – a manager's daughter, the niece of the local doctor, two plant workers' children, and "Fifthly, Charles Mackenzie…"

The hall fell silent.

I was waiting for the punch line, but it never came. My heart raced as Miss Fordyce announced, "These are the five finalists chosen by the panel, and they have unanimously decided that out of these five fine students, the winner is Charles Mackenzie!"

All the staff rose to their feet and applauded while the students sat dumbstruck. A girl who didn't make it to the final five broke the silence. "Miss, he forgot his lines," she said.

Two teachers stood up, when Miss Fordyce held up a hand and spoke on their behalf.

"Charles spoke with passion and feeling, Lindsay. My dear, your rendition was, what's the word you used, Miss Campbell? Oh yes. Cardboard."

At the annual award ceremony two months later, I gave my best salute to the headmistress and a sly wink to my mum as I collected the coveted Burns Certificate for Poetry.

The following year when I was nine, our teacher, Miss Bellingham, announced another free poetry competition with a cash prize to mark the birthday of our national poet, Robert Burns. All those early years spent with Mum at home reading her poems and singing Highland melodies with her had prepared me. I started rehearsing immediately, refusing any help from Mum and Dad. We had a week before we performed in front of the school assembly and the judges' panel. On the day, my heart was pounding but bursting to perform.

The boy in front of me recited, *The Red Berets*, a poem about the famous British Army parachute regiment. I thought he had delivered it well, despite the content being a bit gung ho, and so I applauded with sincerity.

I walked forward and spoke in a lilting Highland voice.

"The Spook of the Glen. By Charlie Mackenzie, age nine."

I launched into the poem with all the theatrical movements and intonation that my parents had taught me when reciting other poems.

"It comes oot at nicht
When Naebody's seen
It's the Spook o' the Glen
Frae the wee village Plean

It haunts a' the hooses
The toon hall as well
And naebody's seen it
But all can soon tell.

For when sleeping at nicht,
They awake with a SCREAM!
Cos the Spook o' the Glen
Is just a terrible dream."

The whole assembly went silent. Even the teachers did not know what to say as I took my seat, shyly looking down at the wooden floor as I held back a smile.

Suddenly a girl's hand went up three rows back from me.

"Miss, he copied that from the library, it's not his own poem."

Another girl jumped in. "Yes miss I saw him copy it!"

"Me too!" another said.

Miss Bellingham thought for a moment and added, "Yes I think I read it somewhere before as well!"

The first thought that pierced my mind was, "They think my wee poem is good enough to be in the school library?"

But that thought was soon wiped out by the horrible sense of injustice. I protested, "But miss, I don't lie, and I don't cheat; my mother taught me how to write poems."

"Be quiet you thieving Highland vermin," Miss Bellingham hissed.

14

"No play time for a month."

I wept as my poem was snatched from me and ripped up on stage, to the delight of the other children. My indignant parents marched up to the school the next day and Miss Bellingham strangely took early pregnancy leave two days later.

It was only one humiliating incident out of countless others at the school, but it was a very public one with a lasting impact. Their message was clear: you will always be an outsider.

CHAPTER 3

The busy Carron Road was opposite our small second floor tenement flat. Tucked across the road and behind the bus stop to Larbert village was what we affectionately called "The Hut" which was a small wooden shop standing alone and selling such delicacies as Penny Dainties, Black Jacks, Cinder Toffee and Lucky Bags (a small paper bag with a candy and a toy inside). The road itself was too busy during the week for a young boy to cross by himself, but at the weekend, especially on a Sunday, it was do-able with caution. And so, on one such afternoon I ventured across to "The Hut". I had my sixpence pocket money and I was determined to spend it all in one sumptuous and extravagant go!

I looked both ways before weaving in and out of the few cars and a taxi that were lazily making their way back towards Falkirk center. Having reached my destination, I produced my shiny coin and watched in awe as I was presented with my prize in a brown paper bag.

The engine of the large blue double decker bus churned as it stood at the empty stop. I took no real notice. Buses often waited there for 10 minutes, while the driver bought a pack of cigarettes or a newspaper. I meandered past it so I could look at the traffic from both directions. Meanwhile, the distracted driver leapt into his bus and accelerated noisily.

The force of the impact threw me across both large lanes of Larbert Road where I landed on the opposite pavement unconscious.

I looked up to see a large circle of concerned faces of different shapes looking over me. Some asked, "Is he dead?"

"That's the Mackenzie boy."

"Call 999."

"Get an ambulance."
"No it's too late for that, he won't make it."

I closed my eyes and thought it all very strange, before giddily standing up and walking home unscathed. After telling my mother, "I think I have just been hit by a bus," she took me to bed and called Dr Reekie, the family GP. Dr Reekie examined me thoroughly then closed the door and spoke with mum. Through the muffled low tones I heard him say, "No marks, no breakages, not even a bruise, this wee laddie should be dead, it's a miracle."

"A miracle," I said, before falling into a deep sleep and dreaming about Penny Dainties and Lucky Bags!

Those "miracles" were to happen time and again in my life. Now looking back, I believe that God had His hand on me for something special still yet to be revealed.

The Dawson Mission was (and as far as I know, still is) a gospel hall more than 200 yards east from "The Hut" but thankfully, on my side of the road. Every Saturday afternoon some adults dressed in (what appeared in our eyes to be) *fancy* clothes, would invite us all to Sunday School the next day. As far as I can remember, no one from our tenement ever went. Until that is, the day *I* decided to go. "The Mission" was holding a Summer Club with prizes and free food! I dressed in my cleanest clothes and my mum combed hair cream through my hair and reminded me with a kiss that I was a Protestant but to keep it secret.

But when I approached the hall, a large hand stopped me and said, "You're too young. The Summer Club is for over 11s only". Deeply disappointed, I waited until the burly gatekeeper was inside before walking around the building and discovering a small window halfway up the low wall. To my delight, it was slightly open. Borrowing a few spare clay bricks to stand on, I clambered up the white stone wall and fell head first onto the tiled floor below me. Shrieks followed my clumsy landing on the floor below, and I felt a strong hand wallop me around the ear. I stumbled out of the room and into the packed main hall. Looking behind me, I noticed that I had actually climbed in to the ladies washroom!
Inside there was the bustle of children's laughter, the voices

belonging to no-one I knew,. On a brightly lit stage with dark red velvet curtains, a quiz was in progress. I shrunk into one of the small plastic chairs. The boy on my left whispered in my ear, "Put your hand up and say Jesus, the answer is always Jesus." And so I earned my first candy bar by answering that the person who turned water into wine at someone's wedding was Jesus. I also tried to convince the pastor that Jesus parted the Red Sea, healed Naaman and explained the Bible to the Ethiopian eunuch... but he wasn't having any of it!

After experiencing the warmth and friendliness of the mission people and Mr Bain, the Canadian pastor, I was there every Sunday evening. The format was an hour-long gospel service followed by where if you sat still through the hour-long service you were treated to a cup of steaming hot tea in a green cup and saucer and a rich tea biscuit. No one patronized me and I was made to feel just as important as the regular mission people.

Most Sunday evenings consisted of visiting groups from Glasgow or Edinburgh with glowing faces and strange accents sharing something called "testimonies" about how Jesus had changed their lives and how we all needed to be "saved". The songs they sung were easy to learn and fun to sing.

Running over, running over
My cup's full and running over
Since the Lord saved me
I'm as happy as can be
My cup's full and running over.

There was also:

Thank you Lord for saving my soul
Thank you Lord for making me whole
Thank you Lord for giving to me
Thy great salvation so rich and free.

It only took me a few months to start wondering if this Jesus could really love and save me like He obviously had done for all the other people there at the "Mission". One Sunday evening when Pastor Bain led everyone in "The Sinner's Prayer", I said it with sincerity and hoped that it would work for me too.

My encounters with an aggressive, foul-mouthed peer, Jim McKinlay, were one of the most memorable parts of living on Carron Road. The never-ending spate of fresh bruises and cuts on Jim's face fanned talk of his reputation as a troublemaker. Jim had a head of wavy, tousled hair and always wore hand-me-downs that never fit him. He lived with his older brother, John, and their father in the sprawling Langlees council estate across the park from the aluminium works. I was always wary of him and had good reason to be.

Like the time when I was 10. Jim broke in to the Cash and Carry goods warehouse near "The Hut" on Carron Road and took thousands of pounds in cash. Next day in class he was passing 10 and 20 pound notes around the class under desks. I received a 20! I had never *seen* that much money before!

It only took two days for the Criminal Investigation Department to trace Jim and compile a list of everyone whom he had passed the money on to. Guessing all this newly acquired wealth was too good to last, I had hopped on a bus to High Street straight after school and bought a brand new blue and white Chelsea Football Club kit with jersey, shorts and socks. When the police came calling the next day I was proudly wearing it!
"We need all the money back, Mr Mackenzie," they told my father solemnly.

"Well," Dad said, stifling a huge belly laugh, "My son came by this in good faith, not knowing where it came from. Therefore he has broken no law. So I'm sorry officers, no can do... unless you have change from a football sock?"

The two police officers shared the joke and admitted that I could keep my new kit, adding for my benefit, "I don't know who is the craftiest here, you or Mr McKinlay."

As most of the cash was returned - well, apart from 20 pounds of it - Jim was allowed to go free with a stern warning. The police cautioned his father severely about keeping Jim on a strict curfew until further notice! But Jim began to follow me around school and frequently asked to walk home with me (which was in the opposite direction to his own home). I took short cuts and run home fast to avoid him. I was sure he was going to beat me for spending those 20 pounds. A year later I was at high school and I did not see Jim again.

Well that was until eight years later. I bumped into a well-dressed, gentle, friendly Jim McKinlay in Falkirk town center after a night out. We chatted without any fear or tension and I heard Jim's heartbreaking story. Apparently the reason he wanted to walk home with me all those years ago was because he wanted to be my friend, and maybe play with my toys. At his own home, Jim wasn't allowed any toys and was constantly bullied by his older brother. The endless series of bruises and cuts on his face, weren't from fights with peers; it was where his father hit him. All he wanted was a bit of love and kindness. I gathered that this desperate yearning was also behind the Cash and Carry venture. He was simply trying to buy friendship, be it in a misguided way. I learned an important lesson that evening: always look for the best in even the seemingly lowliest of humanity.

CHAPTER 4

When I was nearly 12, Dad told us that we were moving to a house with two gardens and my own bedroom. We'd be leaving Carron Road for good and I'd be finishing up at Langlees Primary and enrolling at a much friendlier high school. My dad had been misinformed by a mile. Camelon High School was the toughest school in Falkirk and the fourth year students ruled. Even teachers were afraid to teach some of these 14 and 15-year-olds for fear of their families attacking, maiming or murdering them.

These thugs subjected all new students to a hazing ritual called riding "The Bubble". This was my initiation into Camelon High. "The Bubble" was a ramp down into the technical storeroom surrounded by a barrier. There was only one way in….*and* out.

Once thrown down there, the older students screamed insults and spat on you. If you tried to escape, then you were kicked back down again. The only way out was if you cried. Once humiliated, you were allowed to "Run for it", while being kicked every step of the way. I refused to cry. I stayed down there until the thugs grew bored and dragged me out. For now, I was accepted, or as accepted as a "Highlander" could hope to be.

At lunchtime, the entire fourth year and whoever else they could coerce into joining them, fought their fellow thugs from St Modan's Catholic school under the railway bridge a few hundred yards away. Armed with sticks, knives and bricks, we rushed at each other. If you limped back to school bleeding, grazed or broken, you were "hard". I am certain that I wasn't "hard" but I did get dragged into this meaningless barrage of bigotry several times and indeed on a few occasions came back to school wounded!

One of the instigators of these pitched battles was John Galviston. John was also one in a crowd of bullies who took great delight in hurting weaker students. Every day he'd seek me out, tower over me and demand my dinner money in return for not getting flattened. I used to go home feeling hungry and humiliated. I never told Dad because I felt he would blame me for giving over my money so easily. So I stayed silent, weeping inside, hating Falkirk and determining in my young head that one day I would escape and never return.-

School life at Camelon was a daily routine of dodging the thugs and avoiding mathematics, which was a waste of football time. I joined the school band and learned how to play solo trumpet. The tutor was so pleased with my desire to learn that he let me borrow the keys to the music room so I could practice any time. And so I did… for nearly every math lesson for two years. I only attended class enough to guarantee myself the bare minimum required to pass exams. I secured a place on the football team as goalkeeper which drew the attention of the prettiest girls in the school and the ire from the other players.

Regardless of whether I had a girl on my arm or was walking home alone, a group of bullies would lie in wait ready to pounce. But what they never reckoned on was my speed. I would run like the wind until I reached my Dionach again. This time, Dionach wasn't a wooden box that I hid inside at the end of my garden; it was a stretch of iron railings encircling an old decaying building called the Camelon Centre for the Mentally Disabled.

Camelon Centre was a home for children with intellectual disabilities, and it was situated on a busy main road with factories on one side and housing schemes on the other. The center was an old decaying building surrounded by a wrought iron fence. As soon as I came within a foot of the pavement outside the center, I was flooded by peaceful, joy-filled thoughts. Even if was surrounded by traffic and passing pedestrians, I could have been on a mountaintop or lush valley. Even if the thugs were only a few feet away, I knew they couldn't harm me as soon as I reached this place. Afterwards, everything around me felt so much brighter and more colorful. Once I left, the thugs would be nowhere to be seen.

On one occasion the gang of about six almost caught up with me but I reached Dionach intact and turned, faced them and smiled with both welcoming arms open. Not expecting this, they stopped in their tracks and slouched off in the other direction. I had no idea that this was a holy place, a place of God's presence, a place where angels ministered. I only knew that as a young boy from the age of 12 to 15, I had serene thoughts there and while I rested within these boundaries, nothing would hurt me.

School came and went. I graduated and did what everyone else at Camelon High did. I got a job. My first job was as an apprentice heating engineer. It meant crawling under floorboards and running copper pipes from one end of a building to another as well as installing radiators and oil fuelled heating systems. Sounds interesting, yes? Not a hope!

Apart from getting some nice smiles from the pretty hairdressers in salons where we worked, it was exceedingly boring. The foreman would do all the technical stuff and I would be the gopher. I stuck it out for three months until he barked at me one afternoon, "Go make my tea, that's what apprentices do." We were under the floor of a five-star upmarket ladies hair salon at the time and he was too fat to climb back up just to make tea, so I was ordered to make it for himself and the whole crew of eight workmen.

I collected my things and never returned, leaving them all waiting for their tea. On the way out I booked appointments for every one of them at the salon's reception for the most expensive perm, blue rinse and haircut in the place. I even booked the foreman for a perm and he was BALD! I wish I could have witnessed the scene at the end of the day as they tried to explain themselves to the big blonde lady who owned the place.

CHAPTER 5

Glam rock was "in".... in the mid '70s! With it came high platform boots, white Levi jeans and dyed long hair! But it was the same old pricey story. A pair of platforms could set you back $200, white Levi's, $150, and a feathered haircut and green dye, $100 plus. When one was burning through jobs faster than a Ferrari on a racetrack, one had to improvise!

I decided if I bleached my blue Wrangler's ($15 from the factory surplus store), then that would be just as good as the white Levi's in High Street. A small investment of $1 for four bottles of bleach compared to spending $150 seemed worth the effort.

I laid my blue jeans in Mum's bath and poured in the bleach, leaving them there for just over four days. The noxious fumes from a pair of jeans marinating in a tub of bleach made the whole house reek. You had to be lightning fast using the toilet and getting in and out of the bathroom if you didn't want to retch. (Afterwards, no one could take a bath for almost a week!) On the fifth day, I rinsed my jeans with a cold water hose and they were pure white!

Next I fixed the snapped heel of a second-hand pair of six inch platform boots ($3 from a mate) that had a big silver star adorning the metallic blue leather uppers on each of them. In Dad's garden shed, I hammered a five inch nail into the broken left boot.

Lastly, I bought a bottle of peroxide bleach and poured it all over my head several times until my hair began to lose its fair brown color. After an hour of this torture, my hair was pure white! (Dad said I looked like a chicken because my scalp was bright red underneath from the bleach burning me. But what do dads know...) Using a toothbrush, I brushed a bright green food coloring dye from the baker's shop (a mere 20 cents!) through my shoulder length, feathered hair and then ran Mum's hairdryer through it. Altogether I had saved just over $400 and was ready to party at the La Bamba Disco where we'd been told that a busload of female American hockey players would be coming for a night out.

On the night, I looked like a rock star! My long metallic platform boots zipped up over my spotlessly white Wranglers, my plain white V-necked T-shirt highlighted by a shock of emerald green hair flowing over my shoulders. Sunglasses provided the finishing touch.

I purposely arrived an hour after the gig began. As I walked through the door of La Bamba, rock drummer Cozy Powell was playing a drum solo. It climaxed with a clash of cymbals. At that moment it went silent, I stepped heavily through the center of the crowd and onto the wooden dance floor. Every eye stared at me.

I strode over to a tall leggy American girl in hot pants and white knee-length boots and gave her a coin. "Call your mum... you're going to be late home tonight." I winked. I basked in the attention of every girl present as well as the jealousy and hatred of every guy. I was simply loving it... until, science attacked me, that is.

No one told me that bleach does not just destroy blue Wrangler ink... it also burns through cotton stitches.... RRRRRRIIIIP!

I heard the sound as the stitching in both jeans opened up from the bottom to the top of my legs revealing a pair of unfashionable Superman boxer shorts! I tried to bend down to prevent further disgrace... RRRRIIIIPPPP! All of the seams gave way, the stitching rotted.

Red-faced and humiliated, I was surrounded by hordes of hysterical American girls and relieved Scots guys. I ran outside into the welcoming rain, but no one told me that green food coloring dye was not waterproof! Bright green stripes ran down my face and onto my white T-Shirt. I decided to run home and change, but no one told me that platform boots with six inch heels could not be secured by a common five inch carpentry nail.

As I turned to run, my heel snapped off and I limped almost three miles home, jeans literally in shreds, my hair now bleached white after the dye was washed away and my face streaked with green stripes. My shirt had turned a dirty wet mauve color and one broken, heel-less boot was sticking out of my torn back pocket! If you have ever watched the movie, *Carrie*, or seen an episode of the *Incredible Hulk*, then you will get the picture.

My dad looked up from his paper as I breathlessly entered our house on Ochiltree Terrace. His eyes widened and he looked poised to make a funny quip until he saw my defiant glare. Wisely deciding to keep his lips shut, he dropped his newspaper, ran to the toilet, slammed the door shut and… well, I can still hear him laughing even now!

After that debacle, I decided the pursuit of fashion required cash and so next day I applied for a driver/handyman job in a Bainsford garage. I got the job easily, because the pay was lousy and the garage was on the edge of an industrial site, several miles from a bus stop!

On my first day I was given my orders, "Be on standby to fix everything from broken doors, creaking floors, leaking sinks and noisy fan heaters and on Wednesday, take the pick up truck to Falkirk town center and collect some engine parts from our depot there."

Wednesday morning came and I was given a set of keys and told, "Take Andy the apprentice mechanic with you, he'll show you where to go." I nodded, took the keys, jumped in the pick-up truck next to a pimply faced teenager, Andy Duncan, and then began to sweat profusely as the realization took hold that I had never driven a car before!

I turned on the engine and slowly crunched the gearstick into first. I dropped the handbrake and the truck leapt forward, hitting a trash can and throwing Andy into the seat behind. "Seatbelt mate," I said casually. I quickly maneuvered the truck onto the road and after about three minutes, I kind of got used to its size and position on the road.

Soon we were travelling at 20 miles an hour while still in first gear! "Crrrunch!" into second, "Crrrrunch!" into third, I was hanging on for life as I charged up busy Larbert Road doing 50 miles per hour in third gear. The engine was screaming at me to change up to fourth then fifth, but my sweaty hands were welded to the steering wheel!

I eventually braked outside the depot, stalling the truck and catapulting a dazed and terrified Andy back into the front seat. White as a ghost, his mouth opened and closed but nothing came out. Eventually sound found its way through his quivering lips and he screamed, "You can't DRIVE!" He stared at me as if I had just escaped from an asylum.

"Ok Einstein, well figured out," I said, without batting an eyelid. "Once you've dried your eyes, you can drive this thing back to base."

Andy drove back slowly though confidently without hitting any trash cans or scaring any old people walking their dogs.

Once safely back in the garage, it was only a matter of minutes before I heard the manager's voice.

"Mackenzie! My office, pronto!" he barked. "You almost scared my nephew to death, nearly ran over two pensioners, you went through three red lights and how you never blew up the engine, I'll never know.... You're fired!"

I stood and smiled at him calmly… "I want a week's wages," I said.

"You're getting nothing, get out of my garage before I-I…"

Mr Frankie Rice went from red to purple.

"Asking an employee to drive a vehicle with no licence or insurance… the police would close you down immediately. One week's salary in CASH," I said.

I stood outside while the cashier counted out the money, waited for him to hand it to me, before smiling at Mr Rice . As I left, I waved to apprentice mechanic Andy Duncan who was still pale and hiding nervously behind an oil drum.

***

Falkirk had become too small for an impatient 18-year-old. I decided to travel to Glasgow, visit a hotel agency and sign up as a waiter. I was prepared to go anywhere as long as it was far away from dreary old *Falkrap* as I used to call it. There was an opening in the border village of Otterburn, England, so I packed my bags.

CHAPTER 6

The 90 minute bus ride from Edinburgh to Otterburn was filled with the breathtaking splendor of the lush green Scottish Borders. Sheep grazed serenely on the hills and endless stretches of stunning countryside. Waterfalls gushed from between valleys, forming sparkling freshwater creeks, rivers and tributaries below. Along the route, the bus stopped at villages with cobbled streets, clock towers, horses tied to lampposts and old men leaning against low stone walls smoking clay pipes and laughing to one another.

I'd secured work at the Percy Arms Hotel in a town I'd never been to before. My heart soared in anticipation at the adventure before me. I soon learned that Otterburn was near a British Army firing range. Gunshots and explosions continually invaded the otherwise tranquil environment of this tiny hamlet in the lush hillside.

I arrived one bright, sunny afternoon with one suitcase and a hunger to experience a world outside of the insular town of Falkirk. The exterior of the Percy Arms Hotel featured Tudor style architecture, with its steep gable roof and casement windows with timber shutters. Inside the hotel was dark and full of character, with wood panelled walls and overhead beams. It smelt like an old coat – a mixture of stale beer from the night before, unaired, stuffy laundry with a whiff of spicy odours wafting in from the kitchen.

The owner, a grey haired man in his 50s, greeted me cordially and introduced me to the restaurant manager. The manager escorted me to my small, plain and clean room in the hotel's annexed staff quarters. He told me to collect my uniform from reception and be on duty at 6am the next morning.

I was to be trained on the job as a silver service waiter. In theory, this would guarantee me work in the world's top hotels and restaurants should I choose to travel. Being a silver service waiter meant that you were invisible until required. You serviced your tables silently and respectfully, never spoke until asked and always smiled.

Overall, I enjoyed living in Otterburn and going on long walks in the countryside on my days off. It was a peaceful existence, aside from putting up with the ridiculous behavior of the rich and middle classes as they complained about everything from the room temperature to the number of peanuts on their complimentary dish.

Some of the patrons grew on you, such as the old army veteran "Major Tomkins" who would get drunk every Tuesday evening (when his wife stayed with their daughter) and stand on the table and sing Elvis ballads! He would greet any attempts to pull him down with a whack of his walking stick.

It was an otherwise uneventful existence until one evening after work. I had just gone to bed with a stomach ache after a few pints of beer in the hotel bar. Thinking it was a bad pint, I tried to sleep it off. But the pain became worse. It kept me awake all night. By morning, I stumbled into the kitchen and holding my side, doubled over and collapsed. A doctor was called and arrived within 30 minutes, diagnosing me with acute appendicitis.

I was rushed across the hilly countryside to the nearest village hospital in Hexham where I was sedated and taken directly to theater. I woke, feeling as if I had been kicked by a horse. The young doctor standing over me said, "We have removed your appendix. You were lucky. Any later getting here and it would have burst and you would be dead!"

I'd cheated death again. Miracle number two...

After being released from hospital, the hotel suggested I take a month off and go home. My mum and dad received me as though I was a decorated war hero returning from the trenches in Belgium! I was treated to an evening at my favorite fish and chip restaurant, was gifted with new jeans and shirts and was invited to go on a holiday with them to a Scarborough caravan resort in the ruggedly attractive Yorkshire Coast two weeks later.

Wallis' Holiday Camp was on the main road between Scarborough and Filey in a county that used to be known as the East Riding of Yorkshire. My parents used to take me there as a child. I'd enjoyed the long train ride down from Scotland just as much as the holiday itself. As a child, I loved all the novelties of caravan holidays. Sleeping in a cozy room. Cooking with bottled gas. Even the lights were gas powered, it was different in a nice way.

But experiencing a caravan holiday at Wallis' as a young adult was different. My wound had nearly healed and my re-energized self was inching towards the edge of boredom.

The centerpiece of the holiday camp was still the Pavilion, where dances, fancy dress competitions and other entertainment took place after the kids were put to bed, and that allayed my restlessness just a little.

On the second night there was a talent show. Becoming increasingly bored, I was about to leave when a 17-year-old girl from York took to the stage with a guitar. She had a pretty, smiling face, was on the slim side of tubby, or the tubby side of slim, and wore a brightly colored floral dress. I sat back down and smiled up at her. Her name was Jill Pickard and she proceeded to sing a folk song called *Delta Dawn*. I was captivated. I had never, ever, heard a voice like this. She sung like an angel; her accent was soft and melodic.

As soon as she stepped down, I approached her and told her how amazing she was! I asked if I could walk with her for a while and she agreed. I made her laugh with silly humor and told her about my green hair and my operation and Inverness and the "bad pins". In return, she told me about life in York. We sat outside her caravan and chatted until after 1am, she kissed my cheek. I floated home. I was in love. Or at least it felt like I could be.

We spent every day together for the next 12 days. I got to know her dad, Alan, her sister, brother and her mum. Jill told me she was a Mormon, which I thought was her job. I nodded knowingly, without a clue what it meant, but I reasoned that if Jill liked being one then it must be ok.

As with all holiday romances, the time to depart happened all too soon. The night before we left, Jill cried all evening in my arms.

"I'll never see you again," she sobbed.

"Tell you what," I said, a lump forming in my throat as well. "I'll come and visit you in a few months, when I am fully recovered."

"You promise?" she whispered, looking up at me.

"I promise" I said, looking into her eyes and holding her tight.

"Well, ok then, see to it that you do, you crazy Scotsman," she said gently patting my wrist.

I never said much on the train back to Scotland. "Ships that pass in the night," my dad said, looking out of the train window and staring into the far distance as if remembering some painful memory of his own. 'Ships...' he said thoughtfully.

I found some temporary work at the Park Hotel in Falkirk and saved every penny I earned as a barman for three months. Jill and I would send and receive three letters every week, sometimes more. I counted the days until I could escape *Falkrap* and be with her again. The week before, I went on a buying spree and bought some flared jeans, a fashionable blue woolen V-Neck and some new leather boots. I so wanted to make an impression!

CHAPTER 7

Arriving at York railway station on a train that came five minutes early, I saw Jill at the end of an adjacent platform with her younger sister and brother. She was watching a coming diesel train in the opposite direction. Her little sister held up a compact mirror as she applied balm to her lips while her brother kicked a pebble around the platform. Making my way to Jill's platform, I moved undetected among the shifting crowd. I tiptoed behind her with the expertise of a lioness about to pounce and slipped my arms around her waist.

"Tell me the capital of Moldova or I kiss you in public," I said.

"You are so crazy, she laughed, turning round quickly.

"Sorry, Socrazy is the capital of Charlievakia. I claim my prize."

I had waited so long for that embrace, but it was worth it. We stood bound together, as though we were in the grip of a powerful adhesive that refused to yield. The magic of the embrace was interrupted when her little brother kicked me on the knee.

"Hurry up, I'm hungry and Jill said you would buy us all an ice cream if we came to meet you," he said.

York was amazing! A mixture of old world architecture and steak bars. Jill's dad, Alan, introduced me to the Yorkshire ale, Tetley's, and the Sunday afternoon pastime of driving to the pub and walking home singing after six pints of the awful liquid.

I liked Alan, he was a lovable rogue with a lovable family. My holiday was supposed to last two weeks, but Jill and I got engaged and it lasted two years!

I moved in with Jill's grandparents, Alan landed me a high-paying job at the city's glassworks and Jill and I were on course to buy a small townhouse in the Fulford area of York. Then in a way that only *I* could…

I blew it majestically! I soon discovered Jill's Mormon involvement was a religious thing, not her job! She did not believe in drinking tea or coffee or any alcohol and her taste in music was limited to mostly The Osmonds. (Who were also Mormons.)

The ultimate clash, however, came when I was invited to a Mormon party at the Church of Jesus Christ of Latter-day Saints' recreation hall. I decided to meet Jill at the party a little later. I didn't want to go on time because I was told there would be no alcohol and the food would be organic. So I stopped at the pub on the way and had five pints of Tetley's and a few drams of Glenfiddich. I was red-faced when I arrived, just managing to stay upright. Fifty shiny faces wearing floral dresses and sensible shoes stopped in mid-sentence and stared with open mouths as I tripped over two teenage boys playing chess on the floor.

Oblivious to the lukewarm reception, I walked up to Jill and patted her bottom. "Where's the DJ?" I slurred. A tall man with a Donny Osmond tank top pointed to a rickety record player next to the fruit juice and cookies and forced a fake smile.

I took off the *Osmonds' Greatest Hits* LP and flung it like a frisbee across the room in the direction of a framed photograph of white suited elderly guy, narrowly missing the (alcohol-free) punch bowl. One or two cardigan clad teenage girls blushed as I winked at them, while others stood holding leather bound books with mouths open. A middle-aged blonde lady with ridiculously wide green flares and a full plate of brownies, swiftly returned to the kitchen at the far end of the room. Even the chess playing "spotty" boys lowered their pieces and elbowed each other in the ribs waiting for the inevitable drama to unfold…

I replaced the Osmonds record with David Bowie's *Ziggy Stardust and the Spiders from Mars* and as the drum beat from the first track, *Five Years*, began to fill the room. (Ironically, this is a song about things coming to an end).

Turning up the volume, I danced. A tall thin teenage girl stepped forward to join me but was tugged back by a man in his 20s, sporting a soft, fuzzy mustache, thick black framed spectacles and a bright yellow pullover.

"Dance with him and you won't be allowed back," he said, louder than he had meant to. After 10 more blissful minutes, someone turned the music off.

A fat man with navy corduroy trousers, a blue shirt and bright orange tie addressed me on behalf of "the guests".

"You are not welcome here and Jill will no longer be seeing you," he said. Had he not taken a step back, I would have knocked him out. Instead I pounded the man wearing the pullover and spectacles, who toppled like a lead balloon.

I shrugged at Jill, who smiled at me through her tears and walked me to the door.

"I'm sorry," she said. "It was my fault, I should have warned you that our parties are quieter than what you may be used to."

I loved her all the more for her gentle forthrightness and turned to kiss her but instead missed her by three inches and vomited over a seven-foot statue of the Angel Moroni.

Needless to say, after that incident I never heard from Jill again.

I took extended "sick leave" and went back to Falkirk for a few days, hoping I would feel a connection to the place, but it was as dull and as unfriendly as ever. I put up with the suffocating village mentality for two days before deciding to retreat to England for a while.

I bade my folks goodbye in Falkirk and made plans to return to the city I'd left, via a bus to Edinburgh and then a London-bound train to York.

The bus trip from Falkirk to Edinburgh took 90 minutes. After arriving at St James bus station, I stepped down into the grey but serene afternoon city atmosphere. Walking half a mile to Edinburgh Waverley Railway Station, I arrived at the underground ticket office at 4pm. I paid and pocketed my small red and cream-colored rail ticket and waited on the platform, relieved to be away from the increasingly small place I used to know as home.

As I stood there, I felt a mixture of déjà vu and slight dread flow to the pit of my stomach. A familiar, shrill whistle signaled that someone from a sorrier episode from my past stood on the same platform. A past that I wanted to leave behind.

Glancing over my shoulder, I saw a sight that used to scare the blood from my face. John Galviston. The bully of Camelon High. He used to tower over me and demand my dinner money every day in return for not getting flattened. He stood smoking a rolled cigarette. And whistling to himself. Smug as ever. My heart raced as I relived the memories of this thug's beatings during my days at Camelon High.

I turned slowly and lowered my large black leather clothes bag. Slipping off my blue velvet jacket, I swung at him. The force of the punch (had it connected) would have rendered him at least unconscious, but he saw it coming at the last minute. As he ducked, the momentum of my missed punch made me dive head first onto the railway tracks below.

But something mysterious and wonderful happened. As I plunged head long towards certain death or disability, a sense of peace washed over me. A plethora of colors swam before my eyes as my body seemed to fall in slow motion. Turning over as I fell, I took the full impact on my back and neck on what felt like a bed of feathers. I lay there for a few minutes asking myself if I was dead or in heaven. I couldn't have been hell, because it felt so peaceful; but it couldn't have been heaven because it was very dark down there. But it was certainly a place of serenity, safety and inexpressible joy. (Miracle number three.)

The rattling sound of the train on the tracks made me get to my feet. I climbed unscathed up onto the platform where a shaking Galviston had been looking down into the darkness.

He turned away from the edge in relief and froze, as the train sped past us. I tapped him on the shoulder with my right hand.

John shook visibly, his face pale and drawn. His whole appearance looked slightly ragged, like that of a man much older than his real age.

"I thought you were gone man." He spoke with a smoker's hoarseness.

"Pity I wasn't," I said, seriously.

"You've grown!" he rasped, while drawing hard on his cigarette. Careful not to sound too aggressive, he protested, "You would have broken my jaw!"

"Give me your dinner money, or I'll finish the job," I said.

"We were kids." He laughed.

"Kids." I smiled back before giving him a mock tap on the cheek and in doing so, dismissed the incident and all the pain that came with it, forever into history.

Coughing and wheezing, John Galviston went to meet a relative from Newcastle who was arriving on the next platform. I sighed and stepped onto the waiting 4:15pm train to York.

CHAPTER 8

I returned to York untethered (which was both a good and bad thing) and saw it through new eyes. A haven of stunning architecture and cobbled streets, York was still as majestic as when I first arrived there for Jill. This ancient walled city smiled welcomingly as I took a deep breath and whispered the words "home for now" in the direction of a street juggler dressed in Elizabethan garb, who waved at me through his colorful heavy make up.

I felt the dawn of fresh possibilities. I rented a small bedsit near the city's racecourse and at 19, enjoyed the single life. It wasn't hard to make new friends. Our venue of choice was the city's premier discotheque "The Cat's Whiskers". It was 1975 and Glam Rock was at its peak. My mates and I dressed in flowing silk shirts, baggy dress trousers, huge platform shoes and wide lapel jackets and coats. Wherever we went, people saw us as good-looking young guys, well dressed and oozing with self-confidence.

We were invited to exclusive parties, at stylish locations. We even had competitions to see how many girls we could "pull" in one evening. I hung around the city of York for another year enjoying the nightlife and my pay cheques from the glassworks (where I managed, unbelievably, to recapture my original job and land myself a higher paid position driving a bulldozer there only weeks later!) However, I grew bored with life there and moved south, to the bustling market City of Leeds where I started up my own décor company.

I only hired local unemployed men who needed a few pounds extra on the side. There was Colin Murphy, an amateur boxer who grew up in Belfast among the sectarian gang violence. Colin was good at plastering, painting and protecting me. Although he was a tall, burly man, his nickname "Big" referred to his ability to stay standing in a pub brawl and swing the last (and usually most effective) punch.

Another worker was Ronnie Sales, a small, lean and cunning man with a background in petty crime. He could pick someone's pocket, steal an item of jewelry or con his way into any hotel function, like no one else. He'd spent his childhood with his mother in the sprawling Leeds council estate of Middleton, but had lived most of his teenage years and early 20s in local care homes for disturbed boys.

I paid my men $20 a day and I charged customers $300 a day plus expenses! I always asked for cash, never gave receipts and never paid any tax or the compulsory national insurance. I was wealthy within months! I had a van, a car and was buying a three-storey house in the city's Harehills district.

I even did extra "made-to-measure" orders… like wrought iron gates!

This unexpected endeavor into the world of home accessories came about after a customer whose exterior walls we had just painted, asked if I knew a place that made wrought iron gates measuring 10 by 20 feet. I asked how much he was about to pay and was surprised to hear him say, "Up to $2000." Seeing this as another opportunity to fill my pockets, I sent Ronnie and Colin out at night to measure the gates of homes in the upper class area of Roundhay. They came back with an address the next morning.

Characteristically, Ronnie immediately addressed the logistics.

"The gates weren't on tightly," Ronnie said. "We could just lift them up off the metal hinges and carry them away. They're painted black and in the dark we'll almost be invisible."

"How much of a cut are we getting?" Colin asked. "Hope it's worth our while."

The next night, "my boys" and I dressed in all black clothes and hats, arrived at the said house at 3am, lifted the gates off the hinges and the three of us simply walked away with them. The destination was my backyard, two miles away.

As Ronnie walked, he took deep puffs of a hand rolled cigarette with one hand and while carrying the seriously bulky gates with the other arm.

"It's a good job you told Big Colin and me to do this quickly," Ronnie said. "Otherwise we might have taken offence…get it, a fence?"

All three of us lowered the gates and momentarily laid them against a garden wall as we laughed in whispers at the absurdity of it.

Just then, a police car drove slowly past. All three of us dived over the small two foot high garden wall landing clumsily on top of each other.

"I think I've broken a garden gnome," Ronnie moaned.

"I'll break *your head* if you don't shut up," Big Colin whispered.

"Ladies, ladies…" I hissed. "We are trespassing in someone's garden at 3am and are in possession of two big feckin gates that just happen to be taking for a walk to my house!"

We waited silently, but the patrol car drove on past. Seeing two gates propped up against a wall in Harehills was not the worst they would have witnessed that morning for sure.

To this day, I have no idea what I would have said to the police if they had stopped us! But three days later the gates were painted silver, adorning a detached house in Harehills, and I was $2000 better off!

On nearly all of our many "jobs" I paid one man to stay in the van outside and do nothing. He would get the same wages as the other six workers inside. The men often complained he did "bugger all" until the day we decorated a Chinese restaurant on New Years' day.

We were all severely hungover. The job was a simple two coats of expensive, long-lasting white textile paint. We never cleaned the grease off the walls because we just couldn't be bothered. It was a flat $500 for the gig and we all wanted to be paid so we could return to the pub. We even had a paint fight halfway through the day for fun!

While the lads were cleaning up, I called the owner and told him the job was done.

"Any need to inspect it?" he asked in a thick Cantonese accent.

I persuaded him it was wet and my lads were still gathering their equipment. Meanwhile, huge brown grease marks could be seen through the cheap paint job. The owner paid the cash. I shook his hand and nodded to the men. Outside the van was revving noisily; we all jumped in, throwing dust sheets, paint rollers, trays and empty tins in the back.

I slapped the dashboard and the driver stepped on the accelerator, the 10 year old Ford Transit van screeching like a Formula One racing car. Seconds later, the owner and three hefty men ran out of the restaurant, wielding meat cleavers. Within minutes we were safely on the ring road. I turned to the relieved men and patting the driver (nicknamed Hamster) on the shoulder, said, "That is why we pay him". They never again questioned his role.

As our work became more "diverse", so my hunger for something more grew. I was in my 20s with the world at my feet. In reality I was drinking and smoking myself to an early grave, had no friends because I was worried that they would steal from me, and desperately needed God in my life but where to look?

The longer I worked, the more I became embroiled in grubby underbelly of this cut-throat world. We worked in close contact with rough Yorkshire gangs or the gangsters who owned them (and sometimes, owned us, for a week or two.) We were often contracted to paint over blood and knife marks on the walls of shady looking bars and nightclubs. I learned once there was a contract out on me (someone paid to shoot me or at least maim me) because I had beaten their boss to a lucrative painting job at a brewery.

Our last big decorating job was a huge warehouse near Boston Spa village in West Yorkshire. Our client took us to the storeroom which was packed with "sports wear" - not just imitations but genuine stuff like Nike, Adidas and Umbro. It was a goldmine!

We carefully primed the walls, filled in holes with plaster and skilfully undercoated, painted and varnished to perfection. The manager gave us other offices to complete in the complex, which we decorated with the same commitment and zeal.

You may be asking, why did we take pains to provide an excellent service here and not elsewhere? That's so easy to answer. Now that my business was expanding into factories, public houses and government contracts, these new gigs were making a nice bit of money. And so I was now employing "real decorators" as well as my own "boys".

Also, I did not want any suspicion about our quality of work when several Adidas and Nike track suits were going home most nights in our van and fetching $20 each at our local bar.

After one relatively successful week whereby I was paid for two months' work up front and made $1000 on the side, we decided to all go out and get "wasted". Starting at a few university bars where the drink was cheap and the girls were cute, we moved on to some of the more raucous establishments. These places had sawdust on the floor instead of carpeting. (Easier to mop up the blood stained sawdust than pay for carpet cleaning.)

At 2am we were singing Chelsea football songs at the top of our voices while standing on a butcher's van on The Headrow in Leeds. The polite patience of the on-duty police officers that had answered a call to "investigate a disturbance" soon ran out when they were told in no uncertain terms what I thought of them, their city and their football team (Leeds United).

The police officers hauled me off the van and bundled me into the back seat of their car. Inside I was handcuffed and whacked in the ribs by a baton. In response, I blew the officer a kiss. He struck me again in the ribs. We played this nice game until I reached the central charge office where I was searched and found to be in possession of stolen checks, a false driving ID and wearing an Adidas tracksuit with the price tag still on it!

The police charged on five counts ranging from drunk and disorderly conduct to fraud. They placed me in the holding area until after midnight and then threw me into a van with eight others. I was taken to the notorious Bridewell Cells underneath the Leeds City Hall.

PART 2 – A NEW BEGINNING

CHAPTER 9

The Bridewell, or City Jail, was built in 1858, a year before Charles Dickens published *A Tale of Two Cities*. The daily ration for prisoners at Bridewell was half a loaf of bread and a pint of ale! The prison was said to be haunted by notorious Victorian burglar and murderer Charlie Peace who was incarcerated there before his execution on 25 February 1879. His cell remains untouched.

The entrance to the Bridewell's inner cells.

Three pairs of footsteps made a loud clattering noise as they descended the stairs to Bridewell Jail. With my hands cuffed behind my back, I walked single file between two policemen to the bottom of the stairs and through the narrow stone corridor leading to a plain wooden desk. Behind the desk, the duty jailor asked me, "Name?" without looking up. The policemen uncuffed me and handed a charge sheet to the "uniform" behind the desk. The jailor took out one of several large keys on a chain and opened the large iron gate that led into "the cage" (as the police put it). I looked over my shoulder as I stumbled into the dimly lit communal cell. Having completed their task of escorting me, the two policemen were now talking crudely about a female police officer at their local station.

A pungent mix of stale vomit and urine assaulted my nostrils. I carefully found an unoccupied rubber mattress on the floor in the cell to settle in, avoiding the stares of my cellmates. The stench made me want to throw up. It was unbearable and inescapable.

I woke up bruised and hungover the next morning, having endured a night of a dozen male prisoners boasting about robbing or raping someone. Their crime being someone else's fault was the common thread. I felt that I had hit the lowest pit of my life. All my money, work, car, everything I owned… was outside of a locked door.

I'd profited greatly from my crooked trade in stealing wrought iron gates and now I found myself imprisoned behind gates that weren't too different from the ones I'd swiped. Someone else had paid the price for my wealth, from clients I'd swindled to workers I'd cheated. For the first time, it looked like I'd have to pay and the penalty would be severe.

For the first time in memory, I wasn't in control. For the first time in my life, I felt darkness like never before. A hopeless dark feeling that gripped my heart and stomach and made me want to vomit. I huddled in a corner of the cell, wrapped a blood and puke-stained rough brown blanket around myself and wept. Deep wrenching sobs from the depth of my being. I had screwed up big time and there was nothing left for me. I wanted to end my life. I looked up at the strange orange and red tiled ceiling and prayed for death to come.

I was distracted from my misery by a series of incidents. First, the jailor delivered a large plate of marmalade and jam sandwiches. The other prisoners looked at them in disgust and threw them at the high ceiling above, where the thick jam and marmalade stuck easily to the old Victorian ceiling. I soon realized the orange and red ceiling tiles were the result of jam residue. Sometimes in the night, a sandwich would fall and land with a thud on the black linoleum floor, adding fuel to the myth that Charlie Peace's ghost haunted the jail.

The second incident was a fight that broke out in the far corner of the cell. Two thieves had discovered they'd slept with the same girl. I could not imagine how any girl would want to sleep with either one of them. The men growled and stared menacingly waiting to see who would make the first move. They circled and finally lunged at each other like alpha wolves, each fighting for supremacy in the pack." I picked up a round plastic plate in case I needed to protect myself if the fight spilled over to my end. But a whistle blew and three wardens ran in and took two of the men away and calmed everyone else down.

Five minutes later, a warden returned. He was accompanied by a thin man in his late 30s, who wore a long brown coat, had a thick black beard and introduced himself as, "Fred Anderton from the Leeds City Mission."

"Good morning, gentlemen, I am here to talk about Jesus," Fred said.

His opening sentence was like a red rag to a crazed bull. We glared at this invader in a suit and tie. Who did he think he was? Who was going to rip into him first?

"Just give me 10 minutes of your time," he said in a deep, measured tone.

We looked at each other and someone in the group chirped up, "Ah, it will pass the time for a while, no harm in it." The others mumbled agreement and we all sat on the wooden benches that were nailed to the floor and listened.

Fred began to read from John's gospel, Chapter 1, verse 1. "In the beginning was the Word…"

Suddenly, all hell broke loose.

"Load of crap."

"You're not right in the head."

"Who do you think you are, coming in here and lecturing us?"

I asked questions about the validity of the biblical account of creation given the theory of evolution. How a "perfect" God could create a world filled with war and famine and murder and poverty and greed.

"How does your God let all that happen?" I demanded.

Fred bowed his head and explained calmly, that he didn't have all the answers to these questions but all he knew was that ever since he put his trust in Jesus that his life had known a peace that he could never have dreamed of.

Jesus was the Son of God, who existed with God outside of the time and space. Like a painter stepping into his own painting, Jesus chose to be born as a person on planet Earth. He became a man, but also remained the divine Son of God. Many people did not recognize his true identity, and rejected him, treating him as an outcast, an outsider.

Fred explained that Jesus came to earth on rescue mission; to restore the humankind's relationship with God, which was broken in the Garden of Eden. Ever since then, everyone had fallen short of God's perfect standard.

God's standard could be described as the tiniest center of a bullseye on a dartboard. Even if the dart was 1/64th of an inch off, it still missed the target. Like a dart thrown imprecisely, all of us missed the mark in one way or another.

The penalty for missing the mark was a certain hell because of undealt sin in our lives. One sin; many sins - *any* sin, was enough to separate us from God.

We were *all* in prison, and would never be able to pay the penalty by ourselves.

But there was hope… Jesus had accepted the penalty for OUR sins and paid the price for our freedom with His own blood, by willingly accepting a brutal, unjust execution on a Roman cross. Because He was the Son of God, he returned to life three days later. Jesus had paid for our freedom. He rescued us from eternal imprisonment by ransoming his life.

Now the onus was on us to make a decision – to accept Jesus' offer and be restored to relationship with God or to reject His invitation and try to pay the penalty ourselves.

To accept, we needed to acknowledge our sin before God, believe the Son of God already paid the penalty for our wrongdoing, repent (turn our back on sin) and invite Jesus into our lives as Lord and Savior, We would then become the forgiven, cleansed and adopted children of God. He would change us into His image and prepare us for a place in heaven.

All it took was one decision; such was the extravagant generosity of God's grace.

I was gripped! I stopped asking questions and fell silent, unable to hear the taunts of the others any more, instead only the voice of Fred who was speaking directly into my heart. All too quickly, he arose and headed for the door. After a tap on the iron gate, a warden came and opened it. I seized my opportunity and spoke quietly with him as he motioned to leave. "Can I have one of these books?" I asked nervously.

Fred stopped and searched his jacket pocket. "Here, have my one," he said. "I can get another." And with that, he was gone, and I had a lifeline.

I hid "the book" under my mattress and endured another day of boredom and pretense. Pretense, that I was as unmoved and cynical as the others, to save me from being attacked. Boredom, because their conversations consisted of what they'd stolen, who they'd hurt, and their flimsy justifications. I pretended to sleep most of the day and in the evening, feigned a sore stomach. They left me alone and I was relieved, but it was one of the longest days of my life.

When the last cellmate fell asleep at around 3am, I took out "the book" and began to read, and read! There was something dynamic happening inside of me. The more I read, the more drawn I was to the words. And as I read the words, God began convicting me of my sin and revealing His son Jesus to me, exposing my need for His saving grace. I fell asleep with the book next to me. I slept like a baby for the first time in months!

I awoke on Monday at 6am just in time for "breakfast". This time

I ignored the usual antics of the others who tried to stick their sandwiches to the ceiling, and I ate. I was famished. I was also bursting with unspeakable joy! It was incomprehensible. I was in a filthy pit of a jail and probably going to prison for a year or two. And yet here I was feeling ecstatically happy. This time I didn't feel the desperate urge to run to Dionach… Dionach was INSIDE of me and all around me and shining out through me.

A reassuring wonderful thought came to my mind. I knew that even if I was taken to prison that day, my life was still going to be wonderfully blessed. I had a peace that surpassed even my own understanding and soothed my heart and soul with the promise that even in prison, Jesus would be there with me. I was HIS.

A friend posted bail for me. I left the court shortly after 10am on Monday, 9 October 1983, and was ordered to appear again in three months' time. After a quick shower at home and phone calls to all "my boys" to find out how the jobs were going, I donned my thick furry bomber jacket, my flared jeans and a pair of Adidas trainers ("acquired" from a factory shop that we'd painted two months earlier) and went back into the Leeds city center in search of Fred's office. First I tried an Anglican church and asked the priest, "Is this where the Christians attend?"

"Are you confirmed?" he asked, his tight lips on the verge of a frown.

"I think I am a Protestant, but I was in jail and this guy came –"

"Jail? I think this is not what you are looking for."

My heart dropped.

I had similar responses at the Catholic church and the Methodist chapel, and the Salvation Army, who wanted to know if I was looking for a room for the night!

Deeply discouraged, I wandered in vain down the street, staring at my feet. Just as I was about to give up altogether, I looked up and saw a small blue sign above a butcher's shop:

Leeds City Mission Non Denominational

I had no idea what the last part meant but I knew this was where Fred was from. I climbed the narrow wooden stairs and rung the bell. The door opened and a small, round, funny-looking man answered and asked who I was.

"Here we go again," I thought. But taking a deep breath, I blurted out, "I was in jail and this guy with a beard called Fred came and read from this book and I read it and something's happened and I am not sure what but, it's good and I think I need to be a Christian…"

I stood there, shaking in fear, my nerves pushing me almost to tears. The man smiled and held out his hand. I looked at his hand wondering if this was some sort of deal? I only shook hands in pubs, and only when there was the promise of money involved.

"You'll be Charlie then. Come in lad, we've been expecting you. My name's Dr Coppack and I am the superintendent here, but you can call me Bill."

I froze for a moment. Superintendents were a rank in the police, I had met a few and never on good terms. I shrugged the feeling of doubt away and shook Bill's hand.

Bill led me through a maze of small rooms and a narrow corridor, past several people with smiling faces and into a back room with painted cream colored walls. The room consisted of a few chairs and bare plaster walls covered in posters with Bible verses and photographs of flowers and waterfalls! Seated in one corner was a slim, rangy man in his 50s, hands calmly rested on his lap. Even though he was sitting down, the deep lines on his forehead and his callused, bony hands made it evident that he'd led a hard, tough life. Bill introduced me to him – his name was Paddy Flynn.
Paddy was attached to the Railway Mission. He was gentle and softly spoken. Love burned in his eyes. He lived a life which shone with

his personal relationship with Jesus and a faith that had come to him after difficult times. Paddy invited me to pray with him and asked me to kneel. I felt strange, afraid, and very, oh so very, vulnerable.

He prayed a simple prayer of forgiveness and asked me to repeat it afterwards, which I did, word for word.

"Father I have sinned against heaven and against you, thank you for sending Jesus to the cross to redeem me and reclaim me to yourself, I now repent of my sin and everything that has created a barrier between you and me and receive you into my life as Savior, Lord and King."

Paddy asked me to thank God for what He had just done in my life. I know it wasn't the best or clearest prayer that I had ever uttered, but it was certainly the most important. For in my heart I was pleading at the throne of all grace.

I stood up as the waves of emotion washed over me and the tears began to flow. Paddy shook my hand and called me his brother. Gifting me with a King James Bible, we went through some key verses such as John 3:16. Paddy told me that some things would change immediately and some things would take a little more time. He said that there would be days when I'd doubt my new relationship with Jesus, and those were the times when I had to stand on the promises he'd highlighted in my new Bible.

Furthermore, he encouraged me to tell someone what had happened. "This will strengthen you. Oh and one more thing, Charlie. I will be contacting Bridge Street Church. Here's the address. Be there on Sunday night at 6pm and someone will meet you."

And with that, I was outside in the busy Leeds city center. I walked to the bus station with the Bible in my hand and Christ in my heart. Both invaluable gifts. Clutching the Bible like a precious, fragile trophy, I boarded a double decker bus heading for Harehills and climbed up to the top deck. The bus conductor tapped me on the shoulder and asked for my fare.

"Hold on a minute please!" I said, drawing the attention of the entire upper deck. "I'll just put my BIBLE down, I just got it..." Everyone stared. I gently laid my new Bible on an empty seat and fumbled for the fare, which I gave the conductor.

After I sat down, I counted the number of people on the upper deck and thought to myself, "Right, that's me telling 23 people. Who's next?"

Oh, there were many, very many, waiting.

Fred Anderton who visited me in the
Bridewell Cells Leeds

CHAPTER 10

I started back at my job the next day, with four painting contracts running simultaneously. I was soon back in the throes of ordering materials, staffing all sites, observing all four jobs, and of course, making sure that we would be paid cash upon completion. Things were same-same, but different. For starters, I noticed the foul language that my men were using, the crude jokes and sexist comments. I noticed the blasphemous words spoken every time a brush was dropped or a roll of paper ripped. I also noticed I wasn't using such language any more… and so did they.

The first two to comment were my accomplices in our first gate-stealing stunt.

"You're different," Big Colin said.

"You still coming to the pub on the way home tonight, boss?" Ronnie Sales said.

"I don't think I drink any more," I said, bewildered by my own dramatic internal shift.

"Are you ill?" Fat Pete, Colin's brother asked.

The verse that Paddy had asked me to remember from 2 Corinthians 5:17 sprung to mind, its meaning now dazzlingly clear:

"If anyone is in Christ, the new creation has come: the old has gone, the new is here!"

I was a new person because Jesus had made me new and He was cleaning me up and removing the habits and attitudes instilled in me from my past! I turned to Big Colin, Ronnie and Pete, who were smoking on the third floor office floor in downtown Wakefield.

"I was saved, Jesus is my focus now, and you can cut that language out. I still love you guys (did I just say love?) but I won't have filthy talk in a Christian firm."

Stunned silence filled the room. I wanted to qualify all this and say how blessed and happy I was and that they too should seek and find Jesus... but instead I left for the next job. My heart was racing, yet I felt elated that I had witnessed about Jesus for the first time.

I longed for Sunday to come. I wanted to be free from the cut-throat, dangerous world that I'd become embroiled in - one ruled by gangs, crime scene clean up jobs and territorial disputes. Where successfully bidding for a contract could get you killed by your rivals.

I wanted so much to go to church and wondered if it would be anything like the Dawson Mission Gospel Hall back in Carron Road. Would I be stopped from going in because I was too old or even too young? Did I need to be confirmed or baptized first?

I fed my soul by reading my new Bible. Beginning at Genesis, I waded through each chapter, not understanding much of what I was reading but feeling a sense of lightness and peace inside. God also brought back to my remembrance all the gospel songs that I had learned at the Dawson Mission and they too became my spiritual milk and bread in that long week in between making a decision to follow Jesus and attending church.

Eventually Sunday came around. At 6pm, I paced the pavement outside of Bridge Street Pentecostal Church at the foot of The Headrow, the biggest and longest street in Leeds (and one of the busiest). I waited for another 10 minutes and decided that if no one came out to find me, I was going home.

Doubts flooded my mind as I waited in the cold Yorkshire air. "Was I really a Christian?" "How is it possible that I could ever change?" "How could one small book make me different?" "Is this Jesus really alive?"

I heard singing and clapping inside the large stone building to my right and wanted to be part of it but who was I kidding? I was a nobody. An outsider. Everyone inside that building were somebodies, perhaps brought up in the very homes I stole from and cheated. Maybe they would laugh at my accent, lack of religious jargon or ridicule my long wavy fair hair (even though I washed it for the first time in days…) My legs remained frozen; my jaw tight at the thought of being greeted by the unknown faces who actually belonged there.

I was supposed to meet a young guy called Steve Reilly (who incidentally went on to play a major role in Bridge Street and as I write, is now one of the senior pastors there). Perhaps Paddy hadn't contacted him. Or maybe he had simply forgotten. I took a deep breath, turned and was about to head back up the road towards the familiarity of my unfinished three-storey house in the crime ridden district of Harehills, where nobodies could live for years unnoticed. Maybe stop by my local pub on the way and have a pint or six.

Just as I began walking away, deeply discouraged, I heard a door behind me open. A casually dressed guy in his late teens came over and smiled at me. His hair was short (although not buzz cut short), and he wore a light brown bomber jacket with jeans. He looked genuinely pleased, though perhaps a little apprehensive, to see me.

"Are you Charlie?" he asked in a strong West Yorkshire accent. "I'm Steve, come on in." He led the way, through a light blue painted church lobby with a small table that had piles of red books called *Redemption Hymnals* on both ends. It reminded me of the entrance to a big detached house that I painted only a few months earlier and would have certainly robbed if it hadn't been for its huge Doberman guard dog named "Brutus". There were two sets of double doors on either side of the lobby and two adjacent stairways leading up to the left and right of the doors.

"We'll go upstairs. It's jam packed down here and besides, you get a better view from up there," Steve said.

I was shocked by what I saw. It wasn't all holy statues and stained glass windows. This was a purpose-built place for people to come together and sing to God. It was clean but not impeccable. Bright but not overwhelming; welcoming but not-in-your face. I climbed the stairs, full of anticipation, excitement and a little fear.

A wall of sound hit me as I entered the crowded upstairs gallery of Bridge Street. A band played down below and people sang Christian songs, one or two that I thought I'd heard at Dawson Mission in the Sunday Gospel meetings. People clapped. Some stood, some sat, some shouted, "Hallelujah". Some even had their hands up in the air and a few were calling out praises to God in a language that sounded like Arabic!

Steve led me to my seat and introduced me to a few people in my row who nodded and shook my hand. Here I was, less than a week out of jail and I was sitting beside a policeman, a teacher, a magistrate, businessmen and housewives.

"I am not worthy to be here," I heard myself say almost audibly. And then a still, quiet, reassuring voice spoke calmly into my heart. "This is your family, Charlie, you have every right to be here, just as they are." It felt good to be home at last.

The cramped church was overflowing; I never thought churches were like this. There could have been up to 500 or more there, people of different nationalities, ages and shapes! The message that Pastor John Cave preached was simple, interesting, and easy to understand. It was about Jesus reaching out to a man with leprosy and healing him, when everyone else had deemed him a lost cause and turned their backs on him. I identified with the man in the story instantly. I too had felt unclean, irredeemable – not physically, but spiritually - and Jesus had touched my life with his love and grace and healed my heart.

At the end of his message, the pastor gave a warm invitation to anyone and everyone in the crowd. "If you are here tonight and you do not know Jesus personally, then make your way to the front of the church and I will pray with you and our counselors will talk with you and show you how to start this wonderful new life. Just come now."

I looked at Steve, he nodded, and I made my way to the front. As I passed the hordes of brightly dressed worshippers wearing "sensible clothes", I felt more and more self-conscious. My furry jacket and baggy jeans and my long wavy hair stood out. Yet as I walked to the front, some patted me on the shoulder and spurred me on, others shouted "Praise God!" I was carried to the front in a wave of encouragement and prayer.

Pastor Cave prayed for the many who had gone forward and then we were guided through a door at the right of the large wooden platform. In the side room, I met a young man in his early 20s called Mark. I shared what had happened in jail and the events leading up to it. He smiled at my complicated quest to find the Leeds City Mission office especially when I said, "Isn't it difficult to become a Christian?"

After listening to my story, Mark leaned over and said, "Charlie, I don't need to pray for you to be saved, I believe that has already happened. But I want to pray that you will be grounded in Christ and know His assurance in your life and grow in strength and in His grace." Mark prayed a simple, practical and thankful prayer for what God had done in my life through Jesus and all He was about to do. He encouraged me to read my Bible every day and gave me a booklet called, *Every Day With Jesus* which consisted of a month's daily Bible reading notes by the acclaimed Christian psychologist Dr Selwyn Hughes. Mark encouraged me to attend the Bible study at Bridge Street and to be involved with evangelism at the Leeds City Mission.

Mark also explained about the Holy Spirit. He said, "God exists in three persons - God the father, God the Son (Jesus) and God the Holy Spirit. We pray to God the father, through God the son, in the power and strengthening of the Holy Spirit. He is the one that enables you to understand the Bible, Charlie. It's like reading Shakespeare and having the author sitting next to you explaining what each sentence and paragraph means. The Holy Spirit also enables you to be holy and turn your back on things that are harmful to you and walk closely with Jesus. And the best thing of all, Charlie… the Holy Spirit lives inside you!"

He made it sound so simple and exciting. I was already a Christian! I was a son of God, I belonged to the heavenly king and was part of His holy family. My heart swelled with pride.

After that first exposure to Bridge Street Pentecostal Church, I couldn't get enough! I attended the prayer meetings and Bible studies whenever the doors were open. And under the expert and spiritual guidance of Pastors John Cave and Stephen Thompson (the latter becoming one of my dearest and closest friends to this very day), I began to grow. A few months later I was baptized by full immersion. (The best bath I have ever had!)

Meanwhile, God was still chipping away at my old life. I had stopped swearing, drinking alcohol (I do not believe drinking alcohol in itself is wrong, but I was abusing it, and so it had to go completely, as well as smoking. If my body was "a temple of the Holy Spirit", then no way was I filling the top half with tobacco smoke.) Instead of getting drunk and fighting on a Saturday afternoon at Chelsea matches, I joined the Bridge Street football team and this helped me to channel my energy and save money at the same time.

One Saturday afternoon I arrived slightly late. I pulled up next to a parking meter next to the playing field that was only a few hundred yards from Bridge Street Church where the rest of the team were waiting. I quickly took out an old parking ticket and slapped it under my windscreen wiper. (An old trick I had learned from "my boys" to stop me getting another!) Some members of the football team were walking onto the field in the direction of the changing rooms, a small tin building at the far end. As I walked casually to join the rest of the team, one of the lads went bright red and couldn't look me in the eye.

I joked, "What's up with you mate? Anyone would think you are a cop…"

Steve Reilly inched towards me and spoke cautiously. "Emm, he *is*, Charlie."

I turned red. It didn't take me long to re-park my car and I never played that trick *ever* again. As I said, God was chipping away the rough edges, and it was as coarse and rugged as gravel. As I grew in God, He would gradually show me certain areas of my life that needed refining. Some things in my life would disappear quickly, others would take longer, but the work of building up Christian character had definitely begun in me.

My work made me lots of money, but a lot of what I was doing was illegal and morally wrong, and therefore did not belong in the new life I was now growing in

So on 22 March 1984, I walked into the Inland Revenue office on The Headrow and waited in line. Ahead in the queue, people moaned and asked why they had to pay so much tax and some people utterly refused because of a myriad of excuses. And then it was my turn. The tired clerk sighed, expecting another tirade, and looked up into my beaming face.

"Good morning," I said, "I am Charlie Mackenzie, and I was saved in jail a few months ago, so I am now a Christian. I have my own decorating business and have made a few dollars from it over the years but I have never paid you a penny in tax. Instead I have lied, cheated and avoided paying tax altogether. Now the Lord wants me to live as a citizen of heaven and I have no problem with that, so I have calculated that I owe you this amount."

I wrote the figure down and showed him.

"Now I don't have that much in cash at home but I can pay you monthly over the next year. When would you like me to start?"

"This a sick joke, sir?"

The look of hurt in my eyes assured him it wasn't.

"You are serious, you really mean this." He looked concerned. "You could go to jail for this."

"If that's what I have to do, then I guess that's fair."

"Wait there," he said, and with that, he was gone.

A woman came back and asked that I repeat my story to her slowly, which I did happily.

She eyed me suspiciously. "Can you write all this down? We will be in touch."

I gladly obliged there and then, submitted my written account to them and was told that they would be in touch and criminal proceedings might follow.

My friends at Bridge Street and the Leeds City Mission prayed. Three days later, I received a short letter and a payment form stating, "First monthly payment due on 31 March."

I never missed a payment and always shared a scripture or two and some nice words on the back of the payment slip. On my very last payment a year later, I wrote:

"Dear Mrs Hobbs I am so sorry that this lovely friendship has now come to an end, but please feel free to stay in touch and I hope one day to see you in heaven."

A similar thing happened when I visited the National Insurance office and told them I owed them thousands of pounds in missed compulsory payments. The clerk looked at me and screamed "Harry! We got a crazy guy here in cubicle eight, shall I call security?"

Team leader Harry Boswell entered with two security officers and barked, "What's all this trouble you are causing here?" I calmly explained what had happened, relishing the amazing opportunity to share my testimony again.

The clerk looked at Harry for direction. Harry pondered all this, before saying sheepishly, "Do you know how much paperwork you are going to cause me if I go along with this?" He turned to leave, saying, "Wait there, I'll be straight back."

Harry returned with a sheet of typed paper. "Just sign and date it," he said, pushing a pen urgently into my hands and looking around to see if anyone else was looking or listening.

"What exactly am I signing?" I asked.

"Trust me, Mr Mackenzie, you will be glad you did." He gave me the faintest glimpse of a smile. I stuffed the copy he gave me into my jacket pocket and left.

On the way home, I stopped at a garage for a packet of mints and a newspaper and as I searched my pocket for loose change, I drew out the receipt from the National Insurance office. I uncrumpled it and read it, gazing at the bottom of the sheet.

> *National Insurance contributions arrears up until April 30th 1984 Nil. Penalty incurred Nil. Signed H. Boswell Supervisor and countersigned by Charles Mackenzie.*

I'd been ready to pay for my mistakes, even to be tossed into jail, and was now told the debt had been waived in full. Again, I'd received grace instead of punishment. I had been let off scot free and this was all due to grace. I welled up in tears.

While the Lord was still cleaning me up physically and morally, I now had the burning desire to share the good news with others. After all, if Jesus could save *me*, he could save and change anyone!

I prayed earnestly, "Please Lord, use me to reach out to others, I am prepared to go anywhere: Africa, China, you name it, I am ready."

After a few days of intense prayer, God said, "Anywhere Charlie? OK, then I want you to go back into the jail where I found you and tell the others about me."

I was gutted. Anywhere but that horrible, filthy, dark, putrid dungeon!

"Lord," I pleaded. "Anywhere but there…"

"But you said ANYWHERE AT ALL," came the firm, quiet reply. (I have since discovered that we need to be specific in prayer and not to make vague pledges with God that we are not prepared to follow through totally.)

Only weeks after I was saved, I returned to Bridewell Jail on a wet Sunday morning before church. My hair was now a sensible length, my fur lined bomber jacket and designer jeans replaced by a smart suit and dress shoes. And instead of fear, I was returning with faith. The Leeds City Mission informed the jailor that a *missionary* would be visiting. The jailor smiled and opened the iron gate that led into the community cells that had been my lodging place a short time before. The walls and ceiling screamed at me to leave. I felt like a Christian about to enter a gladiatorial arena in Roman times and be torn apart by lions.

I walked purposefully into the cell and motioned with my hand to the gang of a dozen men of various ages and sizes to come and join me. They grunted and slowly shuffled over and sat in rows next to me. I took a deep breath and began, "Good morning gentlemen, my name is Charlie and I am from the Leeds City Mission and -"

"Fuck off!" a small wiry man shouted, drawing sniggers and whistles from the rest.

"Yeah," another man spat. "We need lawyers, not Bible thumpers like you. You have nothing we want. Get lost, preacher man, before we get angry."

More laughter and mocking sounds. I stood to leave but instead turned round.

"Who slept in bed four last night? Does it still smell of sick and have that damp patch near the wall? Who actually ate the breakfast here?"

The group fell silent.

"Or did you fire them up at the ceiling above me? Who stayed awake until three this morning because you couldn't sleep for the sound of the wardens playing cards? Answer me!"

Eventually one of them spoke into the stillness, slowly, staring at me. "How do you know about the cards at night and the sandwiches?"

"And how can you see the damp patch next to my bed from back here?" another asked.

I began to see their attitudes changing, and felt God's empowerment and the love in my heart swell for these men, and I even noticed a distinct difference in the spiritual atmosphere. This was what my friend's at Bridge Street called the "anointing" of the Holy Spirit. I had been reading in my Bible how God "anointed", or supernaturally empowered certain people at certain times for certain ministry. And here in this dingy group of jail cells with people no better than I was a few weeks earlier, I felt this anointing as I rose to speak.

"Only three weeks ago I was a prisoner here myself and I stayed awake listening to the sound of wardens, and I had to eat the stale jam and marmalade sandwiches like you, and I know about the damp patch in bed four because *that was my bed!*"

"You were one of us?" the wiry man asked.

"Of course I was," I said. "Do you think I would have come here to face you lot of animals if I wasn't?"

The jeers now turned into laughter and the men came closer. "What were you in for then? What happened? You get bail? When will you be back in court?"

"It doesn't matter what I was in for, it matters that I returned. And

I am here because this doesn't have to be the end of the line. If Jesus can do it for me, then He certainly can do it for you too."

The silence meant I had a few more minutes before they would be distracted so I pushed on. "Jesus was a man like us too, He left heaven to come to this sin-cursed earth. He went around healing and forgiving and giving hope to the hopeless and they put him in a jail worse than this, without even crappy bread and marmalade! They put Him on a cross and crucified Him, but even as He died, He forgave a thief dying next to Him. They buried Him yet He rose up. Two weeks ago in this very cell, He came and spoke to me and now I am healed, forgiven and saved! And what He did for me, He can certainly do for you if you will only repent and believe in His name."

I watched them wrestle with anguish and desperate hope, as my words sank in. I almost felt the pain and hopelessness of their situation, as I had recently felt that as well.

"Ah, load of crap," a tall man shouted. The rest followed suit, forcing dismissive laughs.

"You're a ****ing dreamer," another shouted.

I tapped the gate and the jailor let me out. "You don't remember me do you?" I asked.

"But I do sir," the jailor answered. "Indeed I do."

I left Bridewell jubilant. God had used me. The gospel would not return empty. As the prophet Isaiah wrote in Chapter 55:10, "I had faith that as the rain fell from heaven, inevitably saturating the soil, the gospel would produce a result." I visited the Bridewell every week for as long as I could. Many were moved and listened to the simple message of the gospel, some stifling tears as they heard it for the first time.

One young Newcastle man even repented on his knees in cell two and testified to the others straight afterwards. And when he was released we met up in my home as brothers. Praise God!

After this taste of evangelism, I threw myself into everything the City Mission was involved in, while at Bridge Street. I drank in Pentecostal doctrine and loved every minute of it.

God soon told me that my "job" was not glorifying to Him and this was further bolstered by a vision He gave me one night. In the vision I saw the whole population of Harehills Road in Leeds wearing decorators' overalls. And into this picture God spoke clearly and said, "There are enough of these in Leeds, Charlie, come and work for me instead."

The vision was enough for me to hand the business over to my lads and simply walk away from it. Three weeks later I was working for Leeds City Council managing a team of community workers in projects around the city.

My weekly involvement with the City Mission went like this:

Monday PM:	Prayer Meeting
Wednesday AM:	Handing out tracts at the LCM book stall in the Leeds Market
Friday PM:	Visiting the homeless on The Soup Run (more about that later)
Saturday AM:	Preaching in busy Bond Street, the main shopping area of Leeds.

We would also be called on to take part in evangelism crusades at various churches and deputation meetings in and around West Yorkshire.

I was "buzzing" until a police officer visited me with a reminder that I was due in court to face charges for the crimes that had landed me in Bridewell in the first place – drunk and disorderly conduct and fraud. I had stupidly hoped they would have been forgotten. But this was it. I was summoned to appear at the Crown Court for sentencing.

I asked my Senior Pastor, John Cave, and Dr Bill Coppack, the Director of Leeds City Mission, to come with me for moral support and to even speak on my behalf. Both decided to attend and support me. Dr Coppack addressed the court, speaking about how I had been active in the city mission since leaving Bridewell. Pastor Cave stood in the dock and introduced himself and then said, "I have not known Charlie too long, but in the short time I have known him, I have seen a dramatic change in his life and appearance and therefore conclude that something miraculous has taken place in his life."

After this, the Crown Prosecutor carried out a swift character assassination, dismissing my new belief as a con to try and escape prison. He suggested a two year prison sentence would be in order. My heart sunk as I was told to stand and face the judge.

The judge towered above me in his red robe and white curled wig. Peering over his half-rimmed spectacles, he said, "Charles Mackenzie. You have acted recklessly without due thought for anyone but yourself. You are guilty of all charges laid before you and have even admitted so. The due penalty for your misdemeanors is two years' imprisonment."

He paused and let me feel the full force of the law I had broken. Tears welled up within me and the lump in my throat became a tennis ball! I looked teary-eyed to the gallery where my new Christian friends smiled confidently and reassuringly.

The judge continued.

"However, in the light of your newfound faith and contribution to the city in which you have transgressed, I am willing to suspend sentencing for six months. Do you understand?"
I nodded.

"If you are arrested for even the slightest offence in this time you will go directly to prison and serve out two years."

With that, I was released. My friends patted me on the shoulder and

I floated home on wings of prayer and relief.

After that, I threw myself harder into the evangelism program of the Leeds City Mission. My favorite two modes of outreach were the Saturday open air preaching rallies and "The Soup Run". The Soup Run involved four to six of us putting on old clothes and meeting at the upstairs office of the Mission at 10pm on a Friday and praying. We would fill our flasks with hot soup, grab our Bibles and split into pairs or trios.

Our walk would take us into derelict buildings, condemned warehouses, under railway arches and onto the bus and railway stations looking for people sleeping rough. We had our regulars like Harry Bendon, a once-talented concert organist who hit the skids when his wife died, finding solace in a bottle. He was now an alcoholic wandering the streets of Leeds by day and sleeping in broken places by night.

On one occasion, "Mick the Brick" (called that because he was a bricklayer who wanted to serve God in Africa by building churches) and I were carefully walking over a pile of rubble in a darkened factory opposite the Leeds General Infirmary. I was holding onto Mick's back because he had the torch. Suddenly he let out a scream and leapt up in the air, and then ran for the hole in the wall we had climbed in through!

Outside we both stood doubled over, hands on knees breathing fast. "Wh- wh- what, was it you saw Mick?" I asked breathlessly, my words turning to thick vapor in the icy cold air. Mick looked at me in terror. "A rat ran up my leg," he said scratching himself all over! From then on, we tied string around our ankles before entering derelict buildings!

Some of our "outings" ended with us getting chased, bricks thrown at us, and knives being thrust at us. One wintry week, we were offering soup to the gentlemen sleeping under the benches at the city bus station when a large brute of a man, Clint, turned on me. As Clint's mixed breed dog bared its teeth at me, he loosened his grip on the rope-leash around the animal's neck, as though he were ready to let go. Icy fear began to take a hold of me.

"You church people?" Clint said.

Mick and I nodded together.

"Then name me 12 parables!" he growled. "Or I rip you apart."

Mick bowed his head in prayer while I tried to remember even one parable. Enduring below freezing temperatures at 1am while being threatened did not exactly stimulate my memory!

Clint turned to me triumphantly, stinking of cheap vodka. "Matthew, Mark, Luke and John… ha ha, beat you to it!" He laughed.

"What a plonker!" I thought to myself. He meant 12 disciples, not parables! I thanked him for his knowledge and was carefully maneuvering around him to where Mick was still praying and shivering. But Clint blocked me with a big menacing hand.

"You really a Christian?" he asked.

With all my resolve now gone and resigned to an inevitable beating, I answered, "Yes I am, and I am here in this freezing cold because God loves you, ok?!"

The snow was gently falling, and I was glad that I was wearing the new fleece lined beige anorak and hood that I had bought that week for nights such as this.

Clint sniggered, enjoying the audience of men who'd gotten out from under the benches and watched us closely. "If you were really a Christian, you would give me your jacket."

"Here," I said, as I removed my jacket and threw it at Him. Clint hesitated and stared, the garment hanging limply in his arms.

"It's yours," I said.

"But… it's your jacket." Clint sounded as sheepish as a small boy who had been caught looking at his dad's magazines!

Now it was my turn to growl. "If you don't take it, I will -"

"Take it," Mick said, stepping in. "It's a gift from God."

Clint pulled the jacket over his hulking frame and hugged me. I smiled and told him he was a "tube". (A Scottish word of endearment for a loveable clown.) I walked through the snow until we reached Mick's small Ford Fiesta. And the strange thing was that I felt even warmer than if I had been wearing my new jacket.

Another character we met on the "Soup Run" was the legendary Snowy O'Neil. Again, our encounter was after we had walked by the railway arches in search of the lost and lonely who often slept there. In only the previous week, we had been chased here by a weird man who made animal sounds!

Snowy O'Neil liked to tell stories. One night, this rough looking man with battle scars all over his face and knuckles, was addressing a group of about seven younger dropouts. Nearly all of them had a short thin cigarette dangling from their mouths. While recounting one of his escapades, Snowy drank from a large bottle of cider with another several bottles lined up next to him ready to be devoured. "So I picked this guy up and head-butted him while I put the boot in his face and…."

As we paused on our journey to listen, he stopped, annoyed.

 "Go on," I urged. "Finish your story."

"What do *you* want?" he sneered, brandishing the neck of his bottle threateningly and waving it at us. "We are not buying your religion, are we, boys?"

"No way, Snowy," someone called out.
"Go on," another one of his boys called out. "Snowy, tell us what

happened next..."

Snowy resumed his story. "Well, I got my knife and, and... will you Bible boys beat it or I swear I will -"

Suddenly, I felt the Spirit of God descend. "Snowy, we are here to tell you about Jesus and how you can be saved," I said. "God loves you and He wants to be part of your life and give you a new life. You are so much better than this."

The others slid back and waited to watch the impending slaughter; they had seen Snowy O'Neil in action many times before and they all knew what he was capable of.

Snowy, turned and faced us front on. His stare would paralyze even the most hardened thug in Bridewell. He paced slowly, saying nothing. What was actually only a few minutes seemed like hours. His "boys" whispered to each other and elbowed one another with silent delight. Another Snowy conquest to brag about, they thought. He menacingly brandished his half-consumed bottle of cheap cider in my direction.

Smash! He'd dropped the bottle. "What do I need to do?" Snowy asked.

His boys behind him stirred, agitated. They never expected this.

"Go on, Snowy, kill him," one called out in a hoarse, smoker's voice.

"Yeah, rip his throat open," hissed another, moving slowly towards Mick and I from the left.

Snowy gave them a quick glance that rendered them immobile.

Aware this was God working in Snowy, Mick and Andy, our new part-time missionary, prayed. Snowy and I kneeled on the ground beside each other, and I led him to Jesus.
We left Snowy O'Neil there, calm and in his right mind and with a

new story to brag about while we went on our way rejoicing. Weeks passed before when we bumped into another city missionary and heard the news.

"Did you hear about Snowy O'Neil?" he asked.

We looked at each other and said, "What happened?"

"Well… apparently, he was spoken to by some Christians at the bus station and afterwards, he smashed all his cider bottles and ran off telling his mates that he belonged to Jesus. He is staying at St John's Christian Hostel."

I paid a visit to the hostel and found him. The last time I saw Snowy, he was sober, dressed in clean clothes and donning a neat haircut. He was living in a small room with his Bible lying open on the bed. I was able to encourage him and pray with him before leaving, telling him that if I never saw him again in this life, I would look out for him in the next.

As I left the hostel, walking along the foot of The Headrow past the outside of the huge Victorian era City Hall and the entrance to the Bridewell Jail, I recognized Detective Sergeant Toowie (one of the police officers who had arrested me two months ago). Detective Sergeant Toowie was walking a few yards in front of me. It looked like he was off duty and in no particular hurry to be anywhere. He stopped, lit up a cigarette and continued walking towards Leeds City Market. I wanted to thank him for being an instrument in God's hand. So I shouted to him and ran towards him.

Upon seeing me racing towards him, he fled. Confused, I chased him, eventually cornering him in an alley. With only two feet between us, he raised his hands to cover his face.

"I just wanted to thank you for sticking me in the Bridewell," I said, slightly out of breath. "I got saved there, you know."

"You don't want to swing a punch at me?" he said, his hands still in front of his face.

"Whatever gave you that Idea?" I said, laughing on impulse.

I waited for him to relax, to acknowledge my thanks. But Detective Sergeant Toowie looked like a cornered animal, so I turned and headed back up The Headrow.

I thought about it from his point of view. Here's a guy that he put in the stinking Bridewell Jail for a weekend, identifying him in the street, shouting at him in a Scottish accent, and running towards him at speed! I chuckled to myself, "I think I would have run too!"

It was around this time that God first called me to China. The call came as a clear, almost audible voice. "China? Really?" I thought...

"CHINA," came the response.

Thinking I was imagining it, I threw it to the back of my mind and left it there. But it never went away. The following weekend I was handing out gospel tracts in the Leeds City Center when a tall gentleman took one and pushed it back in my face and remarked, "Why are you giving this to me? I don't need it. Go give it to those in China."

My heart began to race. "Lord, is this REALLY your calling?'

Two weeks later, I attended a church rally in West Yorkshire. The speaker was a well-known evangelist by the name of Roger Carswell. Towards the end of his message, he stopped and looked out at the crowd.

"Someone here has been called to China," he said. He carried on with his message.

At the end of the meeting I managed to get close to him. "Roger," I shouted, "That's me that God called to China."

He looked up and smiled. I thought to myself, "There's no way he thinks God really spoke to me…" But I knew He did. The next day my reading was from the book of Habakkuk.

"The vision is for an appointed time, though it tarries in wait for it…"

I busied myself reading every testimony I could find on China. I even joined the Chinese Christian Church that met on a Sunday afternoon. I used to sit through the services and not understand a word, but one thing I *did* understand, and that was at some time in the future, years and even decades from then, I *was* going to China.

CHAPTER 11

The summons came for me to attend the Crown Court for sentencing. I decided to go alone and quietly accept whatever was handed out. I refused any counsel, having already admitted to breaking several laws. For all intents and purposes, I deserved to go to prison.

I arrived at court early, surprised to see a few of my Bridge Street family already there. I smiled nervously at them as I entered the court. My name was called and I once again stood in the dock. After identifying myself, the charges were read out and I was asked how I pleaded.

"Guilty," I said, head bowed.

The judge spoke. "Charles Mackenzie, by your own admission you have broken these laws and deserve to spent the maximum two years in prison for your offences."

As I braced myself for the sentence, he said something that shocked both me, and my brethren in the gallery.

 "But I don't want you to worry about that!" he said.

I looked around to smiles and closed eyes from my silently praying friends.
"You have complied with your probation impeccably but I still need to sentence you.

"I hereby, sentence you to 180 hours' community service within the Leeds city boundary. You will serve this sentence at five hours every week as follows:

"On Mondays you will attend the Bible study and prayer meeting at Leeds City Mission.
On Wednesdays you will work on the Leeds City Mission book stall at our City Market.
And on Friday nights you will take part in Leeds City Mission's visitation to the homeless.

"You are free to go Mr Mackenzie, good luck and I do not want to see you here again."

"Thank you, your Honor," I said, bowing slightly and mouthing a silent, "Praise God". I left the court to go to coffee with my friends and then to share the news with my pastors.

Driving home afterwards, I was ecstatic, and then it hit me... 180 hours of community service? I could have been digging holes in a field, scrubbing graffiti from walls or even removing trash at the local hospital, but here I was serving my sentence while serving my Lord! I pulled over to the side of the road and wept. How kind our God is.

A week later, I was testifying with the City Mission at a little upstairs Gospel church in Otley in West Yorkshire. I loved the deputation meetings, as we would share as a team all the amazing things the Lord was doing in Leeds. I usually shared some of my testimony before giving a report on the work. Usually I felt comfortable and at ease with this. I loved the Lord's work and to talk about what you love is never difficult. Usually.

Something was not quite right this evening as I stood next to Mick and Paddy singing a hymn, waiting to speak, My heart raced. The hymn book shook in my trembling hands.

As the music finished, an overwhelming sense of calm fell upon me and like English theologian John Wesley reported hundreds of years earlier, "I felt my heart strangely warmed". A still small voice spoke deep into my heart. I turned to Mick and grabbing his hand excitedly I said, "Brother! God has just called me into full time service to be a pastor."

I gave my report (not the best I had ever given) and sat down, staring at an open page in the hymn book. The words, "If he is calling, you must go" leapt out at me. I prayed "Lord, here I am in in the heart of England, if it is really you that's speaking to me, then show me my home in Scotland before I leave this hall tonight." It was a strange request and an impossible one. Satisfied that I had put these strange fanciful notions to rest, I tried to settle down and enjoy the rest of the reports but I was full of electricity; it felt like I was wired to the church's power supply! Eventually, a small friendly looking "elder" in his mid 50s gave the benediction, and tea and delicious scones were handed out. Mick placed a brotherly arm around my shoulder and I relaxed a little. But as I vacated the stairs of Otley Evangelical Church, I looked up at the wall and right in front was a large poster with a photograph of Edinburgh Castle. It read simply, "Visit Scotland".

When I saw Dr Bill Coppack two nights later, he looked at me and said, "What's up Charlie, you look worried."

"God has called me to be a pastor, and I'm not sure what to do next," I said.

"Well, you'll need to go to Bible college lad. Get in touch with the Faith Mission College in Scotland." He patted my back.

Now Mick (The Brick) had already been accepted into the Faith Mission College in Edinburgh and was leaving in a few months so I already knew a little about its standards, teaching, missionary focus and fire! The wife of the Principal, Ms Mary Peckham (née Morrison), came into a relationship with God during a revival in the north-west Scottish Hebridean islands that took place between 1949 and 1952.

One famous principal of the Faith Mission College, the Reverend Duncan Campbell was called by the Holy Spirit to lead the Lewis revival in the late '40s and '50. This was no liberal training school, it was a place where people met GOD! The Faith Mission was also a college that ran on faith. You prayed for everything you needed and God provided. It was soundly biblical and fervent in evangelistic training.
I approached Pastor Steve Thompson at Bridge Street the following Sunday and shared my heart. "Should I apply to the Elim Pentecostal

College, Pastor?" After all, I was a member of the Elim Church and it was courteous to apply there first. Pastor Steve thought about it for a few moments, and then said softly in his lovely Lancashire accent, "Knowing you as I do, I really think you would feel slightly claustrophobic there, Charlie. Why not consider the Faith Mission?" And so, I applied. A month later, Mr Joe McNeely, the Faith Mission District Superintendent for the North of England, visited me. At first glance, Joe seemed like a small slip of a man with thinning grey hair, in his dark blue suit with a Faith Mission necktie. He had a soft (but firm) Northern Irish accent. I would hear Joe preach in mission meetings in the years to come and as soon as he spoke, he no longer looked or sounded like the small man I met that day... he was a spiritual giant!

I shared my calling, my desire to lead souls to Christ, to study, to learn and to go wherever God wanted me, and Mr McNeely listened. He didn't ask much, just silently listened. Several weeks later I received a letter with the Faith Mission badge on the envelope. I went into my "prayer room" or to be more accurate, the half finished front room in my Harehills terraced house and heart racing, I carefully opened it. It read:

Dear Charles

After prayerful consideration, we have pleasure in accepting your application to undergo theological training at The Faith Mission Bible College in Edinburgh. However, we would like you to start your training next year. This will give you the opportunity to prove the call that you have received. We look forward to seeing you next year, and will be in touch in due course.

My heart rose with delight that I had been accepted but sank at the thought that I had another whole year to wait. But glory to God... I *was* accepted and right now, that was all that really mattered.

I busied myself between the outreach of the city mission and my commitment to being a member of Bridge Street Pentecostal Church. Pastor Steve enrolled me in an International Correspondence Institute course run by Elim College. I completed subjects on New Testament survey and Old Testament survey, which looked at the content, structure, historic setting and themes of the Bible. I did further subjects on the work of the Holy Spirit, and evangelism. As I was doing all of this, my 180 hours of community service came to a close. I took my card into the Leeds City Missions office for Bill to sign off on and cheekily asked for another 180! Church was teaching me so much, the fellowship was amazing and through the Mission's outreach ministry, I led people to Christ.

At a "social/spiritual" gathering at a friend's home, a group of us relative newbies to the Christian faith, decided to stand in a circle and sing praises and prayers to God.

We began the night singing a few favorite songs. After about 20 minutes of singing familiar Christian songs praising God, worship tunes that we regularly belted out at Bridge Street, we began to feel our spirits lift and be filled with overflowing joy.

After more time passed, Chris, the leader of the group, encouraged us to open our mouths and speak in a tongue that was not our own. Slowly, intermittently, like water coming through a tap for the first time, one by one, group members began to praise Jesus in a new language. It sounded strange but warm and deeply spiritual as the chorus widened and grew stronger until everyone was worshipping God in a new language. That is, everyone but me.

I was sincerely pleased for my friends, but as we hugged at the end of the night, I went home with a heavy despondent heart. "How come Lord?" I moaned. "How come everyone but me?" I returned home to my house in Roundhay Terrace, Harehills and went straight into my prayer room and sunk to my knees. I took a deep breath then prayed out loud… in a different language! My heart was hot. It was like I was breathing fire. I stayed there, praising God until I became too tired to pray any more and fell asleep. The burning within me grew stronger over the next few days until it was Saturday afternoon and the Leeds City Mission met to preach in Bond Street, the busiest street in Leeds. We were gathered around a small wooden portable platform, ready to step up and preach to the crowds of shoppers. Normally, we would take it in turns to stand and preach the gospel for a few minutes as the hecklers mocked and a few shoppers stood for a short while to rest their shopping bags and try and figure out what the noise was.

I was due to go on second. Paddy Flynn had just finished his six minute stint and smiled as he saw me moving up to preach. I raised my Bible, opened my mouth and preached with authority, fire and defiance to all who were mocking. It was different from any other time I had preached. God gave me a clear gospel message and I delivered it with loud, clear passion. I was told afterwards that at one point there were as many as 200 standing still, listening. I stepped down, face glowing. Itching to get straight back up again!

My pastor shared with me the next day that the Baptism of the Holy Ghost, was also a Holy "go". It wasn't just about praising in tongues, it was about the ability to love and reach out to others with power and passion. Not in my own strength but in the power of the Holy Spirit! Using the Bible he was holding, my pastor explained that the Holy Spirit enters us and dwells in us the moment we accept Jesus as our Lord and Saviour. But as we hand over areas of our life such as habits, ungodly relationships, things we say, read, watch and do that are not honouring to him, the Holy Spirit occupies the spaces that are surrendered to Him. He added that God wants to "baptise" us and fully saturate us with His Holy Spirit. When that happens for the first time, it was an unforgettable experience. "This is only the beginning, Charlie," he said. "When the Bible talks about being filled with the Holy Spirit it is not a one-off experience. There will be many other times of filling, refreshing and immersion in the Holy Spirit, as God wants to reign in every area of your life, every day."

I wanted more of this transformational power in my life. I felt on fire in my heart and almost invincible, but common sense is not always present within a young believer.

Not long afterwards, Chris suggested we all go to a graveyard at midnight on a Sunday near his home because he had heard that Satanists were using that particular part of Leeds to worship. A few of us turned up and prayed in the eerie-looking cemetery. If there were Satanists there, I would not have known as I was shivering with cold and fear! Walking around this ancient dark enclosure for 10 minutes felt like being there for a month!

A voice, whether audibly or in my head said, "Get out of there quickly!"

I turned, stepped off the cemetery step onto the road and a huge heavyweight transporter truck careered past me, missing me by an inch! I was nearly dead.

I learned a vital lesson. We are supernatural beings not super heroes. There would be many times in the future when I would be at the front line of spiritual warfare, but for now, I decided I would not go looking for evil. Especially at midnight in a graveyard!

On 3 July 1985, I left Leeds with two large suitcases and set off for my new life as a Faith Mission student or, a Pilgrim, as we were more popularly known as. I had given away my business months earlier, sold all my furniture and belongings to pay for my first year fees and buy a second hand blazer, as the uniform was compulsory at the college. A dear old widow and friend to the Leeds City Mission, Mrs Lawson, bought me a new gray suit to wear on Sundays. I was arriving with nothing but the call of God and childlike faith.

It didn't take me long to settle into college life. Because I had been a supervisor with the Leeds City Council, I had access to the housing department and through intercity cooperation, was able to secure a small apartment in the Saughton area of West Edinburgh, a few miles from the college at Gilmerton Dykes and a stone's throw from the prison. I bought a second hand bicycle with the little I had left. I only needed one meal in the evening as college lunches were included in the fees.

The first thing I learned was that I did not know much about the various subjects. Even after a year with Leeds City Mission as a street evangelist, I knew nothing about homiletics (the art of preparing sermons and preaching), the Second Coming or Messianic prophesies. But I *did* know the Bible. The International Correspondence Institute correspondence course I had taken in preparation for college had given me a "leg up". And although most of the students at college came from "good Christian stock", namely the farms of Ireland and the Highlands of Scotland, I was able to hold my own. I tried to work harder than everyone else during my first term to compensate for my age. (At 29 years old, I was ancient!) and my lack of a good Protestant nurturing. It paid off.

I looked at the exam results lying in front of me after my first term. I could hardly believe it... 82, 89, 85 per cent. My project work score was 98 per cent. I was among the top students in the college! Buoyed by this, I propelled myself to be the best that I could be for God, and if truth be known, to feel the satisfaction of seeing those exam marks again!

I always felt slightly hungry in Saughton. In fact, one wet weekend I opened the cupboard, and like the children's nursery rhyme, my cupboard was bare. As a good pilgrim, I decided to shut myself in the room and pray for food. "Dear Lord," I said, "You have brought me here and opened up this amazing door, but your servant is hungry and - "

"Bam, bam, bam!" went the front door.

"Kids," I thought to myself and carried on praying aloud. "Lord, I love you but -"

"Bam, bam, KICK!"

I prayed louder, trying to drown out the noise at the door but eventually I gave in. I stormed to the door at the end of my hallway, moaning, "This is so not right, here I am on my knees praying for food and those kids are just not letting me get through to you."

I pulled open the door and looked at the large smiling figure facing me. His name was Alistair, and he was another student at the Faith Mission.

"Hi, brother Charlie," Alistair said. "My freezer has broken and all this is starting to defrost and will go to waste." He nodded at the two plastic carrier bags he was holding.

God's timing had been perfect. Alistair had driven from the other end of the city to deliver the bags of steak, sausages and sliced beef! Just as I had begun praying!

Another time, I was almost down to my last cent when a huge parcel arrived from Leeds. God had instructed a family in Yorkshire from a Methodist Church who had heard me testify a year earlier and knew I had sold everything to get to college to put together a hamper and send it to me! Here I was down to my last coin, and eating top quality cheese, crackers, fine meat, caviar and chocolates!

It wasn't just my physical being God looked after. Bible college students get attacked spiritually as well. On one occasion I was feeling depressed and lonely. My spirit felt icy dark and even on the brink of suicide. Again, right at my lowest point, a package arrived. It was from a group of 17 young people whom I had shared my testimony with on an evening in West Yorkshire two years ago. I'd felt a very strong sense of God's presence at the youth meeting, held in the hall of a small upmarket Baptist church outside Leeds. At the end of my testimony, I felt moved to ask everyone to bow and pray. I prayerfully invited anyone who wanted to know Jesus personally to raise their hand and I would lead them in a prayer of repentance. After an uncomfortable silence of about three minutes, a hand was raised. And then another was raised, and another... until 16 teenagers indicated they wanted Jesus in their lives. And then with a slight hesitation, the young adult youth leader also raised his hand! I had the joy of leading the whole group to Christ before leaving them with instructions to pray daily, read the Bible and share *their* testimonies. Now two years later, they had all gotten together and made me cards, sharing their love for Christ and their love for me. I wept with joy at God's providence.

As you can imagine, my faith was strengthened by these God *incidences* and I began to show a boldness that I had never known before. I think it was James Hudson Taylor who once said, "Attempt great things *for* God and expect great things *from* God."

No wonder mouths dropped open and eyes popped at the next Faith Mission students prayer meeting when I prayed, "Lord, thank you for providing me with a bicycle, but the weather is cold here this time of year, so please can you give me a nice car?" The Head Boy took me to one side and had a "quiet word" about the sanctity of prayer and that we do not approach the Lord with a "shopping list", which I guess was fair, but I wasn't being irreverent or selfish. I was merely asking my father for something that would make life a little easier and warmer.

A week later, a letter arrived from a businessman in Bridge Street. He'd ordered a new car and instead of trading the old one in, he wanted to give it to a Bible college student. It was a Saab, solid as a rock, with gears on the steering wheel. I drove the four hours back to Edinburgh in raptures. There was no stopping what God could do; all I had to do was ask.

You would think that life at a "holiness" missionary training college would be dull and somber? Not a hope! We were studious in the lecture room, serious in the prayer room and silly in our free time. At college I learned the art of covering the toilet bowl with cling wrap! At meal times in the dining room, you were not allowed to make a sound unless you were offering a drink of water or passing the salt to another student. Which meant if you were dying of thirst, you had to wait to be offered the water jug. Or if the food tasted bland, you had to wait until someone next to you or across the table from you cared to "kindly" offer you the salt or pepper. Needless to say, that we all had legs that were covered in bruises, from the little hints we gave each other under the table.

The matron at the Faith Mission was a gem of a lady in her early 50s called Miss Anne Smith, nicknamed, "The Blade". She was called this because she was sharp and missed nothing. If you walked by her with your necktie crooked, a hand in your pocket or unpolished shoes, she was onto you immediately. She was one of the most saintly ladies I have ever met, but well nicknamed. When she was nervous about something, she'd rub her right ear while maintaining her otherwise unruffled composure. Apart from that you'd never know that she was stirred by anything. We decided to put "The Blade" to the test.

A group of us were going on an outreach evening at a church in Glasgow and we planned a prank. We hid a large stereo player and speakers in the bookcase just behind Miss Smith's chair and placed inside a tape recording of us singing the Edwin Hawkin Singers' version of *Oh Happy Day* and laughing and shouting in crazy voices. We set the timer on it for the exact time that she would lead the students in the evening prayer before dinner.

In the college minibus to Glasgow, we counted down the minutes until the big moment.

At the college, everyone gathered together for prayer, heads bowed reverently. Just as Miss Smith began praying, a long, slow, deep loud growl went off behind her sounding like a demonic voice from Hell. One of us had forgotten to swap the almost flat batteries in the tape player with new ones.

Meanwhile, some of the women screamed and the men looked at each, other shaken. Miss Smith rubbed her right ear, shrugged and continued praying. What a hero!

CHAPTER 12

As students of the Faith Mission we were all assigned to a church on Sundays, and kids' Bible clubs during the week to give us practical experience in children's evangelism.

I was assigned to help out at the Gorgie Mission Hall in the west end of Edinburgh. During a bout of rain on a Monday evening, I caught an old maroon and grey double decker bus to Gorgie Road. Holding my grey overcoat tight against the miserable east Scotland weather, I tried to stay dry as I walked, and turned the corner onto Wheatfield Terrace.

Gorgie Mission Hall was hidden behind a crescent of tenement buildings just off the depressingly nondescript Gorgie Road. It was a large tin frame rising starkly against a dull grey landscape, made from corrugated iron sheets and painted brown and cream, A warm orange light glowed from inside. It became brighter as I walked towards the doors.

Dripping wet from the rain, Anne, a wonderful teacher who led the "Monday club", warmly greeted me at the door. Anne welcomed me with a huge smile and introduced me to the team of volunteers. She was a small slim woman with a disarming smile and a likeable Edinburgh accent and every bit the schoolteacher. The place smelled of Calor Gas, due to the four large portable gas heaters situated in four corners of the large square rectangular hall. The children were all sitting on tubular metal chairs, the kind that you could stack high, and seemed to be loving every minute of just being there. Straight away Anne had me helping with everything from holding up the Bible verse cards to assisting with games and choruses. As I attended more regularly, I began to share the Bible message, lead the activity and play sessions, as well as praying with the children.

One Monday evening, two primary school girls from near where I lived decided to attend the children's Bible club. A school friend had invited them, and after the initial shyness, the sisters were chatty and happy to be there. Their names were Cindy and Candy McCarron.

On their second visit to the Monday Club they accepted Jesus as their Lord and Savior. I gave them both NIV Bibles and asked them to read a small verse or two every day.

Back at college we rejoiced over the girls' conversion and celebrated in praise and worship to God. On the girl's third visit to Gorgie, I asked if they had been reading their Bibles.

"Not really," Cindy said.

"Our dad is reading them instead," Candy added.

My heart sunk and also leapt a little. I decided to pray and then pay their dad a visit.

Jimmy McCarron was a hard man with steely eyes. He had big broad shoulders, a muscular build and hands like spades! (The local bar where Jimmy hung out is featured in the movie, *Trainspotting 2*.) His wife Sylvia and their four amazing daughters were unfazed by their tough dad, but knew when to tread lightly too. A retired plasterer by trade, Jimmy was a man you just didn't want to get on the wrong side of.

I knocked on the door to his council house on Saughton Mains Loan.

"Good evening, Mr McCarron," I said, offering a handshake as he warily opened the door.

"You must be Charlie," he said, ignoring my outstretched hand, "You better come in."

Jimmy got straight to the point.

"Now what's all this nonsense that you've been putting in my girls' heads? We're Catholics and that's it."

Jimmy gave me a summary of his Catholic upbringing and his views that all faiths were the same but that he and his family just happened to be of the Roman Catholic persuasion so why the need to, "Brainwash his children and to be saved?"

I loved Jimmy from the start as he was what I imagined St Peter would have been like –sincere, straight talking and no-nonsense. Jimmy agreed to allow me to visit him weekly and have a one-on-one Bible study. He was an intelligent man who had questions written down on paper ready to ask me when I visited. We would deal with his many questions first and then move on to studying the Bible.

And all the time, back at college, the staff and students were praying for Jimmy and Sylvia and their daughters before Jesus, pleading for their souls to be saved and nurtured.

Edinburgh was a hive of Christian activity in the 80s. There were always notable Christian speakers and leaders visiting and preaching at Carrubbers Close Mission (founded by American evangelist DL Moody) or Charlotte Baptist Chapel, or St Giles' Cathedral on the Royal Mile. We students were spoilt for choice.

One evening, I was on my way to hear the author Derek Prime speak at Charlotte Baptist Chapel on Rose Street. I'd read Prime's books at college and was thrilled he was visiting our city. Wearing my Faith Mission College uniform and tie, I headed for the bus stop.

But I never got to hear Derek Prime.

As I neared the bus stop, the Holy Spirit spoke clearly into my heart. "Go visit Jimmy, he's ready." I reasoned with God that hearing Mr Prime would be a far better act of service than going to see Jimmy, as I could see Jimmy any time. But the voice became a burden, then a compulsion.

"Charlie?" Jimmy said, smiling as he opened the door. "Come on in. Sylvia, put the kettle on, Tracy, turn off the TV, Charlie's here."

I enjoyed my tea and the banter between Jimmy, Sylvia and the girls. Their jokes and carefree teasing always made me smile. I felt part of

95

their friendship circle now and was always relaxed in their company. Tracy said something to her dad and Jimmy replied with a funny remark and said to me, "But it's ok for us Christians, eh, Charlie?"

The words hung in the air. *"It's ok for us Christians"*, but Jimmy wasn't a Christian. He was religious, loving and hospitable with a heart of gold, but he *wasn't* a Christian. The Holy Spirit settled into the room almost visibly, like a silent wind, and I stopped smiling.

"You're not a Christian, Jimmy," I said, with all the love that God was pouring into me.

Jimmy looked deep into my face and said pleadingly and firmly, "But I want to be."

What happened next was all due to God. I invited Jimmy to get on his knees and asked his wife and daughters to leave the room. Filled with the presence of the Holy Spirit, the room was now a holy place and things bearing eternal significance were about to happen there.

Jimmy confessed his sin before Jesus and heaved big sobs of regret and repentance. And as he did, the peace of God that surpasses all understanding flooded through him.

After some time kneeling, we sat up and I pointed him to Bible scriptures that assured him he was indeed a Christian now. I called out for the girls to join us and I slipped away into the night. As I looked through Jimmy's living room window from outside, I saw Jimmy, his daughters and his wife hugging and crying together. They had a Christian father and husband. Things would never ever be the same in this family.

With Jimmy, Candy, and Cindy all saved, it wasn't very long before Tracy also gave her life to Christ. One evening Jimmy phoned me and said in his own unmistakable way, "Charlie, Sylvia's ready, can ye come round and save her?"

I sat with Jimmy and Sylvia explaining it wasn't me that saved but

Jesus; He was the author of salvation, I was merely an instrument and He could use any other instrument if He wished to. The important thing was we recognized that Jesus took the punishment for our sin and died in our place, and we could repent of our wrongdoing and invite Him into our lives. Jimmy sat politely and then looking at his watch said, "Ok, can you hurry up and save her now, we've got visitors coming." Sylvia was led in a simple prayer of faith and accepted the Lord."

Back at college, our prayer meetings pulsed with excitement, as there were now five McCarrons who were saved and so we all prayed fervently for their eldest daughter Donna. She was the tough one of the family, into the local gang scene, streetwise and highly intelligent. We prayed daily for weeks but still there was no news from the McCarron household. Our prayers took on increasing intensity. "Lord of heaven and Earth, nothing is too difficult for you. You saved Candy, and Cindy, and Tracy and Jimmy and Sylvia. You can save Donna too!!" Still, I heard no word that anything had changed.

Unexpectedly, on one of my frequent visit to this endearing family, while we all sat chatting and laughing and talking openly about the Lord, Donna walked into the living room combing her long brown hair. Jimmy looked up and blurted out, "Donna, when are you going to get saved? They've been praying for you at the Bible college for weeks!" Donna stopped combing her hair and said matter-of-factly, "Didn't I tell you? I got saved weeks ago one Sunday up in my room." She resumed combing her hair and walked through to the kitchen.

Jimmy's brother soon got saved, and his sister, and brother in law, and *their* children… I had the joy of leading Jimmy's mother to the Lord on her bed, moments before she died. Donna became a student at the Faith Mission Bible College and Jimmy and Sylvia began running a drop-in café at Wester Hailes Baptist Church.

As I write this today from my apartment in Hanoi 30 years later, Tracy, Donna and Candy are all married to Christian men and have lovely children. Cindy runs a Christian helpline for gay people that need God's love and healing. (I preached at Donna's wedding and was there at

Tracy's as well). Donna is a pastor in Edinburgh and all three other girls are active in their churches in England. We remain in touch.

Every year our college participated in the Bangor Bible Week in Northern Ireland, where the whole town became one huge Christian convention with meetings, rallies and Christian gatherings in church halls all over this small but attractive sleepy little seaside town.

On one occasion, Faith Mission missionaries, students and supporters from all over the world gathered in a church hall for dinner. After the dinner was finished, it was customary for people to stand up and give a testimony about what God had been doing in their lives. Beginning at one table, a guest would stand up and share a chorus of "Amens" and "Hallelujahs" before the focus moved to the next table. I invited Jimmy over to Bangor for the weekend and prayed he'd testify. When it was our table's turn, our circle couldn't help but look at Jimmy as he was the only one present who had recently been saved.

The audience's eyes swept to the man who was the focus of our group's attention. Word of his family's conversion had swept through the Faith Mission network, and everyone was eager to hear his story. He sat still as a rock, all eyes on him. A few moments of nervous silence passed as we waited for someone at our table to stand up. Eventually, Jimmy pushed his chair back, stood up and pointed to the back of the hall. "I'm going to the toilet," he said loudly. The place erupted in laughter. God has indeed a sense of humor.

Donna in her first year at the Faith Mission Bible College.

Donna today, as a pastor with the Church of the Nazarene, Edinburgh.

CHAPTER 13

In my last year as a Faith Mission student, I was called by God to be assistant pastor of the Edinburgh City Mission's Niddrie Mission Hall (now the Niddrie Community Church). I would serve directly under the former director of Edinburgh City Mission, Pastor Alec Dunbar, who was an institution in Edinburgh. He was already "retired" when I started at Niddrie but soon became a father, teacher and pastor to me in more ways than this book can ever do justice.

Niddrie was a sprawling council housing estate on the east side of Edinburgh, nestled under the shadow of the majestic Holyrood Park. As a child I used to visit Niddrie with my mother, catching the train to Waverley Railway Station. We'd board a big noisy double decker bus to the terminus at Niddrie Mains Drive. My aunt Elizabeth (Betty) and my three cousins lived in that street on the top floor of a Wauchope Road tenement which looked onto a mostly deserted road that children played in. Coming from a tiny flat in Carron Road Falkirk that faced a busy, dangerous road, Niddrie was like an adventure playground. I had cousins who would stick up for me, and I could run about the streets, climb up onto church roofs and play on swing parks with total strangers. It was a different world altogether.

The Niddrie that I experienced nearly 20 years later as a pastor was, however, a different place altogether. It was now one of the drug and crime centers of Edinburgh, with some of the highest rates of muggings, theft and illicit drug use in Scotland.

Many shops that I used to frequent as a child of nine or 10 to spend pocket money in were now boarded up. Burnt out cars were scattered around the deserted streets and packs of wild dogs prowled the grounds. Many buildings had the windows boarded up, others were charred black with fire or had been pronounced condemned following years of disrepair. Heroin and other narcotics were being sold on street corners everywhere. Children became addicted to alcohol and heroin as young as 10 and were lured by ruthless pimps into a life of crime to help pay for their next fix. HIV and AIDS had hit the UK hard and Edinburgh, in particular Niddrie, was now the AIDS capital of Europe.

Decisions made decades earlier had led to Niddrie gradual decline. Some city councilors in the late '50s decided that to keep Edinburgh's reputation as the "picturesque capital of Scotland" it would be best to sweep all the dirt under the carpet. So they rounded up all the addicts, alcoholics, criminals and thugs and rehoused most of them in Niddrie.

But I'd been called here. This is where Jesus had drawn me to reach into the hearts of others for Him. And this is where I would again see God move in miracle saving power!

I decided to ask a "big" thing from God on my first day at Niddrie. "Lord," I prayed, "Please take hold of the biggest, most wretched alcoholic in this place and save him."

It didn't take me long to realize the person I was praying for was actually a woman! In her late 20s, Isobel Peacock lived on the top flat in the building next to Niddrie Mission with her young son Martyn. I heard Isobel before I saw her. Her crude language frequently spewed from her window onto the streets below. Often the believers who were on their way to the Sunday evening service would be the target of Izzy's abuse, other times it was her boyfriend, or no one in particular. Isobel was a dear soul in need of kindness and love. And after softening her initial suspicion towards "Bible people", I was allowed into visit her.

Her untidy apartment was filled with empty beer bottles scattered everywhere. Stale smoke wafted from the overflowing ashtrays and piles of crumpled clothes hung over chairs. She would often be covered in bruises and cuts from a previous fight with another alcoholic whom she had naively allowed into her apartment. Or her injuries were from yet another beating she'd taken from a boyfriend. But whenever I visited her she would listen to the gospel message of how Jesus came to seek and to save someone such as she. Beneath her scars and puffy face, ravaged by alcoholism, there was a beautiful young lady. I could see it, God could see it, but Isobel couldn't. She insisted Martyn attend our youth club and Sunday services and he became a regular at everything at the "Mission".

I volunteered at our furniture distribution depot, which was frequented by bargain hunters and our eccentric regulars. The Niddrie Mission collected furniture from wealthy Edinburgh residents who had lost a loved one or Christians who had bought new goods but then decided to downsize, and sold them on to the people of Niddrie for peanuts. We could have just given them away freely but consumer psychology informed us that charging a small amount would result in the furniture being more valued and treated better.

Another memorable character at Niddrie was "Big Alan", a six-foot-four customer whom I met at our furniture distribution depot. Big Alan would up push his glasses up the bridge of his nose while squinting. He also would rub his giant hands together and crack his knuckles. On the day I first met Alan, he was arguing with a new volunteer who was charging him a tad too much for a wardrobe that he wanted. Smiling, I interrupted him, shook his hand and halved the price. He never forgot this. I visited Alan at his home in a nearby village and was surprised that although he was clearly an alcoholic, his small terraced village home was clean, well decorated and tidy. However, Alan was going through a heartrending marriage break up. Although I met both parties, it was hard to bring trust back into the relationship when unfaithfulness had stolen what was once precious.

I began approaching schools to volunteer my services as a chaplain and offer to lead their weekly assemblies. The overworked teachers and principals seemed eager to allow a new face into their schools to give them a break once a week. I taught Bible stories and led the weekly assemblies at four local schools, with many of the children coming along to the Mission's youth clubs and Sunday schools as a result.

In 1980s Scotland (and probably still today to some extent), Catholics and Protestants did not have a lot to do with each other. Sticking to "your own kind" was permanently driven into you as a child. But one afternoon I was driving past St Francis Catholic Primary School and a prayer about being a witness for Jesus weighed upon me. The Holy Spirit convicted me there and then. "Go ask," was what He laid upon my heart. Again, like the case with Jimmy McCarron the previous year, I tried to wriggle out of the situation. But the voice was clear. "GO ASK." So, a little apprehensive, I walked into the school and asked to see the Headmaster. Instead a feisty petite lady in her 50s came out to ask who I was and what I wanted from her school. Margaret had small, piercing eyes, crazy, wild hair and bony hands and arms. Wearing a long dress and brown leather shoes, she stood with an air of authority and a posture that made it clear that she was in command of the school.

Bracing myself, I explained I was from the Niddrie Mission, which was non-denominational, and that God loved everyone including St Francis students. I was offering to teach some Bible stories on flannelgraph and take whole school assemblies, and the students were also welcome at our youth club and Sunday School if that was ok with the principal?

I waited breathlessly and nervously for the barrage of abuse to come. Margaret stood, hands on hips, looking me up and down before saying in a loud (slightly Irish) voice.

"Those Protestants get all the fun, no one ever remembers us here at St Francis, wait here Father, I'll go get the principal now."

The Principal came downstairs and sat down and all he wanted to know, was it free and how often a week could I come in?

I happily agreed to take three religious education classes a week, looking at Bible characters. I would lead their mid-week assembly every week too.

"Go ask," God said. It was as simple as that. The religious education lessons at St Francis became a highlight of the week. The students were being taught from scripture that faith in Jesus alone was the only way to salvation. On more than one occasion I led several students at a time in the Sinner's Prayer right there in their classroom. *"Go ask."* This was to be my motto in every church I pastored.

Peffermill Primary was where I saw the biggest growth and also the craziest things. I put together a football team there and we conquered the world! Maybe not quite. For starters, people were either too afraid to play us, or too afraid to visit Niddrie. Our captain was a highly talented 11-year-old girl called Gillian. She'd often whisper to the captain of the opposing team before kick off, "Tackle me even once and that big guy watching the game over there will blow your head off with his shotgun!" Gillian and two others had a nasty habit of identifying the opposition's top players and kidnapping one or two of them and locking them in the school toilets until half-time. Perhaps on accident, one school in Falkirk invited us over to play in a Special Cup invitation match. I think they may have got us mixed up with one of the city's establishment teams. But of course our team was up for it!

Returning to Falkirk was uncomfortable. The school that we were playing was Falkirk's championship team. We, on the other hand, were not even in a proper league. After a noisy one-hour journey, we arrived, pumped up for the match, which was a strictly under-11s game. Fourteen-year-old Billy Liddell had asked to come with us and I agreed. Billy was on vacation from a *"Special"* school; in other words he was there because of acute behavioral problems and reading difficulties. Billy was wiry, but boy, could he play football! I agreed he could be our mascot and be the 12th man (another name for a team's fan) cheering us on. He happily agreed, not fully knowing what a 12th man actually was.

It was evident from the start we were going to be the target of abuse. Scores of parents had gathered to watch the game, aggressively brandishing homemade banners and waving their school scarves and flags. To inflame the situation, we ran onto the pitch wearing the green and white kit of Hibernian Football Club, an East Edinburgh football club with strong Irish Catholic roots. The home crowd booed and shouted racist remarks as our students took to the field, a little bewildered by it all (as they usually were the abusers!)

Even the referee (the local sports teacher) was unashamedly biased, giving free kicks in abundance to the home team, whose supporters reminded me of spectators at a gladiatorial arena.

By half-time, the score was two-nil to the home side. We'd been forced to use our only two substitutes due to apparent "bruising tackles", misconduct that the referee had flagged against our players while he *wasn't looking*. Fifteen minutes into the second half, the score was three-nil. Unused to defeat in such hostile surroundings, our young, undisciplined players began to blame each other, much to the enjoyment of the home crowd.

When eight-year-old Sean Casey was elbowed in the face and carried off with a busted nose, crying, I was on the verge of calling the game off. And then I was handed a gift - the referee came to the sidelines and pointed to Billy Liddell.

"If that's your last sub, you better get him on now, not that he will do much good."

Billy looked at me and began to protest. "But, I am nearly four -"

"You heard the nice man," I said, placing a hand over Billy's mouth. "Get your kit on and go play out the last 30 minutes, and Billy, we only need four."

Billy ambled on awkwardly wearing shorts that were too tight and one sock pulled down at his ankles. The parents and home supporters singled him out for special attention, calling him "beanpole" and words best forgotten.

Billy's reply came in the 80th minute. Gillian expertly kicked a perfect cross in from the right. Running at full speed, Billy dived head on and headed the ball high into the net. Running up to where the majority of home fans stood in silence, he started dancing and shouting, "That's just the start." And indeed it was.

He rammed through the home defense like a hot knife slicing through butter. Knocking down Sean Casey's older brother, he launched forward and buried the ball low in the bottom left corner of the net. This time, when he ran towards the home crowd, the rest of our team ran with him. Our opponents were noticeably rattled by his skills and confidence. When their center-half kicked Billy's legs as he pounced to stop a goal, the referee reluctantly awarded a penalty kick. Billy raced towards the ball and kicked it clinically, placing it beyond the keeper's reach in the top left corner. Our scores were now even.

The home supporters were still roaring, but now they were roaring for the final whistle to be blown! Yet we still had five minutes left to play. To their credit, the Falkirk team brought back all the attackers on the frontline to form a formidable barrier with the defenders. Our opponents had seized possession of the ball and were leisurely passing it amongst themselves. Every time one of our team members tried to win the ball, our bigger and taller opponents simply passed it on. The Niddrie kids were starting to swear in frustration.

The referee kept looking at his watch and was about to blow the whistle when one of the Falkirk kids mistimed his kick. Billy seized his chance. He pounced, retrieving the ball and danced a zigzag through the defence. Not expecting this breakthrough, the goalkeeper was caught out of position. Billy stopped for a moment, turned around, blew a kiss at the defending mob, who were sprinting towards him and effortlessly kicked the ball over the stranded goalkeeper's head and into the net. He ran shouting for joy towards the home end and then stopped dead and turned his back to them. The rest of our 10 team members did the same, before diving on top of me in delight.

Suddenly the referee stopped looking at his watch and even began cheering the home side on! I called him over and had a quiet word.

"The longer you keep this going, the more Billy is going to score," I said, shrugging my shoulders.

He glared at me, cursed and blew his whistle.

The Falkirk players were stunned.

"How could *these* people beat us?" a tall thin player shouted to his teacher.

But our Peffermill team was far too jubilant to care. Billy ran around the pitch blowing kisses to the home crowd. It didn't even bother them when the local newspaper, "The Falkirk Herald", refused to photograph them holding the trophy we had just won.

"Falkirk news for Falkirk folk," the photographer said coldly.

(I felt for my kids, this was the first trophy they had ever won and they were being denied even a tiny photo in a small town paper.)

As we packed up and boarded our bus back to Edinburgh, the home coach came over and said loudly so the whole bus could hear, "That goal scorer of yours is not behaved, he's not tolerant and he's got no respect for adults."

I leaned over to the coach, patted him on his shoulder and whispered in his ear, "He's not under 11 years old either."

CHAPTER 14

Door-to-door evangelism in Niddrie was not for the faint-hearted, although the "Soup Run" in Leeds had served as good preparation.

But whenever one entered a tenement building in Niddrie, anything could be inside. Sometimes it was addicts shooting heroin or sniffing glue bags, sometimes it was drunks sleeping on the stairways or even couples having sex. Dogs ruled Niddrie so it was always a good idea to carry a Bible and a piece of meat just in case a hungry rabid hound came lunging at you. On one occasion my Christian friend, Brian McBain, was walking slowly past a garden where a huge dog was growling at him in a low, "I'm going to eat you" tone. I could see Brian was terrified so I decided to help. Instead, I tiptoed behind him, grabbed the back of his thin right thigh and barked loudly! He took off like a greyhound and climbed over the green wire mesh fence. The dog noisily sped after him, leaping over the fence.

Drinking bars were by far the scariest places to evangelize in Niddrie, especially at night. The most ominous was the dimly lit Castle Tavern on Craigmillar Road. Brawl-itchy Patrons eyed newcomers with narrow eyes; a sense of violence hung in the air.

Now, I had drunk, fought, and been thrown out of some of the worst bars in Scotland and England. I could face the toughest thug in any bar and not back down. But the Holy Spirit lived in me now. I was more spiritually aware and sensitive to things that didn't glorify God. I acutely felt any traces of spiritual darkness and oppressive spirits. I had realized back in Leeds that whenever a person gives their life to Jesus, that person steps into the light, and the devil and his cohorts will perpetually be your adversary. So whenever I ventured into his territory, the devil made it clear he would oppose the Gospel message being shared.

One evening I wandered in wearing a brown jacket, jeans and my minister's clerical collar so I would not be seen as a threat. The barman glanced at me and warned, "Leave your leaflets on the bar pastor, there's a bad crowd in tonight."

Foolhardy or fearless (probably the former), I walked around and handed out the leaflets personally. The barman was right about the crowd being a bad one. Whether they had just been released from prison or had returned from an unfavorable court hearing, the atmosphere was tangibly evil. Many patrons took a gospel flyer and ripped it up or set it on fire. Feeling uncomfortable but not quite rattled by this, I noticed a middle-aged man in a secluded dark corner round the side of the bar. I joined him and introduced myself.

"Hi, I'm Pastor Charlie from Niddrie Mission, may I join you?"

He grunted, not even looking up. I pulled up a stool and began to explain why I was there. Suddenly, from the shadows, two scruffy looking men in their 20s, began to take an interest. They whispered to each other and nodded in my direction. One of them spoke.

"On your own, are you pal?"

I smiled but ignored the question. The other spoke. "Nice jacket that you're wearing, and Clarks shoes are they? You must be worth a few pounds."

I began to pray. "Lord, please rescue me from my foolishness, please send an angel to protect me in Jesus' name."

The men were now sitting opposite me within a breath's distance and leaning over. I prayed again, "Lord, I could really do with that angel. Right this very minute would be good please."

"Hi pastor, these little boys bothering you?"

I looked up to see the welcoming face of Big Alan (whom I'd befriended in the furniture depot) smiling at me and cracking his giant knuckles. The two men seemed to know him and moved away instantly to let him through.

"Actually, I was just about to leave," I said, standing up from my seat to shake Alan's hand and whispering a "Thank you" to him.

"Eh, I'll stay here for a bit, if it's ok with you pastor, I just want a *quick word* with your two friends here," Alan said. Glaring at the two slightly nervous men, he sat down, taking my place at the bar.

"Be my guest, Alan," I said, as I walked briskly out of the castle tavern, praising God and smiling at His choice of an "Angel".

As I walked past the lounge window I could still smell the stale aroma of pale ale. I also heard the sound of a large hand connecting with two human cheekbones and concluded that this was Alan's way of having a "quiet word".

Even outside of some of the rougher pubs, I could still feel the gloom and hopelessness in this slum-filled area. On an overcast, wet November day, I was in my vestry preparing the message for the coming Sunday evening and listening to the rain hammer the low roof. In amongst the hammering sound, there emerged another distinct rhythm – an abrupt thudding. At first, I ignored it as sometimes children threw rocks onto the roof for fun, or adults would lob a beer bottle or two if they saw my light on. But no, this was a loud knock, the kind the police gave when they were on "urgent" business. The fire exit door was actually "in" my vestry several yards away from the main entrance to the hall. As it was Niddrie, we were trained not to open the door if we were alone as it could be a robbery.

I thought about opening the fire exit and tiptoeing around to have a peek at the front entrance, stroking the smooth dark brown baseball bat that always lay no more than a few inches from me when I studied alone, I almost did my "Jackie Chan" impersonation.

However, I stood up, walked to the front door instead, put an ear to it and listened. Through the noise of the rain outside I heard crying, adult crying. I undid the lock and opened up the heavy door and leaning against the doorframe crying, with mascara running down her swollen wet cheeks, there was Izzy.

"Isobel!" I said softly, "What's happened?"

I gently pulled her in from the rain and led her inside, sitting her down at the desk next to me.

"I need Jesus," Izzy said.

"I don't want this life anymore, I want to be saved, I want to be beautiful again."

I listened to her story of abuse, rejection and addiction. The tears ran down my own face as she poured out her dear heart. Silently, we knelt together in that tiny room, so similar to the one where Paddy had once led me in a prayer asking for forgiveness, and I led Izzy in the Sinner's Prayer. When Izzy opened her eyes, the change in her was remarkable. Izzy's face was still red with the cold, but was now glowing with the peace of God. Her back seemed straighter when she stood up. God looked down on this broken life and lifted her out of her mess. He clothed her in the beauty of grace and forgiveness. She went home clutching a Bible. Her son Martyn had already accepted Jesus at one of our clubs months earlier.

Word spread round Niddrie like free drink at the Castle Tavern. "Izzy Peacock? Saved? No way."

"Ah, she's in it for the drink."

"See what happens on Sunday, she'll be too drunk to walk."

The comments were cruel and unrelenting and yet the whole of Niddrie waited with anticipation to see what would happen on Sunday.

And then it was upon us. I sat on the platform looking at the clock. It was a minute to 6pm and still no Izzy. I tried to delay starting the service for a few more minutes but eventually had to rise and welcome the congregation. At 6:07, I heard some excited chatter coming from the back of the hall, and then the door opened and

Isobel Peacock entered, walking arm in arm with her son Martyn. She had bought herself a new green coat and had spent time putting on her makeup. She looked like a movie star walking down the red carpet at the Oscar awards in Hollywood. Her face had lost the stress and hard look of a drinker and instead had the grace of a saint. It felt as though royalty had graced us. As she walked up the aisle tears flowed from the eyes of congregation members who had been praying for her. I could barely speak and wanted to step down and hug her. God had heard that prayer, He had listened to my pleading to take hold of the biggest alcoholic in Niddrie and save her. More than that, he had heard the cries of a wretched young lady who desperately needed His love in her life… and he answered!

Isobel quickly became an active member of Niddrie Mission helping in the "Outreach Cafe" and at our youth clubs, and was there every day the doors were open. She confounded the skeptics and the mockers alike. She was a breath of heaven to Niddrie and indeed the whole of East Edinburgh.

CHAPTER 15

The balmy summer weather at the Mission always heralded the annual Children's Camp in the harbor town of Arbroath, on the north east of Scotland. I anticipated feasting on the town's culinary specialty, the "Arbroath Smokie" - smoked haddock made by dry salting filleted fish and curing it inside barrels with a hardwood fire burning inside. (You could prepare mackerel using similar techniques, but it wasn't an authentic Arbroath Smokie). At one time a bustling fishing port, Arbroath had become a haven for holidaymakers from the larger towns and cities and retirees who had settled for a low cost, quiet existence in a pleasant little town. Well, "quiet" until the annual arrival of children from Niddrie!

Edinburgh City Mission was given free use of a well-equipped youth hostel in the center of Arbroath. Along with four adult volunteers, I led the campers on what for them was an adventure, and for me was a test of physical, mental and emotional endurance!

The "fun" began as soon as we arrived on Monday at three in the afternoon.

"I'm bored" shouted one 10 year old.

"I want to go home!" another said.

And so began the quest to entertain a group of 20 children who had rarely been more than five feet away from a TV screen or a PlayStation!

The first game we played was, "Find the Pastor". I would dress up in disguise and hide in the town. The children would then be released from the hostel and if they found me, all they needed to say was "Jesus loves you" and they would be rewarded with a chocolate bar. Simple? If only!

In previous years, Pastor Alec got dressed up in a traffic warden's uniform and went around putting stickers on cars. It worked a treat and no one recognized him, but then police arrested him. There are NO traffic wardens in Arbroath and police thought he was trying to steal cars!

Another year, the children were told that it would be two of the female volunteers who would be "hiding". Standing in plain sight, both volunteers dressed in white overalls and stood at the front of a grocers' shop, backs to the road, writing the words "special offers" on the display window. Our kids rushed past them and instead, found two elderly nuns in the park, badgering them to parting with chocolate bars they never had!

The year that I took them there, I had arranged with the Arbroath town council to provide me with a set of orange overalls, a trash cart and a sweeping brush. For twenty minutes I walked up and down High Street picking up garbage and putting it in the cart. All was going well until a drunk man with a Glaswegian accent stopped me.

"Ho, hey pal, gonnae tell me where the train station is, eh?"

"I don't know," I whispered loudly, keeping my woolen hat over my head. The drunk looked confused and then bent over and leaned forward until his face was inches from mine.

"How can you not know where the train station is? You're a *******
street cleaner!"

"Go… away," I said, walking away from him.

He grabbed me by the arm, but slipped on trash that I had forgotten to sweep up, lost his grip and fell. Not bothering to get up, he lay there, looking up at the sky and shouting, "Hey, everyone, this guy's a fraud, he doesn't even know where the train station is!"

"Ok, ok, you win," I said, bundling him into the trash cart and wheeling him half a mile to Arbroath Railway Station. Where I gave him five pounds and wished him a safe journey. Closing his fist around the cash, he clumsily stepped out of his "wagon", staggered, stopped and stared at the five pound note as I wheeled my cart back into town. As soon as I returned to the city center, one of the taller children a thin clumsy looking 13-year-old by the name of John McArthur recognized me.

"Eh, 20 chocolate bars, please Pastor C and Jesus loves you by the way."

"How did you know it was me John?" I moaned, handing over the chocolate bar prizes.

Eleven-year-old Gillian chirped, "Your socks, you dope... only you would wear bright blue Chelsea FC socks with an orange overall. Fashion police not arrest you?"

We all laughed and we headed back to base for dinner, a movie and an early night.

The next day, we decided to tire them out. Our ploy involved the legendary Rab Ferry, a young athletic Niddrie guy whom I had pointed to Christ after meeting him on the road one day outside the mission hall (who incidentally got married to a Sunday school teacher at my next church and went on to train as a Church of Scotland minister).

Rab wore a loosely fitting shirt with more than 50 foil wrapped sweets, candy bars and chocolates painstakingly sewn to it by ladies from the Mission. The idea was that we'd all go to the park, Rab would hide behind a bush and when he saw the kids he would run in the opposite direction. If any of them happened to get close enough, they could reach out and pull off a treat or two. What a perfect way to spend two hours and tire out our hyperactive campers, right? Wrong!

What I naively forgot was that Niddrie children are the sharpest, most cunning, resourceful kids in the land. They had to be, to survive in the jungle they called home. So, upon seeing Rab take off at speed, they huddled together in a circle and chatted, nodding in agreement with one another. Rab was shouting from a safe distance, "Come on, chase me." I should have known that they were hatching a plan, but how wonderful is hindsight.

Eighteen Niddrie kids set off a full speed (two others had slipped away unnoticed), forcing Rab to increase his pace. They chased him the length of the park, always keeping a distance of about three yards between him and themselves. When Rab slowed, they slowed and so the game of cat and mouse continued. Having come to the end of the park, Rab had no option but to do a large loop back to where he started. This took him along a narrow path that passed between two large rose bushes. As soon as he reached the bush-lined path, he tripped over a large wooden branch that poked through the hedges without warning. Clutching his shins, Rab writhed on the ground while the two branch-wielding Casey brothers ripped off his shirt and distributed its candy to their 18 accomplices!

The evening was a manic mix of children shouting the refrain, "I'm bored," and the older ones playing cards under their bunks. I was beginning to feel demented!

In the morning, after a food fight in the kitchen, one of the volunteers suggested that we take the kids to Edinburgh Zoo for the day.

"It will take at least an hour to drive them there and another hour back, and the whole day will be gone," he said, feeling pleased with his contribution.

"A zoo?!" I said. "A real zoo, with animals and small children? You out of your mind?!"

"You got any better ideas?" the others said.

The reality was that I actually didn't.

The trip down to Edinburgh the following morning was the usual pandemonium of the children making faces out of the window and throwing rolled up paper and snack wrappers at passing motorists.

Eventually after what seemed like a month, we arrived at Edinburgh Zoological Gardens in the fashionable west end of the city. After paying for the tickets, I called the kids together and read them the Riot Act!

"Right, you have exactly one hour. No fighting, stealing, rioting, injuring small animals or climbing into the enclosures for a closer look. These animals are wild," I said.

"So are we," seven-year-old Barry Telford said, laughing.

"Point taken, Barry," I said. "But these animals are slightly larger than you, ok?"

They grunted in agreement. "Ok, I want you all back here in an hour. Now off you go."

And with that, they were gone. I breathed a long sigh of partial relief and headed for the tea room accompanied by my three helper friends. Just an hours' respite was enough to charge my batteries for the remainder of camp. "Luxury", I thought to myself.

Punctuality appeared to be a foreign concept to Niddrie children. They'd often arrive late for football matches, wander into Sunday school halfway through or turn up an hour late for church trips. So imagine my shock as I went to the zoo car park at the allotted meeting time, to find all of my kids sitting in the bus ready to go back to Arbroath! Skeptically, I thought they had been barred, but no, the security told me there had been no incidents that afternoon. I thought perhaps they were sick, but all seemed happy? So I slowly climbed on board, took my place behind the steering wheel and began to drive back.

The journey back was strangely quiet. No foul language, no rude signs to motorists and nothing flying out of windows... not one thing! Big Rab (Not to be confused with Rab Ferry, the candy laden runner who had been the victim of the children's efficient scheming) smiled and said, "Told you the zoo would do the trick Pastor C."

117

I was not fully convinced, but had to admit that the peace I was enjoying at that moment in time was heavenly.

The children disembarked orderly, talking to one another, instead of their normal screaming. "You all enjoy the zoo?" I asked as they trotted into the hostel's kitchen. Tommy Galston asked, "Can we all go up to our dormitory Pastor, we are all quite tired."

I looked at the "told you so" look on the nodding faces of my colleagues and replied, "Sure, on you go, and take your time."

Someone suggested we take a tea break and I agreed eagerly. We all reclined on the torn but comfortable sofas in the kitchen area and relaxed, steaming cups of black tea in hand. After 20 minutes, I thought I heard loud thunder… inside the building! I awoke from my half slumber and realized the noise was coming from the ceiling above me!

I ran up the stairs and burst into the boys' dormitory and there was the whole gathering of them. They were standing in a circle, clapping hands, shouting and stamping their feet on the floor and there, right in the center of the floor was a PENGUIN!

After the initial ice-cold panic lifted, I demanded, "How did it get here?"

"Em, flew here from the zoo," Jimbo said, his innocent tone devoid of sarcasm.

"Yeah, it followed the bus," Harry Blakeny added, nodding earnestly.

"Really?" I said. "Funny that, because Penguins CAN'T FLY!"

"Ok," John McArthur owned up, looking round for the group's consent to tell the truth. "We stole it from the penguin parade when the older of the two keepers was looking the other way".

"But how did you keep it quiet on the bus?" I asked, intrigued and feeling totally defeated.

No answer was forth coming at this point so I chased everyone out of the room until I was left standing alone with a large, angry-looking King Penguin. He seemed indignant and dangerously low on patience, glaring at me with regal disdain. Like most of the King Penguins at Edinburgh Zoo, this one had probably been born into captivity at the zoo. I looked into its cold eyes, before running downstairs as well!

"Hello, is that Edinburgh Zoo? This is Pastor Charlie Mackenzie from Niddrie. I was here today with a group of 20 children from our annual holiday camp and. - yes, we enjoyed the Zoo, but someone - yes, yes, I would recommend the zoo to all my friends, but you need to understand that - on a scale of one to 10? Probably a nine. LOOK! WE HAVE ONE OF YOUR PENGUINS HERE!" I shouted. "Hello? Hello?"

But the zoo had hung up, obviously thinking it was a crank call. After all, who would steal a penguin…? Who indeed!

I had a similar response from the police and also the animal shelter. Eventually I got through to a branch of the RSPCA in Dundee. "A large penguin you say, sir? Can you tell me its species?"

"Eh, hold on Einstein, and I'll go and ask it!" I said. "Look, can you just send someone to pick it up before it hurts itself..?" I pleaded, "… Or me," I added under my breath.

Within 30 minutes a navy blue transit van arrived at the hostel. And two uniformed officers carrying a cage big enough to trap a lion, stepped out and marched towards me.

Slightly short and thin, Officer Harry Bennett and Officer Ray Carmichael, the younger, taller half of the duo, barely acknowledged me as they entered the building.

"Where is the beast?" Officer Carmichael enquired, his imposing figure like a tightly wound coil ready to spring into action.

"There will be charges brought against you if it's hurt in any way," Officer Bennett added, as I led them upstairs and into the dormitory. I had locked the kids in the TV room and put on a movie, *Street Fighter 2*, I think. "Totally appropriate for the audience", I thought. I climbed the stairs to watch two RSPCA officers face off against a penguin. For 20 hilarious minutes, I was entertained by slapstick double-act, Officers Bennett and Carmichael.

Clutching the open cage, the small-framed Officer Bennett edged toward the penguin. Meanwhile, Officer Ray Carmichael walked inched behind the penguin.

"Now!" Officer Harry said and they both lunged forward trying to trap "the beast". Who simply side stepped to the right and enabling both men to catch their fill of air, lunging past each other.

"Ok, next time *I'll* trap it," Officer Carmichael said. Officer Bennett shoved the cage into his hands. Again, on the command, "Now!" the penguin stepped to the left and the "Laurel and Hardy tribute duo" skidded across the wooden floor with an empty cage.

After another 20 minutes of penguin line dancing, I offered to help these experts.

"What do YOU know about penguins?" was their curt reply.

"Probably not as much as you," I conceded. "But I do know a bit about hunger."

I ran downstairs and returned with a fillet of smoked mackerel that I'd purchased earlier that day in Arbroath. I wondered if this poor man's version of the iconic Arbroath Smokie would be an acceptable culinary offering to the Penguin King, I mean, the King Penguin.

Taking a breath, I threw the fillet into the cage. The sharp beaked fish connoisseur waddled over and entered the cage, devouring the smokie. I flipped the wire gate closed and smiled at Laurel and Hardy.

"We would have done the same," Officer Harry said angrily.

'There *will* be charges," Officer Carmichael said, as they carried the caged penguin into the van and (hopefully) back to Edinburgh Zoo. There were no charges. But I did receive a phone call from a parent the next morning.

"Hi Charlie, my boys ok?"

"Sure Malcolm," I answered, surprised, "Why shouldn't they be?"

"Oh, no reason", he said trying hard to stifle a fit of the giggles. "Any black and white birds flying around up there?"

He burst into laughter and was joined by what sounded like half of the Castle Tavern! Apparently in all the local newspapers the next day there was the heading, "Rare penguin kidnapped from zoo." I cringed and wished I was back in Edinburgh, minus the penguin kidnapping ring. Also, I never looked at an Arbroath Smokie the same way ever again.

CHAPTER 16

After the "bird incident", I decided to cut short the children's camp by two days just in case I walked in and found a horse in the kitchen! As we were packing all our equipment for the return journey, I told the kids that they could go to High Street and buy a souvenir for their parents. This would give me time to get tidied up while they were all gone. Again, I naively hoped this exercise would tire them out.

They were gone for two hours and returned just before lunch. There was only one minor incident during lunch, where eight-year-old Gary McMurdo slipped a cockroach into Gillian's liver pate sandwich. This resulted in a black eye for Gary and a broken plate!

After lunch, I sat everyone down and gave the midday talk. It was about honesty, and I used the example of George Washington. I ended with, "No one likes anyone who steals or lies, though Jesus can save you from both if you follow Him."

I asked the kids to go upstairs and pack their things, and they finished more quickly than I'd anticipated, before returning downstairs and wandering around moaning at each other. I began my task of packing my one meager bag a little later. As I was cramming my things into my backpack, Sean Kelly guiltily approached me. Despite his discomfort, he didn't bother to pull me aside, but started speaking in full view of the other kids.

"Eh, Pastor Charlie, I listened to your talk and eh, well, I've choried something." (Choried is Edinburgh street talk for stolen).

"Ok, Sean, thanks for being *honest*," I said, holding out my open hand towards him, palm up. "Hand it over and we'll return it and forget it happened."

Sean looked at my hand confused. "No, I've *really* been chorying," he mumbled, almost in tears. And then he ran upstairs and returned with a pillowcase that was a third full of something…

By now, the whole group was watching us curiously, welcoming the break from the monotony of doing nothing. Even though they were a very close-knit community, they loved to see one of them get into trouble.

I stood back as Sean tipped the contents of the pillowcase on the threadbare carpet. I breathed in noisily, expecting porn magazines, weapons of some kind or small furry animals, and out came 87 pencil sharpeners!

"I collect them," Sean said, feeling pleased as he saw the pencil sharpeners lying in a heap.

"How many do you have that are actually paid for?" I asked.

"Don't be silly, Pastor C, chorying them is the best part," he said, as if stating the obvious.

"But it's wrong," I said, staring at him.

"I know." He stared at his feet.

"Ok, anyone else got anything to return that they have 'accidentally' taken?" I said, throwing them a lifeline.

There was a three second silence before the entire horde ran upstairs noisily and returned with their "stuff".

I stared at the pile in front of me.

As well as the 87 pencil sharpeners, there was three bottles of Johnny Walker Blue Label, six packs of Marlborough Light, a claw hammer… 18 pairs of underpants and a face cloth!

"Where?" I tried to finish the sentence but was interrupted by 10-year-old Fiona Gourlay.

"Woolworths Pastor C, it was easy, the security guard was having a smoke out the back and Jimbo isolated the camera with his penknife. Sorry."

I tried hard to conceal the shock on my face, and eventually said gently but in a tone that no one would argue with.

"Right, we go back now and return them, don't worry, I will speak up for you all."

And so we all walked to Woolworths where I asked a disinterested assistant to take a pause from applying her lipstick because I urgently needed to speak with the manager.

"That's Mr Gordon, the Deputy Manager," she said in a monotone nasal voice. "Mr Duncan is in a conference." ("Duncan?" Where had I heard that name before?)

"He'll do," I said.

Minutes later, Mr Gordon, a young spotty male in a suit appeared, demanding to know what the emergency was. I explained apologetically that although my kids had broken the law, they were returning the goods because they sincerely hoped to make amends.

"I'm calling the police!" Mr Gordon exclaimed so the whole shop could hear.

"Not a great idea," came a familiar voice from behind him.

Mr Gordon held his ground, protesting, "But Mr Duncan, sir. I am sorry, sir, these hooligans have robbed our shop and should be behind bars, sir!"

I turned around to see Mr Andy "the apprentice" Duncan give a dismissive flick of his wrist, as if to send us on our way. In a recognizable Falkirk accent, Andy said, "Charlie Mackenzie, you haven't changed a bit since you almost killed me driving the truck from my uncle's garage."

"Thought you were going to be a mechanic?" I said.

"Nahh, you put me off driving for life," he joked.

And with that, the incident was closed. Within the hour we were loaded up on our bus and heading south towards Dundee and eventually Edinburgh.

But alas, it took less than half an hour for it all to begin.

"Can we stop?"

"I need the toilet."

"Me too, I'm bursting."

"Can we stop at a petrol station, I want a drink."

Eventually I pulled over at a filling station next to a playground underneath the brow of a large green hill just off the City of Dundee's Kingsway.

As soon as the bus pulled to a halt, the kids were running towards the playground having magically forgotten they needed the toilet! Three small boys about six years old were already using the swings. Gillian reached the boys first. "OFF, now!"

"But we were here first," one small freckled boy replied.

"Move, or you are history," Gillian shouted. The three boys ran off in the direction of the hill stopping to shout at the Niddrie kids (who were now dangling four to one swing and the rest diving down the slide).

"We've got brothers and they are bigger than you!"

"Bring them and your fathers and your grandfather's dog!" Jimbo Casey yelled, laughing.

Half an hour went blissfully past without incident. I lay out across the passenger couch of our minibus and snoozed.

I was woken by a finger prodding me. Rab Ferry was pointing up at the brow of the high hill behind the park and saying slowly, "Maybe time to go."

It looked like a scene from the cult movie, *Quadrophenia*. The length of the skyline was awash with around 50 young men and older teenagers brandishing sticks and shouting threats to our kids below. I leapt out of the bus and roared at our kids to get in! Rab started the engine and seeing this, the cliff top army raced towards our children like molten lava flowing down a furiously erupting volcano - hot, terrifying and fast!

I was already on board, looking for a seat to hide under! Rab was trying to reverse the minibus that had gotten conveniently stuck in mud. I lifted my gaze above the seat to sneak a look, expecting to see our kids diving aboard any second, while the gang of angry parents, uncles, brothers and dogs came within twenty yards… and stopped.

We looked on in disbelief as eight-year-old Kenny Munro shouted towards them. "You got 10 seconds before we come at you, so be good and go run back up that hill, we're from Niddrie. We don't run."

"Why you little maggot," a hoarse sounding man in his late 40s bellowed.

Kenny and his "pals" bent down, picked up broken lumps of concrete from the playground and in unison hurled them at the crowd. What followed didn't make sense. First the dogs seemed to turn on their owners, and as the Niddrie kids ran towards them, they vanished! Up the hill and gone. I was now anticipating Hells Angels or paramilitaries with machine guns arriving by helicopter to attack us but it just all went eerily still. Our kids returned to their swings for another half hour, and 90 minutes later we were back in Edinburgh.

"How was the holiday?" one of the mums called out as the kids poured out of the minibus.

"Boring," was the reply she received.

"Yeah, boring!" shouted another kid.

The mum smiled at me and said apologetically, "They are not used to the quiet life Pastor Charlie, that's what it is."

I went to speak but nothing came out of my mouth. So I just smiled and waved goodbye to the kids who were now on their way back home to their PlayStations!

CHAPTER 17

While I was pastoring in Niddrie, I'd been living in a tiny village which on the surface, appeared to be the opposite of Edinburgh's slum-ridden government housing area. My rented home in Wallyford was located in the prosperous East Lothian council area.

The whole area of East Lothian was decidedly middle to upper class; a retirement destination for rich accountants and financiers and upper tier police offers. Bordered by 40 miles of coastline in the north, East Lothian had a golf course next to the sea and many upmarket hotels that catered for "those foreign tourists". (In other words, English tourists).

In many ways, East Lothian was a paragon of affluence, order and healthy living with its fresh air and views. It had even been dubbed "the sunniest area in Scotland".

By contrast, a sense of darkness seemed to hang over Wallyford, an inland village on the western side of East Lothian. Wallyford was originally a mining village consisting of mainly council housing, a row or two of shops, a primary school and a small library. When I arrived there, the coal mines had long been closed and it had become known as a village without an identity and or a real purpose to exist on a map. The village itself lacked a soul; people seemed friendly but were very private and "simply tolerated" outsiders.

Prior to moving there, I had heard countless rumors of child abuse and rampant witchcraft where parents indoctrinated children as young as five into harmful ritualistic practices. Many villages on the east side of Edinburgh had a history of paganism. And sad to say, child abuse was a product of this. So when I decided under the leadership of God to begin a children's club there, I felt a wall of resistance spiritually, but also a sea of welcoming smiles and gladness from the children of Wallyford.

I ran the weekly Bible club out of my rented home in Wallyford. Many of the children would race to my home and were always reluctant to leave, seeing the club as a refuge, a safe place to be, and a break from fear and uncertainty. My friend Irene King played guitar and led choruses and I taught the gospel from flannelgraph. Every week 40 or so children would squeeze into my lounge for 90 minutes of Christian ministry and fun activities and prizes. Several children accepted the Lord as their Savior.

The work was fruitful and joyous, but a few months after it had begun, I was called to pastor a church in the fishing town of Hartlepool in England's north-east. I needed someone to take over. Easier said than done.

In the same village, I had heard of a house fellowship made up entirely of young people who worked in a large department store in Edinburgh. They were talented, enthusiastic and even had their own pastor. I invited the leaders of the fellowship to visit me for a chat, excited by the prospect that they might take it on. After all, how could they not? It was changing the lives of the many kids who were hungry for a relationship with God.

I was greeted by folded arms, tapping feet and glazed over eyes at the meeting. It was clear from the outset that they were disinterested about taking over another person's work. They had many excuses. They had to spend time in worship, they had study classes, and they had prayer meetings and even fellowship times. I had to agree that these all were noble and edifying for young people to be attending but... to have a golden opportunity to reach the heart of young unchurched children with the gospel once a week, was that not what we were supposed to be all about? The evening finished uncomfortably. I shared my disappointment with them and they left a little annoyed with me.

My heart felt heavy as I went to bed that night. God spoke to me in a vivid dream. In it I saw a large boat crossing the River Forth near Wallyford. On board, the crew sang and prayed and preached and had fun. And then I noticed that all around this huge boat, there were young children drowning in the water. From time to time one of the crew members would try and reach out to one of those children, only to be pulled back by the others.

"We've no time to do that," the majority would shout.

"We are too busy practicing for Sunday, and we have to pray and have our Bible study."

"Leave them alone, someone else will save them."

As I watched this disturbing picture, the Holy Spirit then showed me the house fellowship in Wallyford, gathering for worship and praise and He spoke these words into my heart:

"Behold, The Ship."

The heartbreaking sight of the desperate children as their flailing limbs became still and they sank below the current jerked me awake. I tried to get the horrible picture out of my mind, but the Holy Spirit said to me, "I want you to share this vision with them Charlie."

I found out from a friend that the group would be meeting at their pastor's home in the village center the next evening at 7pm. I prayed for courage and clarity about what to do.

On the evening of their meeting, I knocked on the pastor's door at 7:20pm. I could hear the lively songs of fellowship from the lounge as he opened the door.

"What do *you* want?" the pastor called out, looking down at me. He was a year or two older than me, perhaps in his late 30s with grey hair and a slight tan.

"May I come in?" I asked.

He turned to his group of young people who had stopped singing and were looking at me, through the open door. "What do think?!" he said. "Shall I let him in?"

Grunts and a few nods spread around the room and I was ushered through to the lounge. There were no spare seats and so I stood against the far wall.

"This won't take long," I said, my smile belying my discomfort.

I began to share the vision with them as they sat in silence wondering where it was all leading. And then as I reached the climax of it all, I pointed to everyone and allowed my outstretched arm to sweep silently around the room.

"Behold, the ship!" I said solemnly.

There was stunned silence for several minutes, then the sound of whispering and gasps.
"Get out," one young girl shrieked.

"Who do you think you are?" another rasped.

"I think you better leave now," the pastor said, furious. "How dare you walk into our fellowship and disrupt it!"

I made no apology, but solemnly headed for the door and was glad to be back outside in the safety of the Wallyford fresh sea air and wondering if that message really was from the Lord, or was it just my own imagination?

But it became very clear a year later, while I was pastoring the church in Hartlepool, England. I received a letter from one of the girls present at the evening fellowship meeting. It read as follows:

Dear Pastor Charlie,

I was in the meeting at our Pastor's home in Wallyford the night you visited us and shared your "revelation". Had you not left directly afterwards I am certain that they would have torn you apart. But one man stood up and asked the question, "What if Charlie is right? What if God IS telling us to reach out to those children with the gospel?" We decided to fast and pray and seek God's guidance on this and after many days, a group of us, of whom I am part, decided to take on this work. It has been a year now and the children keep attending in good numbers and many are being saved.

Yours in Jesus

I praised God for this confirmation. It came at a time when I needed encouragement. And it strengthened my belief that when the Holy Spirit speaks to us in dreams or visions, we are to share them, regardless of how difficult or hostile the outward circumstances may be.

As it would only be months until I was officially appointed as a pastor in Hartlepool, I stood down from my duties in Niddrie to concentrate on the move south. I spent more time at home in Wallyford packing and preparing for a town center ministry in England, much different from what I had been used to in Niddrie.

CHAPTER 18

One of the first things I did after arriving in Hartlepool was to take a walk around the town itself. Hartlepool is a small town on the north east elbow of England not far from the larger town of Middleborough. At one time it was a bustling ship-building center, but when I arrived in 1989 there was high unemployment among the 92,000 or so citizens. They were nicknamed Hartlepudlians or "Monkey Hangers". I'll explain why in a moment.

As I walked around the area near Sandringham Road where the church manse was, I stopped and introduced myself to a couple of police officers who were "walking the beat".

"Hi, I'm the new pastor at the church in Lowthian Road," I said, extending my arm to shake hands. The WPC and PC looked at my hand, paused, shrugged and shook it.

"I know you police officers have a tough job walking the streets all shift, your feet must be killing you," I said. "I am at number 90, and have tea, coffee and endless boxes of biscuits. Pop in when you are passing for a chat and a break, ok?"

Word soon flew round the local police station about a friendly Scottish pastor who had befriended the police, and nearly every day, there were one or two police officers having a break in my living room.

My inaugural service in Hartlepool was a packed out affair attended by dignitaries including the mayor, local politicians and church leaders. Now, I never really understood just how much the "Monkey Story" actually embarrassed the good people of Hartlepool, although I sincerely wished I had! But alas, isn't hindsight a wonderful thing.

After being introduced at length by the chairman of the Hartlepool council of churches, I climbed the platform, in suit and clerical collar, smiled and said "Good morning everyone, what's all this about a monkey?"

Silence!

Heads looked away, people tut-tutted and a couple of people glared. I quickly moved on and after expressing formal greetings to the honored guests, I gave my first sermon and sat down. The historic background for monkey references being a local taboo is this…

During the Napoleonic wars of the 19th century, a French vessel carrying a large amount of gold was shipwrecked off the coast of the headland in Hartlepool. Now, English law forbade a ship of any kind to be plundered if there were still any signs of life on board. So when the locals found no one alive except a small monkey dressed in a French naval officers uniform, this meant they were unable to take anything away from the ship. So they hatched a cunning, though lame plan to rectify this. They arrested the monkey and brought it into the Hartlepool town center where they interrogated it as a spy. When the poor monkey was unable to answer or respond to any of its interrogators, the town's leaders concluded that it was indeed a spy and ordered its execution. This took place on the public gallows. And the people of Hartlepool to this day are a bit miffed about the whole thing. The town that boasts a league football team, a rugby club and a history of being one of England's finest shipbuilding centers is still known as the town that hung the monkey.

In Hartlepool, I started in children's work, where I left off in Scotland. Often whole families are won for Christ through children. (For example, as in the case of the amazing McCarron family in Edinburgh). I approached the local primary school, which was at the end of my street and not too far from church. They were only too happy to allow me to lead weekly assemblies, teach Bible stories and even invite the children to the JAM (Jesus And Me) Club. The children loved the colorful flannelgraph storyboards and I loved telling them about the Creator and Savior of the universe. When it came time to launch the JAM Club at church, the school allowed me to hand out some leaflets.

We were overwhelmed! The 100 person capacity church was bursting at the seams with more than 200 elementary students. God was blessing the work and it would only get better!

It wasn't long before I began to face spiritual opposition to this work, which reared its head in different ways. I had been telling the Bible story of Jonah the Hebrew prophet and the great fish at an assembly when a young boy had asked if this was a true story or just made up? I assured him that it was a true account, hard to imagine but still, I believed it was a factual account of what happened to Jonah. The boy was the son of the Anglican priest and a liberal theologian who denied the miracles of Jesus. In addition, this man was the school chaplain, the chairperson of the school board and was jealous that the JAM club was seeing more children attending than his own church attracted in a month!

And so, in the next week I was summoned into the principal's office and told that I could no longer speak at any more school assemblies.

The front-page headline in the *Hartlepool Mail* the next evening rubbed salt into the wound. A photograph of me in my clerical collar appeared underneath the headline, "School bans local pastor". The article was a biased attack against Biblical Christianity.

Now, in an area of England where child abuse was often regular front page news, such a heading was not a true reflection of what really happened. But who cared? It sold newspapers. I felt the eyes of the world scrutinizing me for days after the "banning". Whenever I walked into a shop or bank, I heard whispers, fingers pointing and heads shaking. I was tried and condemned without even an opportunity to give a plea.

I decided to call the newspaper and demand an apology. I said, "Your article is giving the public a wrong impression of who I am. If my name is not cleared and a full written apology printed in your next edition, I will sue for defamation of character." Two days later I was in the paper again. The heading read "AN APOLOGY TO REVEREND CHARLES MACKENZIE". The correction piece apologized for its previous article and ended by saying the writer meant no harm to the pastor and that it did not mean to detract from his good work with the youth of the town. But the damage had already been done.

Two days later, I received a flyer through the door of my house asking for "Volunteers of upstanding morals" to apply as a parent governor of the primary school as the existing office bearer was moving to the south of England with her family. Parent governors at the school were like the fire that fuelled the engine. They'd help with concerts, bring food to class parties, support the teachers with "Reading Corners" and help out with everything from supervising playtimes to designing costumes for school performances.

When the school received my application they were livid! How could a pastor who they banned from their school be allowed to even nominate? The whole town was buzzing at this absurd but very controversial topic. A local newspaper ran a survey on who would vote for me. And then there was the biggest problem. Who would stand against me? Apparently no one wanted to. Eventually, the school secretary was press ganged into standing, and thus began an all-out campaign which Hartlepool had never witnessed in all its hundreds of years teaching students. People were carrying out doorknocks, gathering signatures for a petition titled, "Don't vote for Pastor Mackenzie". Meanwhile Christians from several denominations were campaigning in the shopping center encouraging parents to "Vote **FOR** Pastor Mackenzie". The campaign lasted a fortnight and the newspaper's survey results showed opinion was evenly split 50/50.

I arrived at the school office for the result having already pushed by a horde of journalists, camera people, photographers and anxious parents. Once inside I shook hands with the governors, the principal and the stern looking secretary whom I was standing against. After 10 minutes of papers being folded and notes scribbled down in a book, the principal announced the result. Mrs Margaret Smith: 52 per cent. Pastor Mackenzie: 48 per cent.

A huge sigh of relief echoed around the small office and the principal seemed to almost faint as the stress lifted visibly from her shoulders. I leaned over and gave Mrs Smith a hug and handed her a box of chocolates and a congratulatory card. She thanked me, was about to say something else then stopped and thought for a moment before slightly confused words tumbled from her mouth. "You *knew* you were going to lose, didn't you? You planned for this... but why?"

I smiled and held her hand and said, beaming, "I just had to make a point Mrs Smith, God is not mocked, that's all." I walked home happy that 48 per cent of the school parents had stood with me and made a stand for the accuracy of the Bible. I was also very pleased that the primary school now had a really nice lady as their new governor.

After the dust had settled a week later, I saw a small notice in the local newspaper, asking for volunteers to accompany the elementary school students on their annual trip and help with the equipment and food supplies. This year, the trip was planned for High Force, the highest waterfall in England and volunteers were in short supply. A few days later, on the morning of the trip I stood in the reception area of Lynnfield Primary School. The principal came out to talk to me after she saw me through her office window.

"What do *you* want here?" she said.

I smiled and said, "It's simple - if I can't teach your students, and I can't be one of your governors, at least allow me to carry your bags."

Caught off guard, she waved a hand in the direction of the waiting bus and I began to help the driver load up the crates of citrus juice, sandwiches and fruit. On the bus, I chatted with the children about football, TV and why I had become a pastor. When we reached High Force I sat with the teachers and got to know them a little. They asked me what food I enjoyed, why I was in Hartlepool, if I knew any good jokes (I did) and what pastors did in their free time? I laughed with them, told too many corny Irish jokes and showed them the very human side of Pastor Charlie Mackenzie. I returned, having seen towering barriers be pulled down, opinions changed, and hearts healed. I made many new friends that day.

Within three months, I was invited to share Bible stories to every assembly at the local high school, where I was able to teach twice as many students as I had done at Lynnfield Primary. The 11-year-olds whom I had been banned from teaching earlier had now moved up to high school and I was still teaching them! (Including one Anglican vicar's son whose father had no power whatsoever at his son's new school).

CHAPTER 19

The church in Hartlepool was next to about 60 square yards of wasteland. At one time, it had been covered by buildings but all that was left was rubble, broken pipes protruding from the ground and smashed bottles, trash and weeds. "What a waste of a good football pitch," I thought the first time I saw it. I prayed about those 60 square yards a lot, as the church (and this land) was in a busy corner of Hartlepool. The next time my church's District Superintendent visited, I asked, "Can you lend me $30,000 to buy the land and I will raise enough to build an all-purpose sports field and community center on it?"

He thought about this and said, "Charlie, most people look at this land and see danger, eyesore, empty beer bottles, but you are an innovator. You see football pitches, clubs, community centers. I think you really could pull this off."

Within a few months, the land was ours. Now I needed money to build something. My plan was to construct an all-weather football and netball pitch and a building where we could host youth events and teach local immigrants to speak English. But Hartlepool was poor, and raising money was not an easy task… "But if God is for us who can be against us?" as Saint Paul once wrote.

I had noticed that more than a few teenagers were kicking a ball outside the church on an evening. Often during prayer or the message you could hear the thump of the ball on a window, or someone on the roof retrieving it after it was kicked up there. When I asked the elders what to do about this, their response was typically harsh.

"Burst the ball."

"Get the police."

"Have them banned from the street…" and so on.

I decided to talk to the youngsters instead. After all, I loved football too. It turned out they simply had nowhere to play. I asked them that if I opened a youth club in the church, would they come? They assured me they would. Aged from 11 to 15, these Pakistani and Indian boys were desperate for acceptance in an area which had little time or energy for "outsiders".

The youth club began after a few months of prayer. We had rustled up enough money to buy table tennis nets and bats. I harangued the mayor (who was a Pentecostal Christian) into donating enough to buy new table tennis tables and some sports equipment. On the night the youth club opened, I almost wept to see our church hall packed with smiling faces, calling to each other in their native tongue, safe under the Lord's care. Their fathers also came, and I began to visit their homes and share the gospel. Months later, one of those parents designed and built a new pulpit and began attending church with his family.

One thing was very obvious to the trained eye: those boys had amazing football skills.

"Are you in a league?" I asked.

"No Charlie, no one want us 'cos we Asian," Ali said.

"We'll soon see about that."

Our first game was against a local sports club under-16s team. They all looked like mini supermen and arrived at the public park wearing royal blue tracksuits and identical Adidas sports shoes. They seemed irritated that our lads didn't even have proper kits and that we all played in different colored tops and t-shirts. The racist comments from their coach certainly didn't help either. My talented boys were beaten three-nil and it could have been double had it not been for the heroics of our 13-year-old goalie Ahmed.

"What happened?" I asked my dejected players as they sloped off the pitch heads hung low, knowing they never even got out of first gear.

"Look at us!" Ali said, almost in tears. "We're a joke! A bunch of poor Asians whose English isn't great and we can't even afford a football kit to play in."

He had a point. Wearing a decent football kit was like beginning a match with a one-nil advantage.

"You will have a kit for your next game," I promised. I wondered where on earth I was going to find the money. "Phone calls will have to be made," I thought to myself.

"Here's the deal," I said to the boys. "You get your fathers to buy you a pair of good quality football boots and I will take care of the rest."

They seemed happy with this. "What about a name for us?" one of them shouted. I looked at their filthy tops, all covered in the fresh Hartlepool mud they had played in.

"Panthers," I said, "The Hartlepool Panthers."

"Sound name," someone called back as the group walked down the street, around the corner and out of sight.

It only took a morning of calls, starting with the mayor, to finally get in touch with one of the trainers at Hartlepool United Football Club. After hearing my story, he invited me to the stadium the next day.

"This is our training kit, Charlie," he said, handing me a huge kit bag containing 15 sets of yellow tops and shorts and red football socks. "It used to be our team away kit until we got our new sponsors this season and now we are not even permitted to wear it."

I was overjoyed to accept the kit on the boys' behalf and even posed for a photograph for the local paper. The next day, the typically patronizing headline read, "Benevolent players befriend local Asian group", but still, I hoped word would spread that we were a serious football team. My philosophy (or one of them) at this time was,

"Don't let the press intimidate you, use them!" Whenever we had a bazaar, fair, competition or event, there would be a photo of yours truly smiling in the paper with a write up. On one occasion an 'investigative reporter' came around to ask me, "You are hiding the fact that you were previously a criminal, don't you think that if the people of Hartlepool knew this, then you would not be the popular figure you are?" This was meant to scare me without a doubt, but it didn't. Instead I visited the features editor of *The Hartlepool Mail* and asked to be interviewed. I shared my full testimony with the same journalist who had asked the original "scary" question and held nothing back. A week later, the newspaper printed a half-page spread with a photo of me in clerical collar and the heading, "Christianity with its sleeves rolled up." The feature was more or less word-for-word what I'd shared at the interview. I visited to thank the editor a few days later.

The local churches used the write up for outreach and I had it printed as a gospel leaflet to explain how God can change a person's life for the good. The public mostly warmed to the honesty of the article and doors began to open fast and furious.

An old lady asked me to head up a petition to stop a local gangster from opening a night club with a late license next to a group of pensioners' residences in a quiet residential area. In addition to the prospect of blaring live music until 2am or 3am every morning, rowdy drunk patrons and relentless taxi traffic, the pensioners were anxious about the proposed venue attracting criminal activity. We petitioned with relentless energy and the application was eventually blocked and reported about enthusiastically in *The Mail*.

One day I had a phone call from a new shop owner who surprised me by asking, "Is that Pastor Mackenzie? Can you come and pose for a photo with me outside my new shop and I'll give you 20 pounds for your youth club."

"Twenty pounds? For a photo?" I said.

The man was serious. "I looked in the paper and you are in nearly every week, so I thought if you appear with me outside my shop, then people will come and visit it, especially all the Christians."

But this new public awareness had a downside. Two active and generous families in the church came to see me to inform me they were leaving. My church treasurer and my church secretary said the new publicity was too much. Although they had prayed for years to see this, they felt overwhelmed and now weren't sure that this was really what they wanted. They left to join another fellowship. The church had now dropped to 20 members. I asked the Lord if my "up front" approach to community evangelism was what He wanted or should I step back for a while? I sensed I had to keep moving forward and within a year the church had grown to more than 50 members. One evening we were invited to visit, sing and testify at my beloved Bridge Street Pentecostal Church in Leeds. We brought our newly formed choir made up almost entirely of believers who had been saved in the past year!

On the social side, things were gaining momentum. Thanks to the efforts of the talented Tommy and Ruth Orley and their family, who ran a sheltered home for vulnerable adults, we developed a ladies' netball team and a men's football team. Both teams were so successful that we decided to field them places in the annual Nazarene northern region sports competition. The event had never been won by an English church, mainly because the event always took place in Scotland and was always won by the bigger, better-attended and resourced congregations north of the border.

We trained for the netball, football, volleyball, hockey and other field events like competitors fighting for a place in the Olympics. We had custom-made sports tops with the church name printed on the front. As the weekend of the event neared, we were convinced that we were good enough at least to be in the top four.

But one thing hit us between the eyes. "How on earth were we going to get there?" We prayed in church that God would provide transport. One of those, "Dear Lord we need some free transport to attend these games, but if it's not your will then that's ok" type of prayers. For reasons that still completely baffle me to this very day, I stood up and announced to the church, "We will have a new minibus by this time next week!" I am sure angels cringed at this and even muttered, "Not again Charlie…" But it was too late, it was now out in the open. People rejoiced at my (haphazard) faith and I had my neck on the line for the umpteenth time.

I waited all week for a phone call or a gift to arrive in the post… but nothing. I began to feel nervous and afraid that this was where Pastor Mackenzie had gotten it very wrong. The disappointment of not being able to compete would have been crushing for the teams, coaches and our supportive church community.

Just two days before our Sunday service, I was driving home from a business meeting in nearby Middlesbrough when I passed a car dealership and stopped. There in the forecourt was a sparkling, nearly new minibus gleaming in the sun. I got out and had a look. I opened the door and sat inside it. "This would be so perfect for our children's work, our sports teams and especially our trip to Scotland in a week," I thought, almost out loud. My dreaming was interrupted by the beaming voice of the garage owner doing his sales pitch.

"She's a real beauty isn't she?" he said. "Just had a complete overhaul, can fit over 20 with the seats down in the back and only 5000 pounds cash."

I was about to say that there was no way I could afford it, when he handed me the keys.

"Here, take it," he said.

"But - but…" I began.

He smiled back at me and said "You're that pastor person from the newspaper. If I can't trust a vicar, who can I trust? Pay me when you can, no rush."

I called one of the men from church to drive my car home and I drove the bus to my house. On Sunday morning I arrived in a gleaming beige-colored minibus to the smiles and joyous outbursts of the church that had spilled out onto the road to see it.

"You were right pastor," an elderly member chirped. "You said a week, and by George, here it is!"

"Hallelujah," I responded loudly, utterly relieved.

Two weeks later, a member of the local government's Inner Cities Initiative gave me a cash donation towards our youth work. I was gobsmacked. It was exactly the amount needed to pay for the bus.

The bus trip to the sports competition in Erskine, in the West Central Lowlands of Scotland, took less than three hours. This year the competition was being hosted by the Erskine Church of the Nazarene at a schools sports venue. It wasn't just our brightly colored blue, pink and orange polo shirts that made us stand out. As all of our team members had English accents, we were an instant hit with the friendly Scots teams.

Our rigorous training had paid off. Our football team (including yours truly) soon made it to the final, closely followed by our netball and volleyball teams. At Hockey we were outscored by a strong Scots team but hey, we were winning more games than we were losing. I quickly calculated that if we were to win the football final and at least draw a tie in the netball final, the trophy was ours. We won the football final against a skilful and organized Glasgow church by three-nil. Our result spurred on our ladies netball team who convincingly triumphed against a team from Paisley in their final. Our volleyball team only lost by a margin, meaning the trophy was coming home across the border to Hartlepool! As I walked up to collect the coveted trophy and raise it high above my head, our teams erupted in cheering and jumping up and down while the other teams couldn't help but smile at us. We held the trophy at the back of our bus all the way home, waving and showing it off to each car that overtook us on the two and a half hour drive home.

CHAPTER 20

The land next to the church was excavated, levelled and we were ready to lay a strong foundation for the all-purpose sports pitch and community center. But kids were already running through the now reconditioned ground and causing problems for the builders. I needed a huge fence to enable the work to go ahead unhindered and approached several local businesses for help. Surprisingly enough, it was *The Safer Cities* initiative (a government funded project whose purpose was to make our inner city areas safer and more friendly) that came to my rescue. They were happy to fund the construction of a 12-foot high fence around the land as long as I acknowledged their contribution in *The Mail* when the newspaper ran photographs of the fence being erected. I also opened up the church to the local public, putting on a display showing plans and artist's impressions of the finished center and how this would benefit the community. I invited local politicians and, of course, the mayor who was a key figure to build a relations with.

The main objections came from families who had bought the smart new terraced homes immediately opposite the land. They were concerned the new center would be a "Den of Druggies" and were fired up to oppose the plan by the area's town councilor, an atheist who sat on the planning committee and was hostile towards the church. And so, began a lengthy process of meetings with the Hartlepool Housing and Planning Department to seek planning permission. After months of prayer, and petitioning the public for support, we eventually won planning permission to go ahead and build. The approval came with restrictions on how late we could open at night and the condition that the public be allowed to use the premises, as long as it did not conflict with the aims and beliefs of the church. This meant that there would be no alcohol bought or sold in the center and that it would not be used to promote any other religious activities apart from those run by the church

I spent the next weeks and months petitioning business owners, factories, sports manufacturers, in fact, anyone I could think of who could dip their hands in their pockets to help the children.

On one occasion, I put forth my case before David Bell, a friendly, sympathetic senior district government manager who smiled frequently, always seemed to have his sleeves rolled up and wore neckties that were too short for his shirt.

I brought along Ray, a friend who was a police officer, to a meeting with David at a government funding office in Middlesbrough. Ray had started attending church after I met him at one of my daily, "Police pop in for tea and chat" times. (I had also become the Christian Police Association chaplain for the Teesside Police Force.)

I got straight to the point at the meeting. "We really need funding for the all-purpose football surface, around 10,000 pounds should do it, can you give me it?"

Ray almost fell off his chair! Meanwhile, David checked something on his bulky IBM computer for a few minutes, then looked up and nodded. "I can let you have it in three lump sums over half a year pastor, is this ok?"

I nodded thoughtfully. Ray was on his feet ready to leave when I said…

"There is just one more small thing."

My friend was motioning with his head for me to quit while I was winning, but I was having none of it.

"Go on…" David said, smiling warily.

"Well, Hartlepool council has just completed work on the new marina where the old docks used to be and sailing is a sport none of my kids will ever have tried or will try in the future. It's a great discipline and will teach them teamwork and self respect."

"So you want me to buy you a yacht?"

Ray stood frozen to the floor, unable to say a word as I moved in for the kill, smiling.

"Actually, I am looking for three yachts, each big enough to take a dozen teenagers."

David thought for a few moments while Ray was still trying to process all of this.

"Got it," David said, rising to his feet.

"There is a defunct sailing club that own three yachts. They are in good condition and berthed in Hartlepool Harbor, I know the harbor master very well. Leave it with me and I will arrange for your club to take temporary ownership of them."

I thanked David and shook his hand while pulling Ray's arm to leave.

"Did I just hear this right?" Ray said, hands on hips in the middle of the municipal car park. "You have just left that man's office with ten grand and three yachts!?"

"Ask and you shall receive," I said.

Ray shook his head and muttered, "I am in the wrong bloody job."

Back in Hartlepool, I did my calculations and worked out that we had managed to secure enough money to create an all-purpose sports pitch. A local disability center agreed to make portable goal posts complete with nets for football and netball. But that was where the money and good will seemed to end. We would have our sports pitches, but what about our vision for a community center? What about our classrooms to teach English, toilets, recreation areas and a drop-in café? And then I had an idea. What if someone gave me half a dozen portable office blocks? The kind used on building sites? We could join these together and make a large building! The next day I shared my vision with the *Safer Cities* initiative leader in his office.

"You will never find these in the whole of the north of England, Pastor, they are as rare as chicken's teeth," he said. "But, if anyone *can* find them, *you* can. And if you are lucky enough to have someone donate six of these, I promise to pay for a fleet of trucks to have them delivered and fixed into place."

Over the next few days, I searched every builders' yard and factory in the area but the result was always the same: "Sorry mate, these things are hard to get hold of these days and even if we could give you one or two, you're looking at several thousands of pounds."

Through conversations with various people in-the-know, I was guided to a "Mr Fix-it" who put people who needed things in touch with his vast network of contacts. His slight frame, covered in a tea stained light brown cardigan, belied his far-reaching influence. He had excellent relationships in the government and was respected in the town for his commitment towards going the extra mile.

Upon hearing my story, he said, "The only place that *may* help is British Steelworks in Redcar, they have recently finished building a new office block but I think the original portable cabins were taken down south to another site."

"Can you try them for me?" I said.

The man sighed. "Well, I'll try, but it's a waste of time, you know that, don't you?"

He picked up his landline and spoke to someone he obviously knew on the other end.

"Hi Bert, how are you? Yep, fine, fine, I've got this vicar type guy here in my office and he's looking for seven portable office blocks to make a community center in town. Now I told him that I am wasting my time talking to you and that you will have already sent all… What's that Bert? How many? When? Ok, I'll tell him".

He replaced the telephone receiver slowly. "Well, bugger me," he muttered. He sat in silent astonishment, before looking up. "That was the site manager at British Steel. He has six large portable office blocks in perfect working condition, including a shower and toilet block, he's prepared to let you have them for free if you can go pick them up this Friday."

My next step was providing the update to the Safer Cities officer, who laughed out loud when I told him what had just happened.

The whole neighborhood seemed to be in attendance as a convoy of trucks with hoisting equipment, pulled up at the church. Teams of men used a series of chain hoists and pulleys to unload the portable buildings from the trucks. These building were to form our community center, the Jam Pot Center, which we'd fought to make a reality for so long.

Within three months, the Jam Pot Center was open. But those three months were painful ones. I suffered a difficult breakdown. I had been so busy trying to fund the center and build up the church that my health was deteriorating fast. Others noticed, but were too afraid to say anything. My weight dipped and I began to look pale and gaunt. One day I walked into a grocer's shop and picked up some apples and burst out crying. Feeling embarrassed, I ran out of the shop.

"What was happening, was I going mad?" I asked my doctor.

"No, Charlie", he said. "Your body is tired, you have pushed it too hard mentally and physically and it is screaming at you to stop."

I tried to take this all in. "How could I stop now when I have come so far?" I thought. We were within touching distance of the finishing line. But facts were facts. Something was very wrong. My emotions seemed to have their own agenda. Some days were just a numb dark tunnel, while others felt lonely and I just cried a lot. People would try and "cheer me up" but I seemed to take more comfort in the miserable state I was now in. One thing was certain; I was of no use to the church or the Jam Pot project in this condition. I was sick.

I contacted my old friend and pastor Alec Dunbar from Niddrie Mission and went to stay with him in Scotland for a few months. I visited old friends from the Faith Mission and even went to a football match or two. I attended a Pentecostal church in Falkirk one Sunday and when the pastor made an appeal to people to come forward for prayer, I went forward and knelt at the altar. "I am burnt out," I said to the pastor.

Strengthened by the kindness of others, I slowly felt strong enough to return to Hartlepool. I parked my car on the hill overlooking the town and got out. I prayed over the town and felt God saying, 'It's time to go back into the fight but the battle belongs to Me." I felt apprehensive as I drove down into the town. "Deep breath, Charlie, here we go," I said to myself.

The church members were sympathetic and caring in a practical way as I slowly got back onto my feet. I assured everyone I would withdraw from sitting on most of the committees I had chaired and step back from my rigorous activities in schools and in the community at large. The Bible college answered my request for practical and pastoral support and sent an assistant pastor to help with my duties, in addition to the youth pastor that I had taken on a few months earlier But it soon became apparent that I needed a change of location. If I stayed in Hartlepool I would soon be sucked in to life at 500 MPH again.

A year prior to my breakdown, I was approached by Bill, the chairperson of a church in South Yorkshire who had looked at the figures in the church annual reports for England and saw that the Hartlepool church was the fastest growing in the district. Bill drove up to Hartlepool and asked me outright, "Will you come to Barnsley and be our pastor?" I turned him down without even a thought. "Thanks but no thanks," I said politely. "I have a work to do here and will not consider anything else until it's complete."

But now my work was nearing completion and I was reluctantly ready for a change. I called Bill and asked if the church was still without a pastor, and did the offer still stand? Bill said they had been praying without ceasing and still wanted me to come. I drove down to see the church, the town and the fine three-bedroom manse on the edge of Worsbrough Dale. I agreed I'd accept the offer to be their pastor, but only once I had seen the Jam Pot Center opened and was able to smoothly transition everything over to my assistant Ricky.

The church agreed without hesitation. In a matter of weeks, strangely as if in some dream, I was on the threshold of the Jam Pot Center's opening and my last weekend in Hartlepool.

That weekend, an inaugural football tournament that I'd organized took place on church grounds. I had invited the town's top boys' clubs and youth teams to take part. A large trophy and a cash prize were donated by local businesses. The Panthers were excited about playing on their own ground for the first time ever. Parents were invited and relatives, friends and football fans from surrounding areas made travel plans to see the game. Disaster struck. Amidst all the euphoria I had forgotten to tell a lady in church NOT to wash yellow tops and shorts with red socks. But it was too late. I met my boys on the day of the tournament with these words, "Good news and bad news. I have got a set of kits from Hartlepool United, they are ours to keep and you will be wearing them today."

"So, what's the bad news Pastor C?" Ali asked, confused.

"They are all colored peach," I said.

At first, they refused to wear them. Fair enough, back to square one. But then I thought, "No, this is our day and we WILL wear the kits. People have come from miles to watch us in this tournament; we will *not* let them down." I took the boys aside and spoke to them.

"I won't blame you if you decide not wear the kits. Let's face it, peach isn't my favorite choice for a football kit either. You go into this tournament as rank underdogs; the rival teams are all white and you are not, they all play in a league, and you don't, and on top of all that, you now have to face the embarrassment of wearing these

155

kits. Talk about 'up against it!"

They all listened intently as I continued, "But this is OUR day! For the first time ever, you will play on your own pitch in front of a home crowd, you are no longer a bunch of nobodies… you are the Panthers! Now get these kits on, get out there, and play your hearts out, I want that trophy on my desk this afternoon!"

They stood there for a few moments, hands on hips, heads down staring at the ground. The youngest member of the team Abdul Arif looked up. "I believe Pastor C," he snapped. "He's right, look at us, we are Panthers. Panthers are fast and strong, we advance and we beat others." His voice was triumphant, confident, but he looked at the others and wondered if he had overstepped the mark. The rest of the team punched him affectionately on the shoulder. They changed into the peach kits and ran onto the pitch.

The Panthers played like never before. The taunts and jeers from the other teams as they ran on wearing peach, soon turned to applause as they dazzled their opponents with a devastating show of footballing skills. The last time I'd seen such spectacular plays and teamwork was from watching Chelsea as an 11-year-old boy in London. Ali scored twice in the final as they hammered the favorites, four-nil, to win the trophy. In his victory speech, Ali proudly insisted the kits played a major factor in the way they played and from now on, their name would be, "The Peach Panthers."

The second thing that happened at the Jam Pot Center that weekend was my farewell.

During the farewell service on Sunday, all my friends who had helped pay for the center were there. All the dear souls who I had seen come to Christ during my time in Hartlepool were there and of course, the Peach Panthers and their families were also there. The church was bursting at the seams. In his speech, Brian our town mayor and a committed Christian said, "Charlie has a unique gift for asking others for help and expecting it to happen. I am glad that I have no gold fillings in my mouth otherwise I fear that Charlie would have had them taken from me months ago to help pay for his center."

I posed with Mayor Brian for the ribbon cutting ceremony outside the Jam Pot Center after my final Sunday morning service in Hartlepool The months of backbreaking toil it took to accomplish our vision was distilled down to the mere second it took to slice through a light, thin piece of red satin. As we officially opened the doors to the center, the eager crowd clapped, hollered and surged inside. Excited smiles and high-fives abounded all around. The next day I loaded up my car and took the highway out of town to South Yorkshire.

CHAPTER 21

English theologian John Wesley once wrote that preaching in Barnsley was like "plowing sand". No matter how hard you worked, it would all eventually come falling down behind you. Yet Barnsley had produced some noteworthy sons over the years, James Hudson Taylor being one. Hudson Taylor had pioneered the China Inland Mission (now OMF International). After arriving in Barnsley, I sat in the church pew that had been occupied by Hudson Taylor's family, not knowing that within 20 years I would be travelling to China.

I had done my research on the little church on Oxford Street, Barnsley, and knew that it had a troubled history. Yet this sleeping giant was situated in a strategic location only a short walk away from the town center, where it could once again make a huge impact on Barnsley. It sat in the midst of a residential area of Yorkstone terraced houses, not far from a sprawling council estate affectionately called "The Common". The church chairperson, Bill, was hoping my community-focused approach could help breathe fresh life into the church, and I was ready. Sadly, not everyone else was. I was to learn the hard way that some churches are small in number simply because they want to be. Change to some means excitement and spiritual, numerical growth, while to others it means losing power and a lessening of their influence and control over people.

I was brought down to earth quickly at my welcome service soon after The Reverend Dr Bill Coppack (from the Leeds City Mission office) gave the address. Three elderly ladies approached me at the end of the service and said, "We three are all that's left of the original founding members of this church. We've gotten rid of the last two pastors and we will get rid of you too." I was totally unprepared for this immediate show of animosity. It was going to be a mountain to climb but I already had my boots on. (Incidentally, within two years I officiated at the funerals of all three remaining "founding members".)

The first thing that struck me about the church in Oxford Street was its strange, stale smell. I realized what it was... age. This church of no more than 20 or 30 souls seemed stuck in a kind of time warp. Don't get me wrong, they were generous, kind and supportive people. They worked hard and the church was spotless. But the church still seemed, well - old. The elderly pianist would sometimes walk to the window halfway through a hymn and open it with a long pole and return to finish the song. The donated baby grand piano was out of tune and seemed to have a few keys missing, making hymn playing an experience that could bring a sad tear to the eyes of those who loved Charles Wesley's music!

The second thing that struck me was there were no young families in the church. I was the youngest by many years and I was nearly 40. I decided quickly the church needed a youth worker, a new electronic keyboard and an outreach campaign to local homes immediately, or else it was not going to survive the next year. But I needed the members to get behind me on this, and it would take time. I reiterate, some churches are small because they want to be. Change can be a painful thing and so had to be birthed from within.

Our small car park was home to a makeshift football pitch during the week where local middle school and high school boys would play, safely away from busy Sheffield Road. I asked them if they would like to form a team and have me as their coach? They conferred with each other at length, which surprised me, before "Ginner" (aka Ron Sewell) said "Ok."

I told them that I would get them top branded kits and put them in a church league but they would have to attend a Sunday service at least once a fortnight and help me form a youth club. "No problem, father," Ron said, without hesitation. And so the die was cast. I discovered that a representative for the Princes Trust (a charitable organization founded by the Prince of Wales to give small to medium sized grants to local causes) was in Barnsley, and so I approached them and made my pitch: "A grant to buy two sets of quality football kits, balls, bags and training bibs, would get these children and youths off the street and into a church league. It would offer an alternative lifestyle to drug and alcohol addiction and nurture them into responsible adults." The grant funding only took a few weeks to arrive. Later I also made a submission to purchase new indoor sports equipment for the youth club, and this too went through without a hitch.

One of the offerings for girls and young women at the church was a Girls' Brigade club. A highly organized local headmistress ran the active, popular Girls' Brigade like a well-oiled machine. The uniforms were immaculate and the clubs were part of a larger network of church run Girls' Brigade "sections", which were grouped according to age. The programme consisted of a mix of leadership and life skills training, adventurous outdoor activities and community volunteer projects. The Girls' Brigade had my full support.

"But what about the boys?" I thought. There were no organized activities for boys and young men at the church, except the new football club. I had been a member of the Boys' Brigade as a teenager in Falkirk, and recognized its value. I approached the Boys' Brigade organization who informed me I'd need to send men for official mandatory training first. This would take time and money, both of which were always tight.

The '60s puppet show, *Thunderbirds*, was making a comeback and kids everywhere were buying toys, videos and paraphernalia. I decided the church would launch our own version of a Boys' Brigade club and we'd call it "Thunderboys". The ladies at church designed a striking hat and sash with badges for our new club. It was a hit and the club grew quickly. The youth club and the Thunderboys came to church once a month in their uniforms to the delight of parents and members, who swelled the congregation to more than 50.

The youth club was noisy, boisterous and fun. All the teenagers knew each other so fighting wasn't an issue, but I had to step in very fast with language rules. The kids had the freedom to enjoy their own club as long as they respected they were in the house of God. Some of the "elderly members" of church thought that opening it up to "street urchins" was wrong. I wholeheartedly disagreed but respected their views and always made a point of listening to their objections even though it went against every nerve in my body.

I began to visit the families in the area and befriended several of them. One of these families accepted Christ and became members of the local Elim Pentecostal church. Sadly, that church is now closed. Regardless of denomination, I am always sad to hear of a work for Jesus halting. A few families began attending our church. Because of minor doctrinal issues, they could not become fully-fledged members, but they were all committed believers who regularly attended, supported events and gave tithes. Before long, a multi talented new family moved into the area. They played keyboards, drums and electric guitar. We bought a new Yamaha keyboard and a drum kit and after a few months we had our very own church band, which also drew in even more families. The new band also drew the disapproval of some long time church members, who murmured about the overly modern music style and the addition of electric guitars and drums!

As there were about 30 boys in our youth club, we split them into two football teams and purchased kits to match the colors of two popular and fashionable professional Italian football clubs. The Barnsley Royals team played in the blue and black colors of Inter Milan and the Barnsley Monarchs played in the red and black of AC Milan.

Many kids joined just to have the honor of wearing these smart kits and to own a shirt with their name printed on the back.

Our strongest team was the Royals and the Monarchs were our B team. After a few local friendlies (practice games) where both our teams shone brightly, I arranged a match with the top team in the West Yorkshire church league. The top team just happened to be my old team, Bridge Street Pentecostal Church, who had won every match that year. Their captain was the young man who had met me outside of church the week I was saved. I encouraged and motivated the Royals as much as I could and they went to Leeds with high hopes and expected to win easily. They lost 13-nil and for the saving grace of goal posts and the crossbar in the way, it could have been double that!

"We were rubbish!" the lads shouted.

"We were crap!"

"You knew we would get beat, that's not fair!"

"How could you let us play a team as good as that"

"One of them plays with Bradford City." (Which was true).

I waited for their embarrassment and sense of humiliation to die down before speaking.

"That is my old team and they are brilliant. And that is the standard that you will have to surpass if you are to make any impression in this league because although it is a church league, these guys are fit, committed and God fearing," I said. "I promise you that the only way from here is up. You will never lose 13-0 to anyone again. In fact within a year you will beat this team but it will take hard work, discipline and dedication. If you are not up to it, leave now and I will not think badly of you. If you want the glory, then let's go for it."

The atmosphere on the bus ride home to Barnsley was subdued. No one wanted to speak and on arrival they slouched off home without even saying goodbye. "Defeat is a harsh but effective teacher," I thought to myself. They did pick themselves up and trained ferociously twice a week. Some came after school, some after college, and some after work. We recruited a few key players from other clubs and before long we were a club that even professional scouts were watching. That first year we were never ranked last nor did we reach the top; we were in the mid table of a tough league. At the annual presentation of awards at Bridge Street Church, we won the trophy for scoring the most goals that season. (I had already calculated that and personally donated the trophy secretly so that my boys would have something to take home that night).

The next season we played Bridge Street at our home field at "The Common". I actually scored a long range goal from 20 yards as we beat the team, two-nil, that had beaten us, 13-nil, only the year before. We didn't win the league that year but we finished "well high" as they say in Barnsley.

We visited a prison near Thorp Arch village for a league match against a team made up of prisoners. Being a low-security prison, our opponents were mostly in there for theft, minor assault and other misdemeanors but our lads didn't know that. We were taken into the same changing area as our opponents. One of our 15-year-old boys, Neil "Waggy" Wagstaffe, asked a rival team member, "What are you in here for?"

"Mass murder," the older lad sneered. "And if you lot beat us, I'll come for you too."

I winked at the young offender and playfully slapped him on the back of the head. The game ended, one-one, and the Royals were more than happy to be going home with a draw!

On another occasion, a Nazarene church invited our teams to compete in a tournament in Manchester. Apparently they had a few "good players" and thought their victory was a foregone conclusion. The cost of entry was a hefty 90 pounds as well as petrol money to Manchester and back. Both teams were keen to compete. We raised the money and sent it off. The organizer wrote back and asked (in a patronizing way) how good we were. "Average," I replied.

The organizer greeted us soon after we arrived at the packed Manchester sports complex. Holding up two large trophies he was carrying, he sniggered and sneered, "Take a good look Barnsley boys, for this is as close as you will get to them."

My lads were ready to respond in their colorful South Yorkshire language with the associated hand signals, but I stopped them. Still clutching the trophies, the organizer turned away. Before he took off into the colorful throng of teams and supporters from all over Manchester, I called out "Oh well, it's not about the winning," and forced a smile. He glanced at me as I called out to him and I waved at him, but he pointedly turned his back.

It may have been the first time in the competition that my lads were treated with condescension, but it was far from the last. I wondered what my kids, who weren't believers and were from unchurched homes, thought about the "hospitality" and "welcoming" attitudes from these so-called Christians.

I turned to my teams and said, "If you don't win at least one of these gold colored tin kettles, then you are walking back to Yorkshire!"

"Got it Charlie," Big Adie smiled.

As was our fate, we were placed in two groups with the top two teams from each group playing in the semi-finals and then the finals. The Royals and the Monarchs progressed to the semi-finals easily.

Mid-way through one of the semi-finals against one of the organizer's dream teams, he glared at me and yelled, "You cheat! You said your teams were 'average', but look at them! They are way above any other teams here!"

"Really?" I said, pretending to be shocked. "We are *that* good here in Manchester? Wow, back in Barnsley, we are only average!"

The final was between both Barnsley teams and it was guaranteed that not only would we "get close" to both trophies, we were taking them home. The game became a bit of fun. The boys decided they would let each other score three goals to make it entertaining for the incensed home crowd, who for some crazy reason wanted us both to lose?

We planned to go to a penalty shoot out for the thrill of it. For some added mischief, I came on as a sub in the second half and following five yellow cards, was red carded for suggesting to the referee (Mr Organizer) that he was not a nice person and that his parentage was in question. It made the back page of the *Daily Sun* next morning: "Pastor sent off in cup final."

The award ceremony at the nearby Nazarene church was meant to be the climax of the day. The celebration was to be attended by all the teams, coaches and their families. However, when everyone heard we were the winners, only half the teams stayed for the ceremony. After the local youth pastor delivered an eloquent speech on friendship, unity and gamesmanship, the runners up were invited to come on stage to accept their trophy. The audience applauded politely albeit half-heartedly. My lads (the Monarchs) rose noisily to their feet and instead of just the captain coming up, all 11 players and two subs raced to the front, leapt onto the stage, cheering and high-fiving each other. The audience was stunned into silence. Harry Metcalf, the Monarchs' captain, accepted the trophy from "Mr Organizer" himself and threw it behind him to the safety of 14 outstretched pairs of hands. He eagerly grabbed the microphone.

"Ladies and gentlemen," he said, "Thanks for the trophy. I'll keep my dad's tobacco in it when we get home." He winked at the youth pastor's wife and joked (in a tone almost too serious for comfort), "Are all you Manchester birds as tidy as her?"

No one laughed. Mr Organizer, now seeing droves of his faithful walking out of his carefully planned showpiece finale, grabbed the microphone back and shouted, "Now, let's hear it for the winners *this* year – but not *next* year – the Barnsley Royals."

The entire team dived onto the stage and hugged each other amid cat calls, whoops and laughter. They spontaneously burst into a chorus of "You're not very good," while pointing at the 30 or so seated Manchester boys. Both trophies were thrown to and fro across the stage, almost knocking over a bouquet of daffodils and a small glass table with New Testament books. My lads dragged me on the stage and "forced" me to make a speech.

"Thank you, Manchester, you really ought to be careful who you invite to these football tournaments," I said. "You might get a real good team coming one year!"

Our lads went crazy with laughter, hoisting me up on their shoulders and carrying me out of the church and dumping me unceremoniously on the grass outside.

"Animals," a parent yelled as we made our way to the minibuses.

I stopped dead in my tracks and turned to face the thirty-something man, wearing a red Manchester United tracksuit.

"Animals? Really?" I said slowly, in a low controlled voice. "Common, loud, talented, penniless, working class. Yes, we are all of these things and more, but 'animals?' You really know how to share Christ's love, don't you?" I became angrier by the second.

One of my players wrapped his arm around me and calmly whispered in my ear, "Come on Pastor Charlie, he's not worth it. Anyway, Ginner's just dropped some dog poo into his jacket pocket."

A few weeks later, the town's Baptist pastor came to see me. "Charlie, I am leaving Barnsley next month. How would you like to be the new chaplain for Barnsley Football Club. I have done it for five years and I need someone to take over who loves football."

It took me all of three seconds to pray about it. Barnsley FC was in the English first division and Oakwell Stadium was an impressive, modern facility. I asked the church's permission and the answer was, "As if you would listen if we said no…"

I was invited down to Oakwell the following Tuesday to meet the manager, Mr Mel Machin (previously with Manchester City) and the staff and players. It was a wet, cold South Yorkshire evenings where even the cats stayed inside. A reserve game between Barnsley and Bradford City was underway when I arrived. I went for a walk to get to know the stadium and staff. Standing next to the hot dog and drink stand was a lone policeman.

"Ayuup," I said (Yorkshire for "hello there!"), playfully punching him on the shoulder. The lady behind the counter seemed aghast by the gesture.

"I'm Charlie, the new Chaplain... Charlie Chaplain, get it?" I extended my hand, and he shook it, looking a little dubious and caught off guard.

The lady stared at me disapprovingly and was about to say something, when I said, "Give this constable a hot drink on me dear, it's a thankless task being called upon to do overtime in such weather."

"I'm George, and I'm afraid I can't..."

"No need to thank me, my friend, I appreciate all the work you men do. In Hartlepool I was chaplain to the police and have many friends like you in the force."

The policeman looked at the tea lady, shrugged and drunk his free brew. I smiled and continued my rounds. Over the next weeks and months, I became the chaplain to two league managers, Viv Anderson (the first black footballer to represent England), and Danny Wilson, (Sheffield Wednesday's former ace, who was to take Barnsley into the premiership the next year).

A few months after joining the club, I received a call from the chaplain of Manchester United John Boyers, who was now the director of Christians in Sport and based at Old Trafford football stadium. John later became the interfaith chaplaincy coordinator at the 2012 Olympic Games in London, managing the deployment of 160 chaplains.

"Charlie, how would you like to come over to Old Trafford?" (It took me less that one second to pray this time!) John was the chairman of a national network of evangelical football club chaplains and unbeknownst to me, I had become the latest addition.

CHAPTER 22

Match days at Oakwell were filled with laughs. I remember walking into the home dressing room once, just as our striker, Wayne Biggins, was about to give the punch line in a joke. While the others were pulling on their red kits, a shirtless Wayne took one look at my white clerical collar and said, "Ah, forget it."

"Go on, finish the joke," the others said.

"I can't, Charlie's here."

I used to ignore police advice and walk among the visiting supporters, introducing myself to them. Normally they were good humored and would say things like, "You better start praying for your team, Reverend, because they are going to get hammered today!"

The Barnsley FC mascot was a tatty, torn dog suit that looked sewn together by a five-year-old. Called Toby Tyke, the Barnsley Terrier mascot would come on at half time and run round the track while fans from both ends of the stadium tried to knock him over by throwing coins. (A brave, effective yet hapless way of earning a few bucks for the club).

All the other major clubs had professionally made mascots that entertained the crowd and hyped up the supporters and annoyed the visitors, all in the name of fun. Ours was an embarrassment. And then an idea sprung to my mind.

What if, we could raise a thousand pounds and have a large, comic looking, mascot suit made? And then get someone to entertain the crowd for the pure fun of it? I put it to the club board who said, "We'll put up a third of the cost, Pastor, but you'll have to cough up the rest." And so I hatched a plan. If the club chipped in a third, they could use the Toby Tyke mascot on match days. If the police put up a third, they could use it for road safety and school outreach. If our youth club contributed a third, we could use it for advertising the club and special outreach to draw crowds.

Releasing the funds from the youth club wasn't too difficult. We had saved a lot from car washes and weekly subscriptions at the door, but convincing the police that this could work for them? That needed prayer.

I drove to the South Yorkshire Police HQ "B" Division in Barnsley and went to the enquiry desk, introducing myself and explaining why I was there.

"Hello, my name is Charlie and I am the chaplain to Barnsley FC, can I have a quick word with the Chief Inspector?"

"Do you have an appointment? Our Chief Inspector is a busy man, can't just have any Tom, Dick or -"

"Charlie," I interjected.

"Quite," she continued in a monotone voice that sounded both fatalistic and dull, like she was reading from a tedious script announcing the demise of civilization as we know it. "He never, EVER sees members of the public without at least a month's prior notice."

"Can you give him a quick call?" I said, flashing my best smile that I only gave to bank managers and drop dead gorgeous nurses at the local hospital.

She thawed slightly and picked up the large black chunky looking telephone. "Morning sir, it's Julie at reception desk four, I have this priest fellow who says he's some big noise at the football club. He wants to see you. Now I've told him that you never see anyone without - What's that sir? His name? I think he said Garry or Charlie or something, but it's ok, sir, I've told him that you... Pardon, sir? I see. Thank you, sir."

And with that, she replaced the receiver. "He'll be right down," she said, miffed.
"Ayyup Charlie!" the Chief Inspector said, beaming.

To my surprise, it was George from the stadium. Not Constable George. Chief Inspector George.

"Ayyup, George," I said, beaming back.

"Come through to my office for a chat," he said, shaking my hand. "Julie, two coffees please," he said over his shoulder. It dawned on me that on that first wet evening at Oakwell months ago, it was the Chief Inspector's shoulder I had punched and whom I'd casually bought a hot drink for. No wonder the tea lady had tried to stop me.

We spent an enjoyable morning together during the first of many "coffees" and open chats about football, faith and personal stuff. He was only too willing to put up a third of the mascot money. Being an avid Barnsley FC fan he saw great potential in using Toby Tyke as an educational and fun tool to reach children at community events. He envisaged his community constable making use of the mascot. Incidentally, this constable was a Baptist.

The one and only 'Toby Tyke'

Having a friend as community police officer meant that you could borrow "props" from time to time to emphasize a message in talks with young people. Like the time I borrowed a pair of handcuffs to illustrate a talk to teenagers about "Being bonded to Christ in love". After collecting the cuffs, I stopped at the church to pick up some leaflets to distribute at the local Worsbrough Bank End Primary school one Friday afternoon. My good friend, Steve Poxton, was the young Welsh headmaster at the school and a rugby enthusiast too.

Seated in his office, he smiled when saw me in the distance through his open window. "Hi Charlie," he shouted, as I rounded the corner of the playground and breezed into his office. We chatted about upcoming events and I noted down details of the next assembly that I was due to speak at. As I reached into my pocket for my handkerchief, I playfully pulled out the handcuffs. "Watch this Steve," I said. I quickly fastened one handcuff to Steve's left wrist and the other to his chrome tubular chair arm. "Got you!" I said laughing.

Steve laughed. "Ok, ok, very funny, now get these things off my wrist."

I put my hand in my trouser pocket for the key, but it wasn't there. I tried all my other pockets as Steve began to look agitated.

"Very funny indeed. Now, good acting, but you're fooling no one Charlie, now get these bloody things off my wrist. I have a staff meeting in three minutes."

But the look on my face told him I wasn't acting. Meanwhile there were giggles and whispers from behind the principal's open door.

"Pastor Charlie has handcuffed Mr Poxton."

"The headmaster's been arrested!"

More giggles.

Steve erupted, "Get those bloody things off me now or –"

Seeing his staff peering round the door, he composed himself and added as calmly as possible, "Or else I'll call the fire brigade."

Laughter exploded and I suddenly remembered that I left the keys two miles away in my church office!

After a car ride that would have impressed a few Formula One drivers, I returned to find Steve still sitting in his chair. I nervously undid the cuffs and smiled at him. He glared back, before slowly breaking into a coolly menacing grin.

"If this ends up in the *Yorkshire Post*… you know what I'll be using as a rugby ball," he whispered.

CHAPTER 23

I had passed the old Coop building every day for almost two years. It was a four-storey structure with a massive basement, situated less than 50 yards from our church. Most importantly, it stood empty, "begging to be used". I asked my church folk, "How about we take a lease on it and turn it into a community center?" They asked two obvious questions:

1.   Where would we find the money to renovate it?
2.   Who would actually use it?

The first was a matter of trust. The second was simply "advertising".

We sat on the idea for months, praying about it, making enquiries and drawing plans. The idea was to have a fully functional multi gym in the basement and a charity clothes shop and café on the ground floor. The second floor would accommodate a TV lounge and on the third floor would be a designed activity zone (PlayStations and video games). The top floor would be converted into a chill out area and counseling suite.

After four months of praying and discussion with other church leaders, we put together a task force of church members and parents from the youth club and tackled the task with fervor.

We applied for grants and also wrote to every business in Barnsley… and then simply waited for responses. It was a numbers game. For every 20 letters we sent, we received about four or five replies and from these responses, one or two donations.

Within only three months, we had a fully paneled basement and a shiny fully functional multi gym. We had an AstroTurf playing area on the first floor, and brand new televisions, Sega Mega Drive and Nintendo games consoles for the second floor. We also had a fully kitted shop, a cooking area, counters and a cafe eating area. To become a functioning café, we need a free supply of cakes and clothes to sell. The local baker agreed to donate all the cakes, bread and pastries that they could not sell on a daily basis (several dozen trays of them) and a Christian businessman sent us as much soft drinks as we needed.

The last thing we needed were clothes to sell and we were ready to open. An old mate of mine from Bible College, Dave McLeary, came to mind. Dave had married a Christian businesswoman and philanthropist, Ann Gloag who had co-founded Stagecoach Ltd, a multi-million dollar bus, rail and air transport company. The charitable wing of Stagecoach sent medical supplies, funding and clothes to Africa. I contacted Stagecoach and received an invitation to visit their headquarters in Scotland. Upon arriving, I was taken to a large bus garage near Perth that was packed with clothing ready to be flown out to Malawi and other needy parts of the world.

"Take what you need," I was told. "It's all God's work."

We filled a minibus with near-new clothes and what we called bric-a-brac. And drove gleefully back to Yorkshire. The Oasis Christian Center was ready for business.

We calculated we'd make about one hundred pounds on our sales of cakes, coffee and clothing on our first day. We made well over that. Word spread that the Oasis Center was a good place to visit and so a couple of schools came to use the gym. Of course the cookies and drinks were cheap too. We had such a large stock of clothes that we were able to rotate stock and offer fresh near-new garments every week. The youth clubs attracted even more young people because of the space we now had and the activities we could offer. Business was great but I was slowly forgetting one important thing: the church.

I even invited the very talented Ulster singer-songwriter and children's evangelist, Robert Swann over to take a weekly children's mission at the Oasis. I had met Robert the year before and had heard his amazing testimony. At one time he was active in the paramilitaries in Northern Ireland. He told me how on one occasion he was going to plant a bomb in the dark when he stumbled and fell over a wall still clutching the ticking device! Robert spent three years in the Maize Prison outside Belfast before accepting Jesus as his Savior. When he was let out of prison his "friends" were there to offer him some money and have him back in their ranks, but Robert said to them lovingly, "I'll buy a guitar with this, I am a follower of Jesus now." Robert came and ministered to us at the Oasis, our church, and at Oakwell, Barnsley FC's Football Stadium. The Oasis was heaving with joyful, gospel activity.

Meanwhile the church too was growing. On most Sundays, it was more than half full. On our monthly youth Sundays, the football teams would attend, swelling the congregation by at least another 30.

And then it began. It was very unnoticeable at first, and then a little more persistent, the soft sound of neglect. In all my Gospel fervor, I had inadvertently begun to neglect the very people who called me to pastor the church. When people whispered, "Why are all those new people coming to *our* church?" I should have listened. When a few old stalwarts said they disliked the new keyboards and found the drums too noisy, I should have felt their heart, but I didn't. Instead my immaturity prevailed and I become annoyed and dismissive.

When a few dear members shook their heads in disbelief at their pastor hobbling into church on crutches after being injured playing football the day before, I should have taken note. I never saw it coming. When you are young and full of Gospel fervor, you seldom do.

In reality though, I was becoming more drained by the hour. Although I felt nowhere near burnout, I'd learned that it was all too easy to ignore the signs of an exhausted body, and keep postponing rest until it was too late. Unchecked fatigue had a habit of consuming you, until it overwhelmed and conquered you. I began to get weird headaches and was becoming breathless at the slightest of small physical tasks.

I decided to take a holiday, as I didn't want to suffer another breakdown like I'd done in Hartlepool. I went to Ireland and drove a lot, ate a lot, and relaxed a lot. I arrived back refreshed. Only hours after returning home, however, my phone rung. It was Pastor John, the District Superintendent in charge of Scotland and Northern Ireland's Nazarene churches.

"Sorry to hear the news, are you bearing up?"

"What news?" I said. "I am just this minute back from Ireland."

The voice at the other end went quiet. "You didn't know?" John asked.

"Knew what?" I asked, alarmed, "Just tell me what's happened."

"Sit down. Your church held a meeting in your absence. They have taken a vote of no confidence in you. They want you out, Charlie."

I sat with tears rolling down my face, gutted.

"Now, we have got one thing going for us, and I am driving over tomorrow to enforce it," John said. "No one can call a church meeting without the pastor's approval."

"So I am still the pastor?" I said, fighting for my life.

"For now," John said.

John called an extraordinary meeting of all church members and the vote was reversed. But the writing was on the wall. John Wesley had it right about "plowing sand". Despite all I had achieved, still I was being kicked out. But that was it... despite all **I** had achieved, not them! Again, had I the maturity to know better, or someone tough enough to tell me "No", I would not have done what I did, the way I did it. But it happened.

The young people who frequented the Oasis had a hunger to attend weekly church services. I scheduled a Sunday morning service in the Oasis at exactly the same time as the church that had voted against me. Many came with me, some bringing instruments. A local Pentecostal church was only too keen to support me. But it was wrong, very wrong. Our Oasis Christian Fellowship was rocking to the sound of clapping and electric praise. Meanwhile the faithful members of my old church had to pass this on the way to their sanctuary that was now almost void of young people. The young people who I had drawn away from them.

In the end I decided this was not right and told everyone I was returning to Scotland for an unscheduled break. Unbeknownst to me at that time, I had begun on the slippery slope to oblivion. I was like the prophet, Jonah, running away from the voice of God, or impetuous Peter slicing the ear off the servant, Malchus, in the Garden of Gethsemane. But unlike Peter, I had already started to backslide. I just didn't know it yet.

CHAPTER 24

I rented a small cottage outside Edinburgh and began to look for work. What does a pastor who is "resting" do? Answer: He delivers Chinese meals of course!

I worked seven days a week from late afternoon until the early hours of the morning, driving round the Gilmerton area of Edinburgh delivering meals from Paul Mann's Chinese Take-Away. The work was tiring but at least I got paid every day and had decent meals to eat. After some months of this, Niddrie City Mission heard that I was back in town and asked me to return as their pastor. With hindsight, I should have said no. I was in no way physically or spiritually well enough to do this. But I said yes. Niddrie had changed a lot… for the worse. Most of my boys had grown up, so I soon became the football coach, pastor and mother hen of their younger brothers and siblings. I wasn't ready for it and only months after saying yes, I was saying "No" and walked away from the stress.

But one of the strange things about backsliding is that God still blesses you. You are still in His care, His family and under His protection. He does not love you any less than He did before. At times I could feel His love, while at other times He allowed me to feel lonely so that I might begin to search for Him again. I began working for a kidney charity, standing outside High Street shops with a collection can. I was allowed to keep 10 per cent. Within a few months I was earning more than $1000 a week and managing five teams of collectors.

Once, all my teams were fully booked and the manager of a large supermarket in the Scottish borders called to see if I could send a Santa with a collection can to add some "Festive Spirit" to his store and of course make a lot for charity. But there was no one I could call on except one possibility. It was a long shot, but I tried his old phone number.

"Hi Alan, how do you fancy making 20 pounds for sitting in a shop and smiling at kids for a day?"

Big Alan (from Niddrie) answered with his typical cheerful swagger, "I think I could squeeze that into my busy agenda, Pastor C."

And so the weekend before Christmas, I drove Alan to the gig, arranged for him to get changed into a Santa suit and had him sit just inside the entrance. I could hear the pound coins dropping in his tin before I even started my car. It was only 9am and I knew the day was going to be memorable. What I didn't know was that it would be memorable for all the wrong reasons. At precisely 2:45pm my phone rang.

"Come and get your Santa and remove this monster from our shop at once!" a lady shrieked down the line at me. "He is scaring all the children and insulting the ladies."

When I arrived, Alan was lying on his back singing songs that you couldn't sing at Sunday school and waving an empty Glenfiddich whisky bottle in the air.

"What airhead gave my collector alcohol?" I demanded.

"Well, our manager Mr Dimcott thought it would be a kind gesture to donate a fine bottle of malt to Santa for his encouraging words and benevolent attitude coming here just before Christmas," a large round lady said. She was wearing a badge which read, "I'm here to make you happy." She didn't.

"He is an alcoholic!" I screamed at her, causing five trolleys to stop, and the people pushing them, to stare.

"Am I?" Alan said, sitting up and grinning drunkenly.

We got out of there soon after.

"Do I still get my 20 pound?" Alan asked back at his council flat.

"Course you do," I said. Alan was a friend regardless of what had happened. I paid him and put it down to a bad day at Santa's grotto. But with all the finance came the folly.

I began smoking again. Cigars at first, then 20 or more cigarettes a day as well as having the occasional pint of beer after work. This eventually led to a half bottle of whisky and six beers every day just to get by. I drifted from one hopeless affair to another, and soon I was on a spiral of drink, work and more drink. I hurt those who got too close to me and ran from any form of responsibility. And yet, all the time I knew I was still God's child; it was I who had run away, not Him. I pulled myself up by the bootstraps so many times, only to fall flat on my face again, deeper in the mud I had climbed out of. And then my mother, Mary Jane died. My big funny, uncouth, cuddly mother just died. I was with her the night she slipped away. I didn't want her to go. It was not the right time, but she went anyway, double pneumonia. Two years later, my dad, my best pal, was diagnosed with lung cancer. He never even smoked! He was my only hero in life and meant everything to me. He was also a true Highland gentleman. Whereas Mum taught me fun and art and music, Dad taught me manners, morals and how to treat fellow human beings with dignity and respect.

A year after Dad was diagnosed, he too died. I was devastated. I decided to take his funeral service myself. Still thinking I was a minister in service, I went to the crematorium in a clerical collar and gown. The chapel was packed out. The congregation was made up of more than 100 townsfolk - gardeners, cleaners, shopkeepers, old friends and young people whom he had befriended over the years. I got halfway through the address and broke down. In fact I wept for nearly a month, staying in my home, and refusing to see anyone. The sky seemed to have fallen down, the sun had turned black and it was winter again. Donald Mackenzie had died. My wonderful gentle Highlander dad was no longer there for me. How acutely lonely I now felt.

Again I tried to pull myself up and with the money he left me, I bought a house and a car but nothing made up for the acute loss I was now feeling. Eventually, I decided to buy an air ticket and take off around the world. Scotland had suddenly become a lonely place and I needed out. I headed to South America where I spent a week on the Playboy island resort of Santa Margarita, partying all night and sunbathing on catamarans in the Caribbean all day. From there I headed up the coast, to Costa Rica and then Los Angeles, staying in a tacky little room on Hollywood Avenue before eventually flying home. But I wasn't fulfilled by any means. I needed more in my empty life.

I had been studying Radio Broadcasting at a local college in the hope I could carve out a career as a radio presenter. I now enrolled on a Mandarin course for beginners as well and tried to master the basics. I also attended Strathclyde University in Glasgow in the evenings and passed a TEFL (Teaching English as a Foreign Language) course. Again, I was trying hard to pull myself up from the gutter, but it was still in *my* strength and not in God's. The day I walked into the Chinese Embassy in Edinburgh to apply for my one-month tourist visa was a monumental step. I told someone straight afterwards, I was standing on Chinese diplomatic territory!

I told my college in Edinburgh that I was going to visit China for a month to fulfill a dream, and they asked if I would be interested in teaching at one of their sister colleges for a week during that time? "We will pay all of your expenses," they said. For the first time since Barnsley, a small weak voice deep inside of me began to sing a little.

I booked a ticket to Taiyuan in Shanxi Province, northern China, where I would cover classes for a Taiwanese teacher for a week at a Canadian Experimental school. This was a new kind of school, a partnership between the Canadian government and the Chinese. Following that, I would join a tour group in Shanghai and tour Shanghai, Beijing, Nanjing, Xi'an and Chongqing. This would totally eclipse my experiences in LA and South America; it was the trip of a lifetime. My friends urged me, "Go, get this China out of your system and come home and be normal again." But after this trip, I was never to be "normal" again.

I caught the overnight Beijing flight from Copenhagen and fell asleep around 2am (somewhere over Europe!) The flight attendant woke me at 10am to offer me breakfast. I asked where we were and she smiled and said, "We are flying over western China, if you look down you can see the land." I looked out of the window and for the first time I saw China. The tears flowed hot and freely. I sat there praising a God who I had wandered from, but here I was just as HE had promised more than 20 years ago, fulfilling a dream to travel to China! My heart swelled as I sunk back into my chair and ate heartily.

I had decided to wear my kilt on this monumental visit to China. The Danish flight attendants seemed impressed with this and as a result, I was given VIP treatment even though I was cattle class! I landed at Beijing Capital International Airport like a kid in a toy store! I smiled at everyone – police, customs officials, baggage handlers – everyone!

In the three hours I had to wait for my connecting flight to Taiyuan, I busied myself with eating pot noodles, talking to locals using the little Chinese I had learned, and posing for countless photographs! I kept screaming in my head, "Charlie! You are really in China!"

I boarded a very busy local Air China flight to Taiyuan (a city so small in physical size that it's not even on the map even though the population is the same as Scotland's!) and soon got an idea of Chinese travel. People sat talking loudly on the plane next to each other. Some were carrying bundles of clothes, some carried boxes and most were either carrying or eating food. I smiled and received several toothless smiles as my reward.

I arrived at the small airport in Taiyuan at midnight and to my horror there was no one to meet me. I was alone in northern China and did not even know the address of the school! Eventually after two hours of waiting and looking for a sign of recognition in every face that passed me, a Taiwanese-Canadian teacher in his 30s called Mark arrived, flustered and apologetic. Mark spoke with a strong Canadian accent.

"Are you Mr Charlie?" he asked. "I only found out an hour ago that I was supposed to pick you up!"

"But they have known my flight details for a week," I said.

Mark smiled, hugged me and said, "Welcome to China."

CHAPTER 25

There was staff accommodation on the premises of the school. I found myself in a tiny room on the fifth floor in a modern (though poorly maintained) building across from the impressive sports arena. My room had a faulty fridge, a broken TV and a bed. That was it. But I was tired and flopped into my bed, almost breaking my back in the process. No one had told me about Chinese mattresses. There wasn't one!

I was awakened by blaring music at 6am. I stood outside my door, rubbing my eyes in the sunshine, watching Chinese children wearing small red neckerchiefs, marching onto an area for what looked like a parade or roll call. By 6:15am it looked like the whole of the primary and middle schools were present. They began to break into an exercise routine set to patriotic music with instructions being barked through the loudspeakers that seemed to be everywhere - even in the bushes! I left this amazing colorful exhibition of youth and synchronization and wandered back into my room and slept for another hour, before eventually finding Mark and asking him where I was supposed to teach.

I was taken to the impressive-looking middle school building and shown a list of the classes I would be teaching. My subject? Chinese history. Daunting as that sounded, I had been studying Chinese history on and off for more than 15 years and so I was actually excited about the challenge, as long as I could teach in English!

Before long, my 15-year-old students began to pump me for answers about Chinese dynasties. I even had to explain why the Great Wall was built and had difficulty convincing them that it was built as much for communication as it was for defense. Several of my students slept (snoring loudly) during entire lessons. I found out there were up studying until 4am! (Although some admitted to be watching movies on their laptops).

Meal times in Taiyuan provided another type of education. The expats had a lush, carpeted, air-conditioned dining room with a grand oak table and antique style chairs. A chef in his whites personally came in and served the teachers who ate with silver cutlery. Next door the Chinese teaching staff sat on wooden benches and ate rice from bowls with cheap bamboo chopsticks. On my second trip to the dining room for lunch, a Canadian teacher asked us to sign a petition to complain about the poor service they were receiving!

I asked "Why?", totally confused. And the answer I got was, "The Coca Cola is warm."

"Your Chinese colleagues, who probably work twice as hard and get less than half the pay you lot are getting, are sitting next door on wooden stools in a flaming furnace drinking warm water," I said. "You are on about warm cola?! You are a disgrace to your country."

Stunned silence greeted me. I walked out of the room and didn't eat with them again. Instead I went 100 yards down the busy main road and sat outside eating noodles with old Chinese men. When they spoke to me in Mandarin, I smiled and nodded, and they patted me on the head and continued eating.

Towards the end of my week in Taiyuan, I decided to go exploring straight after school. I caught a bus into Taiyuan city, which was about a 30 minute bus ride. I stuck out like a sore thumb. Taiyuan was a nice modern Chinese city but I didn't see another foreigner all day. People stared at me and some came over and poked me and felt my clothes. One old guy with breath that could knock out a horse at 100 yards walked up to me smiling and seemed excited to speak the only English sentence he probably knew. I stretched out my hand to him, offering a handshake. He looked at it, spat on the palm of my hand and smiled again. "I love you," he said, before rubbing my head and walking away!

By the time I finished my week in Taiyuan and boarded the plane to Shanghai, I was tired from the lack of sleep, weak from the lack of food and my back ached from the lack of a good soft bed to lie on. But it was an experience. I had travelled a road less known, and survived. Tasted authentic China on my own and actually liked what I tasted.

Shanghai's Hongqiao Airport was almost as big as Taiyuan! Once I passed customs, I caught a taxi to the East Nanjing Hotel in the city center and 40 minutes later I was at my destination. I was shown to my room in this three star hotel and once inside I shouted for joy! I dived on top of king-sized bed and snuggled into the softness. I lay there for about 20 minutes, relishing my creature comforts again, before a note was slipped under my door:

"Dear meester chales, there is meeting in room 569 for travellers. *On China adventure tour 731,* please attend in one hour at your pleasure."

I showered, shaved and put on my whitest shirt and my kilt. "I am in Shanghai, it's Saturday evening, I intend to enjoy every moment of it," I thought to myself. I purposely arrived 10 minutes late for effect, then swaggered into the room. The young American tour guide smiled and said, "Nice of you to dress for the occasion, I take it you're Charlie?"

"Or meester chales, it says here," I said, pretending to read the card again. Everyone laughed; I was hoping they would, it felt good to be there.

The tour guide asked us to introduce ourselves and explain why we picked this tour. One couple was on Honeymoon, another was celebrating their new retirement. One couple just wanted to try China and two young girls said it would be fun.

When it was my turn, I blurted out, "I have been longing to be here in China for 20 years. I have been studying its history from the Tang and Ming dynasties to the Cultural Revolution to modern day Chinese politics. I began a degree in Chinese history in Leeds and one day I will complete it. I love China, I love the Chinese people and I am looking forward to a plethora of colorful Chinese artifacts and tasting the wonderfully diverse food and on top of that, I want to go out tonight and enjoy Shanghai."

An awkward silence followed. An Australian guy slowly said, "Struth. You're really serious!"

The next person to speak was also Australian and after introducing herself as Becky, she said that she had come just for shopping!

After the coffee and chat we split into two groups. The older members went for a meal and then an early night while the young ones set off on a night tour of Shanghai. I tagged along with the young ones. I had waited 20 years for this and was going to savor every last drop!

The guide led us down East Nanjing Road, which is a paved shopping precinct featuring many western high street stores and fast food outlets. We approached the busy "Bund", a fast flowing waterfront area skirting the west bank of the wide Huangpu River. Some of the most famous buildings in Shanghai are here on the Bund's western side, including: The Peace Hotel, where Oscar Wilde often stayed and wrote, and the Waldorf Astoria Hotel (formerly the "British Club that banned women and the Chinese from entering").

Darkness had fallen as we crossed over the multi-lane Bund and climbed some steps on the other side and up onto the esplanade. There was an explosion of patterned lights across the skyline and shimmering on the river, like nothing I had ever seen before in my life! The view across the Huangpu to Pudong districts is, I still believe, the most breathtaking skyline in the world today. The space age looking Oriental Pearl Radio and TV tower with its huge pink globes decreasing in size upwards along the tower, glowed with an array of fluorescent bright, ever changing colors of green, blue and red lighting up the sky around it. It stood surrounded by odd shaped majestic skyscrapers and space age-looking buildings, some with giant TV screens, advertising cream for acne, deodorant and other romantic products! The bright dancing colors and lights reflected onto the river illuminating the coal barges that were still moving steadily along the river. My jaw dropped open as I silently took in the awe-inspiring scenery.

After lingering there for around 20 minutes, the group moved on to a "bar street" (every city in China has them, and asking a taxi driver for this destination will always get you to the center of the partying culture.) I cannot remember what I drank or how much I drank, but the hangover felt like the Chinese Liberation Army was marching through my head.

The next day, we caught a train to the ancient city of Nanjing. The first president of China, Dr Sun Yat-sen (who was a committed Christian) is entombed there. It was also Generalissimo Chiang Kai-shek 's headquarters during the Japanese war, and home to the Ming dynasty tombs. I was excited and ready but as the group was getting ready to assemble in the lounge and wait for the bus to the rail station, I asked the guide "Can you spare me 20 minutes? There's something I need to do?" The group nodded and continued chatting amongst themselves. I sprinted down East Nanjing Road, over two roads and crossed the Bund. I ran up the steps to the Esplanade overlooking the Huangpu and cried out, slightly of breath, "I'll be back. I promise." And with that, I returned to the waiting group, threw my case on the bus and anticipated what was waiting in Nanjing.

I am not sure what I expected at Nanjing. I loved the pollution-free environment at Purple Mountain where Sun Yat-sen is respectfully entombed only a stone's throw from many Ming emperors. I enjoyed walking through the thoughtfully designed gardens leading to the Ming tombs, but it would be two other places that tattooed this magnificent city indelibly upon my heart forever.

CHAPTER 26

The day that I set off by myself to explore Nanjing, it was raining. I was in the south-western outskirts of the city, near the site called a "pit of ten thousand corpses". Within walking distance of this mass grave was *The Memorial for Compatriots killed in the Nanjing Massacre by Japanese Forces of Aggression*. The museum commemorated an extensively documented wartime atrocity that Japan had tried to cover up for decades.

On 13 December 1937, Nanjing fell to Japanese forces. What happened in these first six to eight weeks of occupation is something that China will never forget, although Japan had denied it ever happened until only recently. More than 300,000 soldiers and innocent citizens were brutally raped, burnt, buried alive and decapitated for sport during one of the most sadistic occupations that any country has inflicted on a neighbor.

I had long been interested in visiting the "Massacre Museum", which documented what has been called "China's forgotten holocaust". And here I was. A bell tolled eerily as I entered. A large poem called *Crazy Snowflakes* adorned one wall recounting the time that the Japanese army descended on Nanjing like snow. Everywhere I walked in this thoughtfully and sensitively designed open museum was a tomb. I walked past excavated open graves. I saw harrowing photos of young girls and old ladies being brutally raped, and Japanese soldiers collecting decapitated heads as trophies. I passed through halls full of recorded and written testimonies of those who witnessed the atrocities and yet to this day, revisionist historians still deny it took place. (For evidence I would encourage you to read the late American journalist Iris Chang's moving account: *The Rape of Nanking: The Forgotten Holocaust of World War II*, published in 1997).

The memorial halls were all dark inside apart from the illuminated glass cases full of recorded interviews from survivors, mostly in Chinese with English subtitles. About 10 feet above the floor all around, huge TV screens showed scenes captured on camera by journalists as well as footage confiscated from the Japanese imperial army once they had surrendered to the Americans. The films showed Chinese civilians, women, men, and children being herded together and marched towards the "killing areas" a few miles outside the city. Photos showed Japanese officers slicing off the heads of Chinese civilian men and posing for the camera surrounded by headless bodies. The "trophy snapshots" taken by Japanese soldiers were of old women being gang raped and teenage girls being mutilated after sex. One photo showed the Yangtze River full of dead children. The signs around me said, "No cameras, keep silent". There were no words to describe what I was experiencing and even if I wanted to speak, anything I said would have been wrong.

Amid the violent graphic images, the photograph series that left me utterly gutted were those of a farmer. In the first photo, the farmer was wiping his brow in the midday sun after a hard morning's work in the field while a Japanese soldier could be seen walking towards him. The next photo showed the farmer smiling and drawing on a cigarette while leaning on his long spade. The third photo showed the Japanese soldier walking away, the farmer lying on the ground with a bullet hole in his head. The gentle looking peasant looked just like my father with his amiable demeanor, wavy grey hair and weathered face with laugh lines around his eyes. The similar slim silhouette and simple working clothes reminded me of the many hours back home in Scotland digging and planting seeds with Dad.

My dad was a peaceful, kind man about the same age as this Chinese man would have been. I had only recently lost my dad to cancer and was still grieving the pointless waste of life, and these photos pierced my heart. Tears flowed warm and freely as I walked from hall to hall. Chinese visitors, some wiping their own eyes, looked at me in bewilderment. Why should a foreigner feel their pain? Why should this tall Scot be weeping over lives he never knew? I could not answer their silent questions. But I could weep with them.

After an hour inside the museum, I went straight back to my hotel. My stomach was churning. The thought of eating made me feel violently ill. With the tragic stories still spinning in my head, the images burned into my psyche, I didn't feel able to face another person for the rest of the day. Back in my room, I lay on my bed and cried into my pillow. I had just witnessed the worst side of humanity ever. I can now relate to people who have visited the likes of Auschwitz; it changes you forever.

The other place of intense historical importance that I wanted to visit was the temple where a famous treaty was "negotiated". The 15th temple was sacrosanct. During the era of British imperialism in China, no foreigner or non-priest was allowed to step foot inside.

In the early 1800s, China was a closed nation and one seen by the "bully" west as a resource to be exploited. Foreign armies took millions of artifacts over the years and in return sold opium to China. The British were the primary instigators of this destructive exchange. The habit of smoking opium had filtered down from the wealthy aristocrats to the common people of China to the point that in the early 1800s, 90 per cent of men under 40 years old were addicts. Opium dens littered every port along the east coast.

Industry was being detrimentally affected, people were dying of overdoses and the East India Company and its British owners were becoming extremely rich. Eventually China said, "No more" and tried to ban opium. They began firing corrupt customs officers and besieged 13 British drug smugglers inside their warehouses, publicly burning any opium they confiscated. This eventually resulted in two costly "Opium Wars" where the Royal Navy and her allies completely overpowered the primitive Chinese Imperial Navy.

Having won a military victory, the British forced the Chinese to concede to a series of unjust sanctions. The "Unequal Treaty of Nanjing" was the first of many of these. The treaty itself was signed on the British warship HMS Cornwallis anchored at Nanjing. Western history books tells us the treaty was signed aboard HMS Cornwallis on 29 August 1842 by British representative Sir Henry Pottinger and Qing dynasty representatives, Qiying, Ilibu and Niujian. What these books fail to impress is the utter humiliation that was meted out to China that day.

China suffered economic hardship from being forced to pay war reparations of 21 million silver dollars. Hong Kong was leased to Britain for 99 years. China's attempt to ban the opium trade failed. The country was forced not only to buy even more opium, but also to open up five "Treaty Ports" (including Shanghai) to the West. Opium use in China subsequently doubled.

I often thought about the cold-blooded pimps in Niddrie who lured 10-year-old kids into drug addiction by selling candy laced with heroin from ice cream vans outside of schools forcing them into a life of crime. These drug pushers had blood on their hands. I couldn't fathom a situation where an entire nation went to war so they could continue to profit from a drug trade that was destroying another country's social fabric and killing countless lives.

Having agreed to the terms of the treaty (China had no option), the British delegation marched through the streets of Nanjing to the city's holiest temple with pomp and arrogance. They entered the sacred Jinghai Temple and forced the Chinese leaders to play host, thus desecrating the site with their presence in a grotesque display of sovereignty. History tells us there were at least four of these meetings prior to the signing on HMS Cornwallis. This itself was a crude reminder to the Chinese of how powerful and sadistically insensitive the British were at that time. No foreigner or even Chinese laypersons were allowed to enter this hallowed temple, only the priests.

I had no idea if the temple still existed and if it did, would the people of Nanjing allow another foreigner to visit it? I began to ask anyway. The concierge at my hotel guided me to some old maps of the city. By cross checking these with local historic records, I was able to locate where I thought this temple would be. I followed the route of the original city wall and I found myself walking through huge piles of rubble and derelict decaying buildings. My maps showed this to be a popular residential street at one point, but not any more. I walked along this road, often tripping over bricks or obsolete plumbing pipes and thinking that I was going nowhere. People would sometimes appear from a derelict building and stare before disappearing again. I had the feeling that I was walking into an ambush. After about 20 minutes of being scorched by the blazing hot summer sun, I came to the end of this crumbling street and saw what looked like the entrance to an old temple, obscured by trees. I followed my hunch and voila! There it was.

Featuring the style of traditional Chinese architecture, the two-storey temple had round windows and a red tiled roof. The entrance was a double wooden door with large brass handles. I had to climb over the huge step that most Chinese buildings had below the door. The ancient (and not so ancient) Chinese believed that demons were only a few inches high and therefore could not climb over these steps to enter a house.

Two elderly ladies wearing red armbands with Chinese writing on them halted me. I held out a piece of paper with the words "Unequal Treaty" written in Chinese and they nodded and pointed to another smaller building in the temple complex to my right.

The place was deserted, possibly because it was so hard to find and there were no useable roads that led to it. And partly because most Chinese would not want to be reminded of this humiliating episode of China's rich colorful history. (Although they would never forget it.)

I later learned that the historic site that I had visited was a 1987 reconstruction, with subsequent extensions ever since. The original temple was devastated during the Taiping Rebellion and the Cultural Revolution, which saw the rampant destruction of traditional architecture. The only part of the original temple that had survived was the stele, a tall upright slab on the back of a large turtle sculpture in the courtyard. In 1990, the temple was turned into a public memorial site, the Nanjing Treaty Historical Exhibition Museum.

I went upstairs to a viewing area where drawings and paintings of the treaty's signing were on display. Local cartoons from the time vividly showed the arrogant British bulldozing their way into sleepy little China and demanding rewards for not destroying her! The full copy of the treaty text in Mandarin and Chinese was showcased inside a glass cabinet, with the caption: "The original treaty being kept in London and another original in Taipei".

I followed the backstairs down into a large paneled room with an informational sign which read: "The Unequal Treaty of Nanjing was ratified here." I entered the room and sat in one of the large antique chairs, tearing up. "Shame on you, England, shame on you Britain," I shouted in a whisper. I tried to imagine the shining uniforms of the fat British delegation squeezed into this room with their slight, silk dressed Chinese counterparts having no choice but to agree to all of their terms. It was an acutely humbling experience and one, which made me more in love with China than I already was.

I am not going to give a play-by-play of those three glorious life-changing weeks in China, but I will pick out a few gems. From Nanjing we flew to Xi'an to see the Terracotta Army, made up life sized warrior statues. My highlight was meeting the old farmer who found the first original statue while digging in his community field. I shook hands with him as presidents and monarchs had done before me!

In Xi'an, I also hired a bicycle and cycled around the impressively intact old city walls. During my peaceful ride, I stopped at a photo booth and paid $1 to dress up as the emperor and pose for a photo. While I was waiting for it to be developed, an old man and his grandson pushed a pen and paper towards me and nodded for me to sign it.

"No," I said, gently pushing it back, "I am not a real emperor, I am just a visitor to Xi'an."

The man at the photo booth smiled and whispered to me, "They not clazy, they know emperor of China long dead, they think you famous Hollywood movie star."

I was about to say something to the contrary, and then changed my mind. I took the piece of paper and wrote, "Have a wonderful day, yours sincerely, Charlie Mac."

They jumped up and laughed as I passed it to them.

"Have a good day y'all," I shouted in a fake American accent, waving as I left.

The photo guy looked at me. "Bad accent," he said, "I think you German."

I collected my photo and rode off on my bike, giggling.

From Xi'an, my tour group flew to Chongqing where we boarded a boat for our "luxury cruise" up the Yangtze River. I spent most of the three-day trip in a tiny cabin suffering from food poisoning. I only left it once to sing Bon Jovi's *It's My Life* at a karaoke session filled with Chinese and Japanese tourists in one of the lower decks.

After three days of temples, toilets and tummy aches, I stayed in a hotel for one night before catching an overnight train to Beijing. Our tour group experienced the majestic genius of the Great Wall (an immensely moving experience) and was taken to the Forbidden City and Tiananmen Square. The guide inside the Forbidden City said he was going to explain everything to us, and that we should stay close. I thanked him but took off alone. I didn't need a guide. I had studied this palace for decades and watched every documentary, read every book and watched every movie on it.

I was lost in the splendor, swept back into a time of imperial courts, travelling folk operas, floating silk kites, calligraphy painting on wall scrolls, the pungent smells of spices and mouth-watering foods at bustling street markets. I thought about the concubines and eunuchs, usually romanticized in western media, and I imagined their elegant clothing and serene expressions that masked their often-tragic, heartbreaking circumstances.

For years I had dreamt of visiting the Forbidden City in China, the older I got the less likely it all looked like it would happen... but here I was! I drank in the atmosphere as I imagined the dynasties that had lived and ruled here. I stood gazing into the

Dragon Throne, the centerpiece of the Forbidden City and by far my favorite part, although every inch to me was special. My heart raced frantically as I remembered that Puyi, the last emperor of China, had sat on this very throne only 70 years before. (Puyi died in 1967 as a humble gardener, after being "re-educated" by the communist government.)

I lost all notion of time. Eventually, I wandered out as the gates were closing. I tried hard to remember where my hotel was but no, it had gone. It was near the east side of Tiananmen but where was the east? I remembered our tour guide saying, "If you ever get lost in Beijing, look for a Japanese guide with a little flag on a long pole. They nearly always end up back at the square." I soon found a small yellow hatted person with a flag and tagged along behind about 50 tourists with red baseball hats and cameras... FOUR hours later, I arrived back at my hotel having visited three temples, two parks and a sushi restaurant!

I flew home to Scotland in a daze. What had just happened to me? I wasn't sure if I knew who I was any more. I had returned a very different person in so many different ways. The day after I returned, I went to watch my local football team, Edinburgh's Hibernian, play Glasgow's Partick Thistle. I sat watching the bleak game on this wet Sunday afternoon as the rain swept in from the River Forth estuary.

The rain was cold, penetrating and unfriendly. Scotland was like a foreign country to me now. Only days earlier, I basked in the summer sun and felt the light warm rain of eastern China fall gently upon me. I tried to console myself with the thought that I would definitely return soon. But for now, I felt like a newlywed husband who had to leave his wife for a short time on a reluctant but necessary business trip. I was bursting at the seams to tell "somebody", "anybody", about where I had just been and how it all felt...

I turned to a teenage girl sitting next to me and remarked, "You know, it was scorching in Beijing yesterday." She swore at me and ran to a policeman.

"What's all this?" he said. 'You telling people you were in China? No more or I'll throw you out!"

I popped into my local pub on the way home and a regular remarked, "Hey, Charlie boy, not seen you in nearly a month! Where have you been?"

I was about to say, "China", but couldn't... how could I say I had stood in the Massacre Museum of Nanjing, sat where the treaty of Nanjing was ratified, sailed down the Yangtze, walked on the Great Wall and roamed the Forbidden City in Beijing... while this guy had probably not even moved off his bar stool!

"Ah nothing much," I said, sighing.

"Aye, me too," he agreed solemnly.

I knew then and there that I had to leave Scotland for good.

CHAPTER 27

As much as I was ready to pack my suitcase and immediately move to China, I still had things to do in Scotland. I was hosting the regular evening show for a Scottish commercial radio station and enjoying it. My course in radio broadcasting at Edinburgh's Telford College had led to a "dream job" as host of the Charlie Mac show, Monday to Friday on River FM. I worked under the expert guidance of the multi-talented Donny Hughes, who would later become a presenter on The Nightshift on Scottish TV.

The radio show was hard work and great fun. I would run through a playlist of popular chart music, chat in between sets, conduct caller quizzes and competitions, and interview guests. I was sometimes called upon to commentate at football matches, review rock concerts, judge talent shows and along with my good friend Keith Reid, appear at the odd roadshow and village event. I had even developed a "radio voice', which sounded nothing like me. "103.4 River FM… This is Charlie Mac on the big evening show," I would say, trying to sound like Donny. It was intoxicating, fast, and surreal.

During the day I worked as a packer at a DIY warehouse. My colleagues used to brag they had Charlie Mac working with them. I would sometimes even turn up for work in the River FM car which was covered in the distinctive orange and blue logo, causing a buzz at the warehouse. But as jolly as this time was, it paled in comparison to what I had experienced in China. I had been wooed, my heart stolen. I did not belong to Scotland any more.

But when you have backslidden from God, you are living in a vulnerable state. You carry a weight of guilt that you were never meant to bear and will believe every lie of Satan whose one goal is to have you remain in this state of spiritual numbness and condemnation.

That accusing inner voice reminded me time and time again that I had walked away from Barnsley. "You have blown it now. God will

NEVER use you as a pastor again." Like a fool, I believed that lie for nearly 20 years. And so I reasoned that if my heart was indeed in the Far East, I needed a profession.

I had enjoyed teaching part-time religious education in several schools while I was a pastor in Hartlepool and Barnsley. I certainly had an aptitude for children's work. I decided that if I was no good to God as a pastor any more, I would become a teacher.

Having already finished my 10-week TEFL course, I decided to gain add a TESOL (Teaching English to Speakers of Other Languages) certification to my credentials. I was impressed by Chichester College in Bangkok, Thailand that offered a six-week TESOL course and guaranteed a teaching position at the end of it. I applied and was accepted. Not long after, I tendered my resignation to the radio station.

And so on 5 March 2004, I stood at Edinburgh Airport with two suitcases and a ticket to Bangkok. I had driven there in my big red Renault Saloon which I'd already paid off and was in immaculate condition. I handed the keys to the car park attendant. "Here, it's a gift," I said, as I walked away from it. The announcement came for the overnight flight to Bangkok. I turned and looked at Donny.

"Go on," he said.

"I can't do it," I said, crying.

Donny pushed me forward. "If you don't go, I'll kick your arse all the way there myself." His voice cracked a little; he too was trying hard to keep it together. I turned, waved, and left.

Chichester College gave me practical opportunities to apply my training, as local Thai adults paid a reduced fee to learn English from TESOL students in the evening. They received English lessons, the college was paid, and we could immediate practise the vital things we learned in class. Following my graduation, I was placed in a wonderful school with amazing teachers and adorable kids called

Chokchai Bilingual School, about 25 miles north-east of Bangkok. I became a kindergarten teacher along with three newcomers. My friendships forged there with foreign and Thai teachers remain strong to this day.

After two years, I answered an advertisement to become a grade two elementary school teacher in Tanzania, East Africa. I received a phone call a few days later, inviting me to do a phone interview. The interview went favorably and although the principal said that she had one more teacher to interview, I knew the job was mine. You just *know* sometimes.

Five days later, my phone rung, it was a representative from the school in Tanzania.

"Sorry to inform you, Mr Mackenzie. But we have decided to give the job to the other teacher that we interviewed. He has more experience than you and he is also more qualified, thanks for your interest in us and we wish you well for the future."

"I think you are making a mistake," I said.

"Begging your pardon," the rep said, indignant. "We are certain that we have made the right decision and would ask you to respect this."

"No disrespect intended," I said. "But you will see that this is an error of judgment."

The line went dead.

I put the whole incident to the back of my mind and threw myself into Chokchai. It was almost Christmas and there were plays to write, classes to teach and parties to plan for. And then something strange happened which I was not prepared for. Unbeknownst to anyone at all, I had been secretly searching for a Bible for months. I missed God. I knew He still loved me and although I was wallowing in a backslidden state, I desperately wanted to read His Word again. I searched high and low, but could not find even a Catholic bookshop in Bangkok.

The Deputy Principal visited me at coffee break, only minutes before my next class.

"You're a Christian, aren't you Charlie?" she asked, assuming because I was a foreigner, I must be. "There's a group from a local church who have come to sing some carols. They are in the front office. Please come now, they are waiting to begin." Before I could answer, she took me by the arm and began to walk me to the room where a group of Thai visitors and teaching staff were gathered. Once in the room, I looked around and recognized that nearly all the expat staff had been roped in. I nodded to them and sat down nervously, not sure why I felt so uncomfortable.

The Deputy Principal translated for the visitors, who explained that the five of them were from a local Thai Pentecostal church. The group consisted of a pastor, her husband, two other ladies and a 10-year-old girl. A woman in the group with a guitar began to play Christmas carols, with the rest of them singing the lyrics in Thai. I knew the tunes but not the language. Nevertheless I joined in at first, and then lost in the joy of it all, sung loudly in English. They performed some of my favorite carols, *Hark the Herald Angels Sing*, *Away in a Manger* and *Joy to the world*. I enjoyed this intermission from teaching but needed to leave for my next class. Just as I was about to go, the Deputy Principal said, "They just want to sing one more time." I sat back down.

The Pastor began to play acoustic guitar in a soft, gentle way. The 10-year-old girl wearing a long dark blue pinafore dress and bright purple sandals stepped forward and started singing. As her soprano voice filled the room, the girl closed her eyes. The melody was hauntingly serene and powerful. The song was not in Thai, nor English nor any other earthly tongue. I closed my eyes as the unfamiliar melody swept over me. As she sung, I felt like a fire had been ignited in my heart. I thought I was going to burst with joy and power and love. The girl opened her big brown eyes as she drew to a close minutes later and her face shone with pure holy pleasure. I looked around to see if it was only me who had been affected; at least three of my colleagues wiped their eyes and one pretended she had a cold. Something had happened spiritually that the others around me seemed oblivious to. They were moved by the emotion but that was all. I felt cut to the heart by the words she had sung. Hauntingly strange words that I longed to know the meaning of.

The Deputy Principal smiled at me. "That was for you, Charlie," she said. "You have some future ahead of you."

"Me?" I said, shaking.

"Yes, that message was directed at you. The pastor's daughter was giving a prophecy that God is going to use you again powerfully in the future."

And so there, in that moment in time, in a small room in a school outside Bangkok, God the Gracious, the Lord of the Second Chance, began to draw this prodigal son back to Him. It was going to be a long painful road strewn with failure and heartache, but this marked the beginning. I was on my way home to Jesus. The deputy principal called for me to come into her office as I passed by later that afternoon.

"Charlie, the ladies left two gifts, I am going to keep this lovely paperweight for my office, but I think you are meant to have this one."

She handed me a rectangular shaped parcel wrapped in paper.

"Thank you, Lord," I whispered. Here was the Bible I had been searching for all these months.

Posing with an untethered tiger in Phuket Thailand

CHAPTER 28

Over the years, I'd learned to expect the unexpected. But when my phone rang at 4pm after I had left work for the day, I can't say I was surprised by what happened next. I was walking through the small housing compound that I lived in and stopped to answer it. A familiar voice spoke at the other end of the line.

"Hello, is that Mr Charlie? This is Tanga International School in Tanzania. We made a mistake, the other teacher let us down at the last minute. We should have chosen you. Are you still interested in working for us?"

I stifled my imminent laughter and the temptation to say, "I told you so," and said, "I would be delighted to come." Chokchai asked me to reconsider and offered a two-year contract but I wanted to taste Africa and these opportunities were not that common. Furthermore, I was excited about the prospect of living in Tanga, a tropical port city located four hours south of Mombasa. The small northern city had swapped hands a few times during World War II. (Both Germany and Britain claimed sovereignty over it). Tanzania, formerly known as the British colony of Tanganyika, won its independence on 9 December 1961. And so there was a small German and a just-as-small community of Brits living there (which added to the mystery of discovering Tanga).

The noise as I stepped off my flight around 4pm and into Tanzania's Dar es Salaam International airport was deafening. The impatient, rowdy crowd tried to push past each other as we all headed towards customs and immigration. We were ushered into a stuffy room with a low ceiling where people were trying to cut what almost resembled a queue and screaming at the black uniformed custom officers to let them through immediately. A French man in front of me yelled, "Do you not know who I am?" Another threatened to have a customs official fired. "I know the president," he said, wagging a finger in warning. I smiled at the brawny guard in charge and shook his hand.

"I am from Scotland," I said. "I am in no rush, just see to those 'important' people first. I am happy to wait here."

I smiled again and stood back a little, allowing the demanding people to push in deeper and shout even louder. Less than five minutes later, I felt a large hand on my shoulder. "Come," I was told. The large guard whom I had been chatting with earlier, bulldozed his way to the front of the line and said to one of the clerks, "Process this man first... he is from Scotland." I felt like royalty. I was fast tracked and within minutes, walked out a side door and that was it. I found myself in the car park, in heavy rain. Across from me, two men in T-shirts and baseball caps frantically waved at me from inside their car. Their car was at least 30 years old and looked like it had been hit several times by rhinos. I smiled as I walked towards them. For the next six hours, this was to be my taxi to Tanga!

I had arrived in the middle of a massive downpour. The road from Dar es Salaam up to Tanga was a bumpy ride and even worse in wet weather. By the time I arrived at my destination at the Tanga Yacht Club around 10pm, I was tired, hungry and motion sick.

A group of governors and the principal were waiting to greet me at the yacht club, and most of them were more than tipsy. As I shook hands with each of them, I was given a bottle of "Tusker" (local beer) which tasted delicious! I stayed an hour before being driven a few hundred yards to my bungalow on the Indian Ocean. The school had filled the fridge full of goodies such as fresh milk, bread and chocolate. I flopped into bed exhausted and switched on the fan... and experienced my first of many African power cuts!

I was thrown into the deep end the very next day. I woke at 7am to prepare for a school open day at 9am! I wandered over, expecting to mingle with the crowd and shake a few hands. Instead the principal shouted, "You made it then? Good, you can lead all the parents and children in aerobics." I was handed a microphone, the music blared from the speakers and it was my cue! Still half-asleep from travelling, I threw myself into what must have been the world's worst ever exercise routine. After eight minutes, the music stopped and I bent over exhausted. "Great stuff," a German parent cried out. "That got us going," a Finnish Doctor called Tommi said. I looked up and smiled at them.

If I said that the Australian principal at the school was not exactly friendly, I would be guilty of a gross understatement. She was a large lady in her late 40s who barked orders at Tanzanian staff and had a constant red face due to the amount of alcohol she had consumed the night before. It was very clear that she did not like Christians. But I was there for the long haul and to enjoy Africa, so I rose above it.

I had already emailed the local Elim pastor, Raphael, weeks earlier and soon became friends with this remarkable man of God. Raphael had turned down a career as a doctor to pastor Mikanjuni Elim Pentecostal Church, a small village church. His church was run out of a small rented room in a simple one-storey detached concrete building and like most of the small houses in the village, it had a large backyard. On most Sundays, the backyard was the church. A red and blue piece of tarp was pulled overhead to shield us from the east African sun's deadly rays and a fan was hooked up to a long extension cable from inside the house. The cool breeze just about made the one hour service bearable.

Raphael was a man of vision and had plans to see an international church in the village of Mikanjuni. Me arriving there was a step in that direction. Before too long I was sharing my testimony and messages at this amazing little fellowship. I still felt like I was very much the prodigal son trudging home, but I also knew beyond doubt that I belonged to God.

Back at school, the principal continually harassed me and enthusiastically sought every opportunity to attack my teaching style. I would turn up at school, take a deep breath and say, "Good Morning Fay," and usually received the gruff reply, "What's good about it?" I sought refuge by spending time with my Christian family and of course, by playing football.

After a few months, I formed a parents and teachers football team. A few local schools were keen to do likewise and so the Tanga Schools League was born. In football, I released all of my frustrations by imagining the ball I was kicking was a familiar face that I encountered daily! I played hard. The team nicknamed me "Babu" (Granddad) because I was the oldest in the team. They even had it printed on the back of my green football kit. Every time I scored, I had to run to the fans, turn and point to the name!

African football is a dangerous game. After being knocked down so many times, I soon toughened up. If there was a 50-50 tackle (where two players both go for the ball at the same time), I won it. I charged, pushed, elbowed and bruised all who opposed me on the field. Winning was everything. Up until the day I left Tanga, we were only beaten once. But being a "bruiser" was like having a target painted on my back. In one game, a huge African guy managed to tackle me to the ground more than once – payback for me flattening his goalkeeper! It was painful, bloody, bruising fun and I loved it. After the games ended and we sat with the other team, it was amazing how much we liked each other and how we'd laugh about the tackles and "unorthodox" style of play!

At school I often turned up for work sporting cuts or bandages or on crutches, and would be greeted by the principal's taunts, "You should stop playing, you're too old." Her behavior became so off-putting that after a year, I successfully applied for a teaching post at a school in Shanghai. I had enjoyed my stay in Africa but I had my limits. I planned to tender my resignation at the end-of-the-year concert and leave for Shanghai a month later.

The school concert in the open grounds of Tanga International School was a glamorous affair and one of the highlights of the city's social calendar. We were the only international school in the region, so everyone got dressed up and invited their relatives. Before the concert, I approached Indra, the chairperson of the school's board of governors and said that I wanted to tell her something.

"Me too, Charlie," Indra said. "I want to ask you something as well, talk to me after the concert." Having made an appointment to talk to her, I felt calm and comforted that there would be no difficulty in sharing my news with her.

After the last song, people made a beeline to the delicious buffet. Indra found me.

"Ok, Charlie, what is it?" she said, smiling.

"You go first," I said.

"Ok then. The board has had another round of complaints about Fay's behavior in and out of school and we have decided not to renew her contract. We would therefore like to offer you the position of principal."

The offer was so unexpected, I was speechless for seconds.

"Now what was it you wanted to ask me?" Indra said. "Go on, then."

I took a breath, smiled and said, "First of all, I accept your offer. Secondly, I wanted to inform you that a school in Shanghai has made me a very generous offer, but you will be glad to know I won't be taking it."

I emailed the school in Shanghai. While disappointed, they were understanding and said they would keep the job open for me for a year. I thought to myself, "One more year in Africa, and then I am guaranteed a high paid job in China! How good God is."

One of the first things I accomplished as the principal of Tanga International School was a better deal for the facilities staff. They received access to free tea and cake at break times, alongside the local and expat teachers and administrative staff. At the beginning of the year, I organized a meal for all staff members and their partners, from teachers to governors and facility staff. The meal took place on our fashionable, elevated school terrace. It was exhilarating to see cleaners and gardeners arrive looking like royalty. Our maintenance manager, who was a senior member of the local Muslim community, commented, "It is clear to see that a Christian is now the principal."

I also established the "Principals' Fraternity of Tanga" where principals from all the major schools would meet weekly over coffee and cake, and exchange ideas on how we could work together as a community of educators, share facilities and promote a united front as friends. (Football was also often on the agenda…)

I began to preach more regularly at Mikanjuni Elim Pentecostal Church and the large city Lutheran church as well. Raphael arranged a gathering of the leaders of the Elim Pentecostal Church in Tanzania and I was formally recognized as an Elim pastor and given a signed ordination certificate, welcoming me as one of their own pastors.

But I was always painfully aware I was living in a spacious bungalow, driving into town in a new Hyundai and eating most nights at restaurants while many Tangans walked around barefoot and only ate rice and "ugali" every day. A Tanzanian staple, ugali was a chewy, starchy dish made by boiling maize flour, however, it contained little nutrients and in many cases, it was all that families had to eat. Walking around my four-bedroom house at the school with servant quarters, a maid and two gardeners, reminded me of this chasm.

After school one day, I drove to Bombo Regional Hospital. This hospital had been a military hospital during World War II and still has the shell holes on the walls of one of its main buildings. It is the largest hospital in the Tanga region and by far the poorest. On many visits there, I had to walk around or step over deceased patients covered thin white linen. There were at least two patients to every bed and no air-conditioning in the wards.

I entered the general manager's office and introduced myself. The manager sprung to his feet like a soldier jumping to attention. "What do you want, sir?"

I spoke slowly and deliberately. "I am very aware that every day I pass this hospital in my car, and many sick people are carried in by friends or arrive here in bicycles. I live in a large bungalow and many of my friends and colleagues live in mud buildings with no electricity. I want to contribute to this community."

He looked at me, confused, so I continued.

"I want you to find the dirtiest, smelliest, most dangerous job in the hospital, and I will come and do it every weekend for free."

The man stared at me, before eventually saying, "Hold on, I need to confer."

He called a number and spoke frantically in Kiswahili for several minutes, before replacing the receiver and saying, "Please return on Saturday morning at seven o'clock, Mr Charles, I have such a job for you." I shook his hand, thanked Jesus and left.

On Saturday morning, a tall elderly man in dark green overalls greeted me. He introduced himself as Mohamed. His toothless grin warmed him to me immediately. "Come," he said, leading me to a one-storey building near the car park. Upon entering, Mohamed gave me a rubber apron, tall rubber boots, rubber gloves and a surgical mask. We each took along 12 black plastic bags and a refuse collection cart. We were the hospital's trash collectors.

From around 7:15am until we finished about two or three hours later, we went to every ward and emptied all the trash into the large black bags, tied them up and took them to the waste dumpster. When I say trash, I am not talking about paper cups and chocolate wrappers! There were bags of blood, used needles, body parts and vomit all lurking in the trash bins in the wards. The theater was the most gruesome collection point. There you could find anything from a placenta to a human limb. The stench was cruel, and soon I had to rub Tiger Balm under my nose to mask the smell. Yet I was overjoyed at being able to help in a modest way. I sung praises to God as I entered the children's ward, the maternity wards and the men's and women's wards. I got to know the low paid staff - security guards, and part-time cooks, who made really good porridge for the patients from maize flour. The cooks were amazing, hard working ladies who had large families of their own in the villages surrounding Tanga. I also had some wonderful conversations in broken Kiswahili and English with one of the ladies who swept the roads inside the Bombo hospital compound. These dear people became friends to me and I to them. I knew their names and those of their families and they all knew my name… Babu Charles!

One day, I was sitting on the end of a bed chatting with a heavily pregnant woman when I overheard a man opposite us talking in Kiswahili. "Who is the Mzungu (white man)?" he asked. "Oh," his friend answered. "He is a missionary, he comes here every weekend."

"A missionary?" I thought. "No, Lord", I prayed. "I am not a missionary, I am just someone collecting trash to show my fellow Tanzanians that I am not above them." The words of Jesus in the Book of Matthew 25:40 came to mind. "Truly I tell you, whatever you did for one of the least of these brothers and sisters of mine, you did for me." "Wow!" I thought. "A missionary!" It felt good to be called by such a noble name. In the weeks following, I made friends with many locals. Slowly, inch-by-inch, I was also drawing nearer to God.

I spent many hours each week in the huge backyard at my house at the school alongside the gardener and got to know him well as a result. He never stopped working and always had the safety and security of my home and garden on his mind. I bought seeds from the local market and began to grow chilies, eggplant, tomatoes and bananas in the fertile soil and they took no time at all to grow. Dad had been right. I did have green fingers.

My gardener invited me to preach at his church. (My gardener was the pastor of a Pentecostal church in a village a long way from Tanga. In fact, he would spend hours cycling there, preach, stay overnight, then cycle home the next day!) I accepted his invitation and drove there one Sunday. Once my car had run out of road, I drove through long grass and then walked the remainder of the way to the church. The church was built entirely out of dry mud and timber then covered in whitewash to reflect the sun. The only ventilation was the glassless windows and the holes in the ceiling. The congregation sat in makeshift pews that were a few rough logs nailed together. The only musical instrument there was a drum. But the church was packed and the worship as good as any cathedral choir and I preached my heart out (as much as you can through an interpreter).

At the end of the service, the church leaders gave me two live chickens as a gift. I was told "Take them home, kill and eat, Bwana (Sir) Charlie." I had never killed a chicken in my life! So instead, I named them Matthew and Martha. Before too long, I had 22 chickens providing me with fresh eggs every morning. People also began giving me tortoises, either as gifts, or as "rescues" from witchdoctors. (Heartbreakingly, the local witch doctors stole several of the tortoises, mutilated them and used their shells for potions and spells). On top of this, my dog, Pookie, had puppies and my "zoo" had grown to 22 chickens, 11 tortoises and seven dogs! The children in my class at school loved doing science!

It was refreshing to walk through my gate after school to be surrounded by affectionate, barking dogs and clucking chickens. Of course, they all had names. The chickens were: Martha, Mary, Elizabeth, Naomi, Ruth, Sarah, Rebekah, Lydia, and so on. The dogs were named after all places: Paris, Madrid, Glasgow, etc… It was fun.

I remember mentioning to my new maid one day that I liked ugali (a thick porridge made from maize flower and water) but would prefer something new from time to time, and not to spend too much money on it. I wanted her to surprise me, and surprise me she did. The next day I returned home to smell the fabulous aroma of a delicious stew being cooked. I sat at my old wooden kitchen table while she ladled out two generous helpings of tender, hot, tasty stew. After a few sumptuous mouthfuls, I asked where on earth she managed to find such a wonderful dish!

215

She shouted over her shoulder. "I only picked the fattest and best chicken, you have just eaten Mary." My face turned pale. I was eating a fowl-friend! Cheeky, vocal Mary was one of my favorite chickens with real character. I never named any animals again after that!

My home in Tanga Tanzania

CHAPTER 29

While most of the doctors and nurses worked very hard at Bombo, it was pitifully under-resourced and understaffed. There were hundreds of sick people to treat every weekend. Each ward that I visited, either someone was dying, or had already died. Tuberculosis, pneumonia, malaria and AIDS were the most common killers. Although my job was an errand of mercy, I was regularly in close contact with infected patients, breathing in bacteria from open wounds and highly contagious lung diseases. My flimsy paper mask did not shield me from all the coughs and hoarse rasping that was within inches from my face at times. I was spat on several times by accident, as spitting was common in Tanzania. When all of this was compounded with the biohazardous and medical waste that I collected by hand each weekend and the weariness I often felt after managing a busy international school all week. It was inevitable I would eventually succumb to illness.

Goodness knows what bacteria hit me, but it was enough for doctors to warn me off attending my duties at Bombo until I felt stronger and able to fight the many potentially fatal illnesses that could target me there.

I found friends in the most unlikely places in Tanga. Some of these friends were influential figures. I became friends with the District Commissioner after playing at a football tournament. I was invited by the Tanzanian president to a meal at the opening of a new cement plant. The new head of immigration was a believer but sadly, not all of the immigration head's officers were Christians like him. Immigration hit squads were the bane of my existence. They would turn up without warning, interrogate my teachers and threaten my ground staff, demanding the slightest sniff of evidence that I was employing any foreigners without proper documentation.

On one occasion, a van full of overzealous immigration officers arrived at school demanding to be allowed into the classrooms. I ran to the front office and confronted them.

"Show me your warrant," I demanded.

"We do not need one," they countered. "We have special privileges as government immigration officers." A few of them sat down, to show that they weren't budging until they had their way.

"Wait here," I said firmly, before turning to my receptionist. I whispered a number to her, and she dialed it and waited for someone to answer. I angrily addressed the six officers.

"You have five minutes to get off this land or I'll make sure that you lose your jobs in 24 hours," I said.

The receptionist held up the phone and nodded to me. "District Commissioner, sir," she said, as I took the phone. I stared at the hit squad. "Hi District Commissioner, it's Charlie from Tanga International School, I have a room full of lizards from immigration here infecting my school -"

The leader of the pack froze. His mouth twitched as I glared at him, my eyes penetrating his in anger. The others fidgeted on their seats while the ones standing whispered to each other in Kiswahili. I kept hearing the words "in trouble" being used. So I upped the ante. "What's that sir? You'll be passing by my way in 10 minutes? I'll make sure they are here to welcome you." My tone was polite, while my gaze was fixed icily on the man the others looked to as their superior.

Eventually he spoke, his voice now far from menacing. "We have a crisis at Immigration House and need to return at once," he said slowly, offering the very slightest of bows. I wanted to make a joke about how he suddenly heard about a crisis without his phone ringing, but as if she was reading my mind, my secretary looked at me and silently mouthed the word "NO."

The leader barked an order at his team and they stumbled to their van outside, tripping over each other in the rush. He pointed his right forefinger at me and motioned to speak but no words came.

"Go now!" I roared at him and with that, he too turned and fled in the direction of their parked van.

The secretary gently took the phone from my hand.

"You *do* know that phone is still not working, Mr Charlie?" she said, giggling.

"Yeah, but they didn't." I replied winking at her.

Within the hour, I had a call on my cell phone.

"Mr Charlie, it's Captain Chenge from Immigration House, you have just scared the life out of my men, what on earth did you say to them?" Captain Chenge inquired in a sharp official tone.

Captain Chenge or "brother Paul", was a friend of mine, as was his predecessor. A fastidious man, Paul always looked immaculate in his government uniform. While the officer who he took over from a few months earlier was a Muslim, Paul was a committed Christian. I'd often visit him at Immigration House, have tea and read the Bible with him.

I smiled as I explained the joke. His voice also mellowed as he heard the full story.

"Keep them away from my school, Paul," I said. "Otherwise I really will make the call next time."

"Consider it done, Mr Charlie," he said.

And then I had an idea. "By the way, how about getting your lads to form a football team and we can play a friendly match at our school next Saturday, I will lay on some free food and drink?"

"Sounds a very Christian thing to do," Captain Paul said.

"Indeed it does," I said, smiling and ending the call.

My secretary leaned over her desk and asked, "Why invite those thugs to our school, Mr Charlie, you can't stand them."

"Well," I said. "If you kicked nine bells out of those lizards in the street, you would get arrested. But if I did it on the sports field, it's called football!"

"You are a terrible man, Charlie Mackenzie," she said, shaking her head.

But she had to agree, it would certainly draw a crowd. I don't know HOW on earth it happened, but word of my plan to have a friendly showdown on the football pitch got back to the immigration department and they never did accept my kind offer and neither did they ever turn up at school again!

A week later, we hosted a football game with Raskazone Primary School. We had beaten them a month earlier in a bad tempered match that left more than a few casualties. They had some of the hardest men in the league and that meant a gruelling 90 minutes of "sport".

We won the game, but at a cost. I hacked and scythed everyone who got near me, I gave away too many free kicks and should have been sent off. It was a brutal game and I was ruthless! When the whistle blew, I punched the air in victory and my teammates slapped me on the back for scoring two goals in the second half. The Raskazone players went away feeling cheated and humiliated. After they left the field, I shouted, "It's a man's game, boys."

Their principal, Mr Kofuku, was a really good mate. I often ate at his table, and he at mine. Nevertheless, he didn't call or visit all week. As the Holy Spirit began to convict me, I knew what I had to do. I drove to Raskazone Primary School as I had done so many times to see my friend, but this time, the guard was instructed not to let me in. I pleaded with him and he (knowing me well) eventually relented. I approached the principal's office and discovered that he was in a meeting with all the teachers. I walked to the meeting room and knocked on the door. When it opened, a towering Tanzanian teacher who I had purposely fouled a week earlier, stood there raging at me. I raised my hand in a conciliatory gesture to ask for a moment to speak and spoke loudly enough so the listening audience behind the door could hear me.

"May I just have 10 minutes of your time?"

He slammed the door shut in my face. I waited for almost 20 minutes until it opened again.

"You have five," the same, large, heavy-looking teacher said, opening the door to let me in.

I walked into a horseshoe of 15 seated Tanzanian male teachers all behind wooden desks with Mr Kofuku at the head and staring directly at me, his face inscrutable. All eyes were fixed on my nervous form. The atmosphere was brittle, I remember feeling this same hostile tenseness at a Chelsea versus Leeds game years before, when it only took one punch from a Leeds fan to end in a blood bath of 500 supporters. I gulped a hard dry swallow of nothing as I glanced around me. The dark wooden meeting room smelled of sweaty armpits and reminded me of a courtroom that I stood in not many years ago.

I took a deep breath and stood in the middle of them. The door was shut behind me.

"I treated you badly, my friends and colleagues," I said quietly. "I behaved like a stupid bull and a racist Mzungu (white person). I paid no respect to your feelings or dignity and hurt you physically and damaged your wonderful Tanzanian pride. If you never want to speak to me again, then I understand. But I cannot live with the guilt of my behavior and beg your forgiveness."

Mr Kofuku spoke into the silence. "Mr Charles, please wait for a moment outside."

I walked out, shaking with emotion and sat on the dirt in tears. Eventually I was summoned back inside and a spokesman, a PE teacher rose to speak on behalf of the teachers.

"You are not welcome here, and we had decided not to speak to you or your brute team mates again. However, we can see that it has taken courage to come here as well as some humility and we Tanzanians admire both. Yes, you were a bully child and cared more about a score line than the friendship of your brothers. But we are willing to forgive you. Now go, and arrange a return match in your school for next Saturday. The matter is closed."

I drove out of the school to a deserted spot on the ocean bank and repented before God. The reputation of Babu had become grotesque. People, not games, matter to God. I vowed I'd never play like a thug again.

Both the population of Raskazone and Tanga International School students and faculty turned out in force for the next game. Wives screamed and waved handkerchiefs as we took to the field. I was purposely taunted and kicked from the start of the game, but for some reason, I felt happy. The Raskazone teachers tried hard to goad me into decking someone, but that impulse wasn't there any more. I held my position at the back as center half and only came forward to pass the ball up field to my team's attacking players. With five minutes left, we were at one-one. I collected the ball from the keeper and ran through the middle of the opposing defense on a late run. I planned to go all the way and score.

From my peripheral vision, I saw two big, fat, defenders swiftly coming at me from both sides with no intention of going for the ball. Crunch! I went down like a burst balloon, the wind knocked out of me as my head bounced off the hard clay ground. I busted my nose. The two fat, muscle bound Raskazone players stood towering above me and pointed at the bleeding Mzungu below them. "Now we even, Mr Charles," they said. I looked up, dizzy from the collision and smiled.

It soon came time to say my goodbyes to Tanga. Indra and the governors were aware that I had inevitably accepted the post in Shanghai. I had only told a few close friends from the Elim and Lutheran churches and no one else. The next end-of-year concert night would be my last, but we would not tell the school until the holidays. That way, it would buffer the shock of the announcement so students and parents would not be too upset. I had agreed to allow a youth group of singers from the Lutheran church to come and sing a song at the concert to add variety and a spiritual dimension.

The night was going smoothly, as I introduced these sincere, talented guys onto the stage.

"We want to dedicate this song to our friend Charlie, it is a song we have written to let him know that we will never forget him as he goes to China next month!" They then began…

"So sad… So sad, So sad you're leaving… We will miss you as you go, as you go. And we sing… So sad you're leaving…"

Mouths dropped open, women whispered, and parents and students looked confused. I wanted the earth to open and swallow me up! Indra quickly grabbed the microphone from the lead singer after the group's performance and in a slightly nervous, lighthearted tone, explained that she was going to share my news at the end of the concert… but that those brash boys beat her to it (no one laughed). So if I had any second thoughts about leaving, they had just been put out to pasture!

Bruce Willis lookalike at a president's Lunch in Tanga

CHAPTER 30

My new school in Shanghai put me up in a hotel in the Minhang district, a residential and factory area along the Huangpu River, with a population of about 2.5 million people. On my first evening, I went for a walk and was bombarded with a plethora of fragrant street food smells. Every food imaginable was there! Roast duck, Shanghai dumplings, stewed pork… everything that would make my tastebuds dance with joy. After two years of having rice, chicken and ugali as part of my staple diet, this was food wonderland.

With my new students in Shanghai

The next day I underwent a mandatory medical examination. The expensive experience was a bit surreal. I arrived at the medical center at 9am and changed into a robe. And then I had to work my way through a series of rooms and examinations including: an ultrasound, heart monitor, x-ray and finally, blood tests. At the end, I was told that I had two large masses in my abdomen. I explained that they were probably just a few of my fatty lumps. The doctor considered this and consulted the radiologist, who nodded his approval. Cue the stamping of my medical record.

I began work two days later, but not before I caught a taxi to the Bund. I walked across its multi-lane promenade, climbed the steps up to the esplanade and shouted at the spectacular Shanghai skyline, "I'm back… I told you I would be."

To be honest, I was like a kid in a toy shop. Living and earning an income in China was a dream come true. Shanghai had completely stolen my heart and senses. It was a totally modern city, yet it was still a part of ancient China. I loved the people, the food, the subway and even Shanghai United International School where I worked

After a few weeks, I began to look for a church to attend. I was told of a few "established" churches that foreigners were permitted to attend but continued to search for one that was a little "less established". One afternoon, I was walking past the hotel I had previously stayed at and I saw a bakery on the other side of the road. A voice within me said, "Go buy a donut." Nothing strange about that, except that I didn't like donuts. But the voice persisted. "Go buy a donut." I relented and crossed the road.

"I don't know why I am here," I said, smiling at the girl behind the counter, "I am here to buy donuts and I don't even like them."

She smiled back and I made small talk. "Nice bakery, who owns it?"

"We are a Christian bakery," she said. "We are part of the Korean Community Church which is the biggest evangelical church in Shanghai. There are 5000 members. The church is on the fifth floor of this building. Please check us out, our services are in Korean, Chinese, Japanese and English."

"Go buy a donut." What a strange request, and yet here was the church I would worship in, for the foreseeable future. I began to enjoy donuts from that day on and to this day, still do!

A few days later, I was sharing this story at school with my 10 year old students when a young Hong Kong boy who was aptly named "Christian" asked if he could punch me hard! I braced myself and

226

said in a deep voice, "Go ahead, give it your best shot." He punched me hard in the stomach and I pretended I felt nothing. The things you do to make kids smile. On deep reflection had God not allowed that young boy to punch me that day, I may not still be here to write the story. His punch was a blessing in disguise, as it led me to going to hospital before it was too late and probably saved my life.

On a weekend visit to Nanjing, I began to bleed from the bottom. Upon my return, I went to see my GP. Dr Mike said it was probably food poisoning picked up in Nanjing. He put me on some antibiotics and painkillers, but the pain grew worse. I continued to bleed. I also lost my appetite and 33 pounds in about two months. Something was definitely not right. I eventually booked some time off school to get to the bottom of this. Dr Mike booked me in for a colonoscopy at his clinic in Minhang. Several friends offered to go with me but I declined. There are times in life when you need people around you for support and comfort, but I believe there are also times when you have to walk alone.

After the anesthetic wore off, I woke to see the senior nurse shaking her head and saying, "Not optimistic," to the radiologist. I asked what was up? She pointed to several round patches on her screen and two large multicoloured circles the size of tennis balls. "Not optimistic," she repeated, and said I needed more scans. After two hours of tests, CT scans, and then even more tests, the senior doctor explained. "You have 32 tumors in your large intestine and at least two are malignant. Mr Charlie, I am sorry to inform you that you have colon cancer."

No one prepares you for this moment, no matter how tough you are. I walked home in a daze. Once I reached my lonely apartment, I called a few friends before crumbling to the floor and weeping. I woke early the next morning next to two empty wine bottles and an empty pizza box. A friend called to say she had discovered that the second top colon cancer expert in China was working at the Fudan University Shanghai Cancer Center. She booked an appointment and I went to see him. Professor Cai and Dr Peng Jun Jie saw me at their clinic and showed me the scans.

"You indeed have cancer and we need to remove it," Professor Cai said.

Dr Peng took me into a side office and explained, "We want to kill this disease so here's what we need to do. I will cut away 90 per cent of your colon. That way, I will have gotten all the tumors."

I began to sob uncontrollably. "I am scared," I said.

"Mr Charles," Dr Peng said, his tone polite and reassuring in its calmness. "Some people fix cars, others houses, here… we fix cancer. Let me do my job."

"How soon can you do it?" I asked.

"Oh, a week or two," Dr Peng said.

"But I might die before that," I said urgently.

Professor Cai leaned over his desk and said. "You have had this illness for at least two years already, what difference will two more weeks make?" He smiled and I felt strangely comforted.

Ten days later I was admitted to Fudan University Shanghai Cancer Center, or as it was known to locals, "the tumor hospital". A week earlier, Professor Cai had asked me to choose the hospital where I wanted to have my operation. I could have chosen five star expat hospitals that would put the Hilton to shame. Instead, I said, "I want it here in Fudan. This is your hospital. You know the staff, the theater, I believe this is where I am meant to be." Was it brave or foolish? Who knows? Fudan was a state hospital with basic but adequate facilities. However, the staff were amazingly friendly and that mattered a lot. But I still felt very alone and afraid in a place where I did not know the language and was uncertain that I would still be alive by the end of the month.

The day before my operation, I gave the front desk at the hospital my medical insurance card and they refused it. "You pay cash and reclaim," they said without any hint of emotion. "I do not have all that money in cash (around $6,500) and if you do not operate, I may die!" I said. But in China, "rules are rules". I had to pay for the operation, the room, food, medication, everything... up front. I called Watsana, a friend in Thailand and got her to sell my truck for around $10,000. Before I'd left for Africa, I had lent it to a friend and every time I visited Thailand on holiday, I had a set of wheels to travel with. Within two days, Watsana arrived with the cash. I was operated on three days later.

I apparently woke up, swearing at the doctor. Two beautiful ladies were standing at the end of my bed when I woke. One was Watsana and the other was Anna, a good German friend. They both visited me every day, and in later weeks, took me for small gentle walks along the corridor. I wept when Watsana had to return to Thailand. Very few of the staff or other patients at the hospital spoke English, adding to my sense of isolation.

Recovery was painful. Chinese doctors do not like to administer painkillers as they believe that pain speeds up recovery. Nurses constantly turned me over in my bed to reduce the risk of clotting and developing bedsores, but it was often very painful. Depression would overcome me like a thick fog. I was forever being taken down to rooms in other parts of the hospital for CT scans, x-rays, and ultrasounds. Often I had no idea where I was being taken. On one such "trip", I was on my back, being wheeled along a corridor, coldly afraid. I prayed a silent, "Where are you, Lord?" prayer, and as I did, I looked up and a sign above me read: "I C U." I knew it stood for Intensive Care Unit but to me right then, I felt that God had heard and understood my fear and was saying "I see you Charlie, it's ok."

That simple answer to prayer gave me enough hope and courage to get through the rest of my time in hospital. I was I was not allowed any food for days. Instead I was fed through a pipe down my nose. I continually pestered Dr Peng to let me have a McDonalds. He would laugh and say "NO". Eventually though, once the tubes were removed and I was just resting to heal my wounds... I sneaked out.

There was a McDonalds three streets away from Fudan. Walking slowly, trying not to injure myself or tear the stitches along the huge gash on my abdomen, I made it to McDonalds in 25 minutes. I was slightly nervous about walking in wearing my pajamas, hospital wrist tag and slippers. I was almost certain someone would call the hospital security. But I gingerly pulled open the heavy door and entered. To my joy and surprise, the whole restaurant was full of patients! Most were in pajamas like me and many had no hair as a result of chemotherapy. To date, that was the best meal I have ever had... ever!

I returned to work far sooner than was wise. I had been told that I would never play football again and that was strengthened my resolve to prove them wrong. I was not only going to play football, I was going to be better than I ever was before!

I resigned from my job at Shanghai United International School and took on an English teaching job at a French school in Shanghai. It was closer to home and my remit was slightly less demanding than at SUIS but nonetheless, with the benefit of hindsight, I should have taken at least three to six months off instead off one!

While teaching at the French school, I suffered one of many life-threatening obstructions in my bowel. I went to the nurses' station one morning with constipation and a crippling pain in my abdomen. By early afternoon, my stomach was swollen and I was in agony. I was rushed to Fudan by taxi with the school nurse next to me. The join attaching what was left of my colon to the lower part of me had closed. No waste could pass through, and though my intestine kept processing it, it just built up until my insides felt like they would explode. The pain was so intense I turned blue and shook. I lay in this state at Fudan for several minutes until I saw Dr Peng coming towards me. My heart leapt in relief. Up in the ward Dr Peng gave me a cocktail of chemicals to dissolve the blockage and I eventually vomited brown liquid all over my bed. The pain ceased and I was allowed home later that day. Dr Peng suggested they insert a wire mesh stent inside to train the join in my bowel to stay open. But a day after the operation, the stent broke inside me and needed to be removed. A date was set to insert a larger stent, but this time the operation was carried out without anesthetic. After several painful attempts to insert this deep in my bowel, they gave up. The stent they had brought was the wrong size. Every 10 days or so I would get blocked again, usually in the middle of the night, and I staggered to hail a taxi to hospital alone.

At one time at about 2am, I asked the security guard at my home to call an ambulance. I thought I was going to die. The nearest hospital had no beds so I was left on a trolley next to reception at the front entrance. The pain was so excruciating that I howled every few minutes as my gut tried to push waste through my blocked intestine. A young doctor tended to me and asked me to swallow a rubber tube that was inserted down my nose and into my stomach. It was painful and I wanted to vomit, but kept taking deep breaths until it was in place. This released a little of the pressure and took the edge off my pain. The same doctor later came by, as I was being transferred to Fudan at 9am and said, "You are the bravest foreigner I have ever seen in my hospital." "No," I replied, "I am a coward, I HATE pain… I just don't want to die yet." It was a lighter moment in the midst of agony. At Fudan, I was given one of many dilations (a balloon is inserted and inflated to open up the join) and the pressure was released. I was back at school the next day.

Shanghai 2 weeks after my cancer operation

231

To avoid the agony of sudden blockages, I decided to have scheduled dilations at Fudan every two weeks. I turned up at the colonoscopy department and sat in a queue. The medical staff would call me in, stick an IV line into my wrist and administer (as I called it), "the white juice". They would ask me to count to 10, and then I would pass out well before I'd finished. I used to make them laugh by fighting the "juice" until the very last moment, but by nine or 10 I was out cold. I would usually wake up to see my friend, Dr Peng, standing next to me, reassuring me that all was well.

Around this time, I began to teach at weekends in a language center. The extra money was handy (I needed it to pay off hospital bills), and besides, I liked meeting the young adults and having fun with them too. I got a lot out of those lectures including a wife…

CHAPTER 31

WEB International is one of the better English language schools in China. I was not rostered to teach the Saturday class on a certain weekend, but a teacher had double booked. I was called in to facilitate his "social club" (an informal gathering of around 20 to 40 young adults where the teacher picks a random topic and discusses it with the class to improve vocabulary skills). My topic was "Christmas" and I proceeded in my usual enthusiastic, fun way to share how the modern Santa myth was actually a clever sales drive from the Coca Cola company in the '50s. I ended my session by singing a Christmas-themed love song with the backing track, "Wonderful tonight" by Eric Clapton. As I sung, I noticed the pretty lady sitting with her friend at the back again. She was young (early 20s I guessed) and had a very attractive face. Her beige woolen V-neck pullover and form-fitting jeans highlighted her slim figure. She had looked up and smiled at me once or twice, but only to acknowledge my presence as I walked around the classroom. As a professional teacher, did not speak directly to her at the end. I later found out from colleagues her name was "Jasmine", she lived with her parents and worked in an office.

The next week, she returned. The topic was, "How to discover your ideal partner". It was a tongue-in-cheek look at how and where we look often determines the type of person we will eventually marry. Little did I know that the same woman who I had noticed the week before was at the end of a tumultuous long-term relationship. This time, I did speak to her, but only as a teacher eliciting information pertinent to the lesson.

As a rule, I always wrote my email address on the board for my students to copy. If anyone needed help during the week, whether it was filling out a form or writing a job application in English, I could reply with advice. I met up a few students, mostly to prepare them for job interviews, but I enjoyed their company and like to think they benefited too.

Two days after my "ideal partner" lecture, Jasmine emailed me with a request. "Please can you send me a copy of your PowerPoint on *finding an ideal partner?*" I sent the PowerPoint and suggested we meet if she wanted to chat about it. We arranged to meet after my lecture on the following Sunday at WEB. However, that Sunday was hectic and I had a horrible flu. I suggested that we meet some other time as it was not a great day all round. Jasmine took my number and said she would arrange something in the week.

During that week, we exchanged several emails and I managed to get Jasmine to part with her phone number. She even sent me some photos of herself. "I wonder where this is going?" I asked myself. Jasmine arranged for us to meet at a "chilli" restaurant. There were certain things I could not eat following my surgery, the main thing being spicy food!

Wearing my leather jacket and jeans, I turned up late to find Jasmine standing at the top of the subway steps. "You are late," she said. "I had to buy a phone card on the way," I said, truthfully but unconvincingly. We sat and chatted in the restaurant and the time flew. Jasmine was a young woman of 24 with a vibrant personality. She loved life. Hailing from a working class background, she had saved her modest income and paid for an English language course that would enable her to leave a dead end office job and train to be a teacher. I instantly liked her.

She kept asking why I wasn't eating the hot chilli volcano bubbling in front of me. I explained that I wasn't really hungry. (Truth was I was starving! But if I had one solitary mouthful, I would have been on the toilet all evening!) I discovered that Jasmine was struggling with a nine year relationship that had started at school. Her boyfriend was cheating on her and had no intention of stopping. She was lonely, felt neglected and in need of encouragement and friendship. And that was really all I could offer. I, too, was now in a relationship that had been tarnished.

We decided to become friends. After leaving the restaurant, we walked slowly to the subway. Jasmine stopped as we approached the steps leading down to the Shanghai Metro Subway. "You will need to catch Line 2 to East Xuxing and I will go the opposite way to People's Square," she said. I thanked her again and gave her a "buddy hug" - you know, a sort of "Hey, we are just friends" type of hug. I smiled and was just about to go when (although Jasmine insists that she never said this), she smiled and said, "You're quite handsome you know." If I had just been punched on the chin by Muhammad Ali himself, it would have had less of an impact than this did!

From then on, we met once or twice a week for coffee and Mandarin lessons. Jasmine was a thorough teacher. She insisted that I do homework and if I didn't learn or memorize the sentences and words she gave me, I would have to pay for the coffees. I knew I had to bring a certain subject up with her. Taking a deep breath, I shared how my last Chinese tutor began to get "too close" and wanted me to live with her and marry her and it scared the life out of me because I had no real feelings for her at all! I looked into Jasmine's eyes and asked her sincerely, "Promise that you won't fall in love with me?"

"You wish," she said. "Why would I fall in love with an *old* guy like you? I am pretty, intelligent and ambitious, I can do much better than you."

"Ok, ok, ok," I said, feigning hurt as Jasmine over emphasized the "OLD" part. I felt awkward and silly after that conversation, but the expression on Jasmine's face told me that it was safe to say anything to her. Our friendship was becoming stronger.

We would always part with a friendly hug in the afternoon or at the end of the night. As we got to know each other, the hugs became more regular and spontaneous. We held hands crossing the road, and Jasmine would often slip her arm inside mine when walking along the street. We were still just friends, but increasingly close ones. Upon discovering I was recovering from cancer, Jasmine volunteered to accompany me to my tests and treatment. This was more than friendship; this was dedicated commitment as I usually went to hospital alone and scared. Our friendship was deep, natural and trusting.
One evening, our friendship took on another dimension that

neither of us was fully prepared for. We had been for a pizza meal on East Nanjing Road and were walking hand in hand to the Bund. It was raining and I shouted to Jasmine in the midst of the busy crowd of evening shoppers passing us on both ways, "Let's dance!" She shouted back, "You are crazy." I threw my arms around her and began to waltz; her face was one of shock, horror, embarrassment and delight. We only danced a few moments but it was enough to set the tone for a night we would never forget. In less than 15 minutes we reached the Bund and crossed it, climbed the steps to the esplanade and gazed at the skyline across the river. "Isn't she beautiful?" I said, lost in the wonder and splendor of what I was seeing. "Isn't WHO beautiful?" Jasmine laughed. "Shanghai," I said. "I lost my heart to her years ago, and every time I look at her, I feel more in love with her." To my surprise, Jasmine snuggled into my side as the rain gently fell around us. We both silently gazed on the illuminated skyscrapers across the Huangpu River. I turned to brush the rain from Jasmine's face and stopped. Her eyes connected with mine and I kissed her. I hesitated for a few moments and then kissed her again. And there, in the glow of "my striking Pudong skyline" we moved from being friends to "special friends".

We walked to the subway with arms around each other. Jasmine whispered that special friends meant that we could hug and kiss. Although our bond was deepening by the day, she still had a boyfriend and I was still seeing someone. The fact that these relationships were broken beyond repair didn't make things less complicated.

We now met for coffee every second day. We went for train trips to the nearby city of Hangzhou and its romantic West Lake, which ran alongside gardens and pagodas and temples. The lakeside was a romantic hangout for countless courting couples with its artistically paved patio and "lovers seats" among bushes of sweet smelling roses. Jasmine's relationship with her boyfriend had ended for good and I'd broken up with my girlfriend. There is no easy way to say this, but our partners took it hard. Jasmine's boyfriend offered her a house and a ring if she'd stay, while mine enlisted her friend to persuade me to stay, but both to no avail. Jasmine and I were in too deep to stop now. We were still "only" special friends. Although I think we both knew it was substantially more than that now, we had not yet crossed the threshold into it being an official relationship yet.

One day I asked her, "On a scale of one to 10, what would you say your feelings are towards me?" It was a stupid question and it deserved a stupid answer.

Jasmine thought for a few moments and then said, "SIX." I noticed the faintest trace of a mischievous smile on her lips that disappeared as soon as she saw me looking at her.

"Whaaaaat?" I said, disappointed. "Only six, we have been friends for so long and all you feel is six?"

Jasmine spoke softly. "I am in love with you, Charlie. I didn't plan to be, but I am. I love you 100 per cent. Charlie, I am yours."

My mouth hit the ground. "I love you, too, Jasmine, I am done for."

She placed a finger to my mouth and we gently hugged. We had now moved into the blissful realm of boyfriend and girlfriend.

"I want you to meet my family and friends," Jasmine said. "If we are going to be married, then it's important that we do it properly."

The thought of marriage did not scare me in the least. The thought of meeting her parents terrified me!

Her adopted parents (Jasmine had been bought for $20 by a kind couple who could not have any children) had been briefed to expect someone a "little older". I had heard horror stories from friends who had been "grilled" by Chinese families prior to weddings. In fact, some had broken off the wedding because the parents were so rude or intrusive.

I arrived with Jasmine at the upmarket restaurant, and the end of East Nanjing Road and opposite People's Park sweating nervously. Jasmine laughed at this and pulled me into the bustling restaurant.

I walked past tables where uptight middle-aged couples sat with faces like stone, having booked specially reserved tables so they could ignore each other. Each time I whispered, "Is that them?" as we slipped past, she would just giggle and shake her head. Feeling more anxious than ever, I quickened my pace and I was about to walk past an elderly couple in the corner table, when Jasmine stopped me. The pair looked working class and ruddy faced and relaxed in contrast to the other couples we'd passed, slightly out of place in the grandeur of the restaurant. The gentleman was wearing a black leather jacket and I later learned was about six years older than me. His wife was small and slightly round with kind eyes and short hair. "Meet my mum and dad," Jasmine said. This threw me off guard. They were nothing like the hellish interrogators I was expecting after reading countless blogs from people who had undergone stern first encounters. Her mum smiled naturally and shook my hand. "Nice to meet you," she said with a strong accent. I guessed she'd been practicing all week! Her dad stood up and took my hand in both of his. "Me too," he said, smiling. I glanced at Jasmine and almost melted with relief.

Neither of her parents spoke English apart from the initial greeting and Jasmine's mum's repeated smiling requests for me to "Eata..." (In Chinese culture it is polite to eat well when invited as a guest). Her father had worked in Russia as a shipbuilder many years ago. To my surprise I actually remembered some Russian from goodness knows where. We spent an hour communicating in broken Russian and pigeon Chinese. Jasmine's mum spoke once, asking her daughter to translate her question. "Mum wants to know one thing only: 'Will you love my daughter and treat her kindly?'" I assured her that on my life I would look after Jasmine, provide for her and love her always with kindness and commitment. She smiled at my translated answer, looked me in the eye and said, "Xie xie." (Thank you)

Neither Jasmine nor I wanted a huge wedding as it was a waste of money (of which we had little) and we just wanted a simple ceremony and then our honeymoon.

Three months later on 15 May 2012, we married at a Shanghai registry office in a ceremony that lasted no more than 15 minutes.

Afterwards, we returned to work. Jasmine was now a teacher at Disney English language school and I was at the Singapore International School.

Before long, the inevitable happened. I was called to a dinner with the extended family that included uncles, cousins and the dreaded aunts. We sat at a huge round table in a restaurant and I felt like I had a huge target on my forehead as the aunts fired questions.

"How old are you?"

"Are you in good health?"

"How much do you earn?"

"Do you own any houses?"

"How much you have in the bank?"

"Will you give us a son?"

I smiled through it all (with gritted teeth). Jasmine nudged me. "Go on," she whispered, "Say it." She had been teaching me a phrase for days to impress the aunts. It was a compliment about their kindness and hospitality. So I stood up, bowed slightly and said it with a smiling face. The aunts gasped in horror, the uncles looked away offended, and Jasmine's parents stared at me. Meanwhile, the cousins were rolling about in fits of hysteria and Jasmine was crying with laughter, tears streaming down her face. I had been set up. What I actually said was, "S**t, I am not happy here!" From that day onward, the aunts (whom I refer to this day as "The Witches") sought to break us up. They told Jasmine she had made a serious mistake and that I would fall ill and die soon. But we already had a plan to escape those aunts and start afresh. We would teach a summer school at an American school for six weeks, travel to Bali, Indonesia for honeymoon and then on to Borneo to take up positions as teachers in one of Asia's top international schools. We were off on the adventure of a lifetime!

CHAPTER 32

What the tour companies and travel agents don't tell you about Bali (billed as the most romantic island in the world) is that many of the towns are full of beer swigging Australians, and the best beaches are privately owned by expensive hotel chains and not open to the public. Undeterred by this revelation, we hired a car and took off around our honeymoon island. The guesthouse we had booked was… basic. And when the travel agents say "near the beach", trust me, they are joking!

But the drive north on this amazing island was majestic and breathtaking. We spotted a secluded picturesque sandy beach and turned off the road to drive down to it. A few hundred yards down we came to a red and white barrier with the sign, "Members only, cards must be shown". A limousine pulled up at the barrier and flashed a membership card at the security guard who snapped to attention and saluted, allowing the driver and his family to move through the raised barrier. Jasmine looked at me and smiled. "Give me your supermarket members card," I said. She handed it to me, put her sunglasses on and lay back on the seat. I drove purposefully to the barrier, held my card to the windscreen for a few seconds and waved confidently. The same guard saluted. I nodded and Jasmine gave him a big smile. We were in! We sunbathed on the soft golden sand and swam in the clear blue ocean for free; well, after all it really belonged to God anyway!

Back in the town of Kuta, we patiently endured swarms of hairy chested, fat Aussies who crowded out the fast food restaurants and the German bierkellar bars, knowing we'd be off on another adventure the next day. To the north of Bali, we discovered a network of magnificent (mostly private) beaches with shimmering turquoise blue water and glamorous holidaymakers. Our honeymoon swept by with gorgeous sunsets and romantic evenings. It wasn't quite what we had expected, but then again, nothing ever is.

Refreshed from our perfect honeymoon, we prepared ourselves for our next adventure: living and working in Borneo, Malaysia. We landed in Kuala Lumpur and took another smaller flight to Miri city in the state of Sarawak. Miri was an oil city; in fact the original oil drill that brought the first oil from the Malaysian coast is still there. It is a clean city, with well-stocked shops and fine restaurants. My new employer, Tenby International School, put us up in a modern looking five star hotel. In fact, it was Miri's newest hotel and our room was almost palatial. We would stay there for a week until we found accommodation.

I was riding the lift down to the ground floor one day when an elderly man in a rumpled jacket spoke to me. "What do you think of the hotel?' he asked in English.

"It's really nice and very comfortable," I said. "Best I have stayed in the whole of Asia."

"That's good to know," he said, "I am the owner."

I wondered if he really was the owner, but was pleased I treated him respectfully anyway. Later that month I discovered that not only was he the owner of the hotel, but also a large chunk of Borneo! I would shortly be teaching his grandson, and his son and daughter-in-law would become close friends.

The home we chose was a tasteful bungalow on Miri's northside, close to the airport. It had a carport, electric automatic gates, a TV lounge, two bedrooms and a huge modern kitchen. It was only five minutes from the beach.

We both enjoyed life at our school where I happily taught grade two and Jasmine taught Mandarin. It was while she was teaching Mandarin that her colleague Siong Siong, a friendly and instantly approachable Chinese Christian, started to witness to her. Jasmine was taken by her honesty and the fact that she prayed about everything.

I was often in pain from abdominal adhesions, a type of internal scarring and inflammation, which commonly occurs after bowel surgery. On one occasion, the cramping and swelling was so severe I had to fly back alone to see Dr Peng in Shanghai. I didn't know that while I was in China, Jasmine was praying, "in Jesus' name," that I would recover. I returned a few days later without pain. Jasmine accepted Christ upon my return from China. We decided it was time to start attending church. We found the Borneo Evangelical Church in Miri, which was pastored by a saintly man called Pastor Dicky. He and his wife welcomed us into their homes and listened to our testimonies. We became regular attenders at the little church above the bookshop and began reading our Bibles together and praying.

But lo and behold, as we began to get closer to Jesus, we began to experience spiritual opposition. Anyone who chooses to follow Jesus has a spiritual enemy who can stir up mischief in unlikely ways. Yvette, the school principal (who was an excellent leader) became noticeably more critical of our work as teachers, ready to jump on the smallest infractions. On one occasion she scolded Jasmine for entering my class to return my phone, her tone caustic and biting. I spoke to her in private straight after the class. "Never, ever, speak to my wife like that again" I said. To her credit, she went straight to the Chinese studies room, found Jasmine and apologized.

But apart from the odd verbal skirmish at school, we enjoyed Borneo a lot! We were only 30 minutes' drive from the rainforest and an hour's flight to the coastal city of Kota Kintabalu where we could boat out to the islands and swim in the clear ocean. We also went for barbeques with Siong Siong in the cleverly designed Taman Awam, also known as Miri Public Park. The Shell Oil Company who designed and paid for the park, had created it to look like a rainforest. It had a flowing waterfall and an overhead walkway that stretched the full length of the park. Every 100 yards, there were barbeque sites with tables, benches and cooking areas that lacked nothing except the charcoal, fire and food!

Our trusted friend, Siong Siong, well knew that Jasmine and I were trying desperately for a baby. But because of my low sperm count due to intensive post cancer radiation therapy, there was not much hope. Siong Siong faithfully kept her ear to the ground and told us a local clinic called the London Fertility Centre. Her friend had fallen pregnant following IVF treatment there and the doctor was trained in London. We decided to give it a try.

The center, which was located above a small row of cafes, was a shoddy affair. The "doctor" was a thin unshaved little man in his 50s who spoke more about the cost (around $5000) than the procedure. Yes, he could get Jasmine pregnant and no, it would not take long but she should begin treatment immediately. I could see that Jasmine wanted this, so I hesitantly agreed and paid him in cash as requested. Over the next several weeks, Jasmine took all the tablets and the injections that we paid extra for and we drove hundreds of miles to his other clinic in Sibu for check ups.

On the day of her egg withdrawal, I stood outside the round glass window of a makeshift fertility theater and watched Jasmine being injected with painkillers that didn't dull her pain. God only knows how many eggs they took. Jasmine later said they took at least 10 but told her they only collected five. I later heard her "surplus" eggs were probably frozen and sold to others. Two days later, we came back and they implanted five fertilized eggs into Jasmine's womb. We returned to Miri and waited. Less than a week later, the small blood stain on Jasmine's side of the bed told us there would be no baby. Three months of travelling up and down East Malaysia, a lot of pain and suffering for Jasmine and anxiety for me, to say nothing of six months' worth of savings, had resulted in nothing. We felt empty and numb. Jasmine did not want to stay in Miri after that; it was too traumatic to relive the memory every time friends at school asked, "Did it work then?" So we accepted a post at an international school in Beijing where I would be the principal and Jasmine would teach Mandarin. We put in our notice and left our tropical paradise, Malaysia.

I had previously visited Beijing on my "holiday of a lifetime" and loved every inch of the hutongs, the narrow alleyways strewn throughout the city. However, living there was a different story altogether. Beijing was seriously polluted and from day one we

244

tasted and smelled the result of years of unhampered industry. We were working and living in the Shunyi district, which was an hour and a half out from Tiananmen. Our accommodation was a small eighth floor apartment in a compound where 50 per cent of its tenants were foreigners. We bought a small electric scooter to travel to and fro. In the summer, it was delightful but in the cruel winter of northern China it was freezing! Jasmine found the Beijingers' Mandarin unusual and a lot different from Shanghainese people who have their own dialect. We also found out that Shanghai accents are not exactly welcomed in Beijing.

The rivalry between both cities is similar to that of Glasgow and Edinburgh, but more aggressive. Even taxi drivers will often not take you on a fare if they hear a Shanghai accent. Once when we were trying to find McDonald's, Jasmine asked for directions from a young man delivering McDonald's on his custom-made delivery bicycle with the McDonald's hot box on the back. He shrugged and said, "Wǒ bù zhīdào." ("I don't know.") I said, "How can you *not* know? You work for McDonalds!" He mumbled and rode off.

Being an ardent Shanghai Greenland Shenhua football club supporter was always going to be a recipe for disaster in Beijing. When Shenhua came to Beijing to play Beijing Guoan FC in the Chinese Super League, Jasmine and I decided to attend with Gerry, one of our American teachers. We took the subway for an hour into the city center that evening, with me wearing my blue Shenhua top. The green clad fans of Guoan were everywhere. I purchased our tickets on the street (as one does) and asked, "Are these for the Shenhua end?" The tout was respectful and quick to reply, "Oh, yes, Shenhua, yes indeed, good seats, all blue."

We walked past the scores of Beijing Guoan stalls, selling all sorts of branded merchandise from scarves to clocks, kits and videos. It was a mass of green and yellow and I stuck out like a sore thumb! After countless security checks, we found our seats. We were in the upper tier, right in the middle of the noisiest Guoan fans in the workers' stadium. The Shenhua supporters were miles away at the other end! For entertainment, the Guoan fans set a Shenhua top on fire and let it float down from the highest point of the stadium's seating area to the crowd nearest the pitch. Every few minutes it would land on someone who would quench the flames to avoid being burnt before relighting it and throwing it up in the air again. My American colleague, Gerry, told me to tie my jacket around my blue top. Instead I took off my jacket and began to shout, "Sheeeeeennnnhhhhuuuaaaa!" Jasmine told me to "Shut up" and my friend slid down into his seat trying to hide (which is quite difficult for a six-foot-four former US Marine!)

The game began with 60,000 Guoan fans pointing at the 200 Shenhua fans and screaming what they were going to do to them! I stood up and took a bow. Again, my friend was almost under the seat. A couple of Guoan fans threw water bottles at me. I ducked and waved to them. They laughed and continued to goad the Shenhua fans at the far end. Even if I tried, I could never be silent at a football match. I cheered, roared, complained at the referee and teased the home fans all through the game, which ended with Shenhua getting convincingly beaten, two-nil. As we were walking out, a large black car sped towards me, expecting me to jump out of the way. I stood my ground and pointed at the driver. "I dare you!" I shouted, dispersing all the frustration of losing! The brakes screeched as the car stopped only two inches from me. A head stuck out the window and the man mouthed "Sorry," and raised an open hand. I stepped aside and he sped off.

Gerry looked like he had seen a ghost. "Don't you know who they were, Charlie? Didn't you see the number plates?"

"Yeah, some idiots in a hurry to the bar," I said.

"Not quite," Gerry said, lowering his voice. "You just halted the Chinese Special Forces!"

CHAPTER 33

The mainly Korean and Chinese students at the little primary school in Shunyi were desperate to be part of a football squad but no one had ever taken ownership of team sports. I asked the school owner for cash to buy a set of fashionable red Puma football kits and within two weeks we had two teams. The new team members were joyful and enthusiastic and that almost compensated for their lack of skill and little sense of direction!

Out of the blue, I received an email from the prestigious British International School, the second largest foreign school in Beijing. It was hosting an under 11s football tournament and would we like to participate? I asked the students if they were "up for this" and both our teams said a resounding yes. I figured that if we managed not to concede more than six or seven goals in each game, I would be more than happy. So we went. British International School was like the Hilton of international schools. Its large campus included several football pitches and a massive running track. There were state-of-the-art classrooms and the students walked silently between classes wearing immaculate uniforms that wouldn't have looked out of place at Eaton!

My kids gazed with envy at the lush surroundings. A large gentleman who lived in my compound, and was one of their sports masters, met us.

"Welcome to BIS, you will be?" He looked down his clipboard and absent-mindedly said, "Springboks."

"Springboard," I corrected him.

"Ah yes, well best of British, I mean, well, good luck anyway."

He bounced off to the next group of students. We were up against the American school, the Brits, and several other international and bilingual schools that dwarfed us in number and size. I gave my kids the same speech that I'd given to a group of young Pakistanis and

Indians in Hartlepool many years before. "You are underdogs, you are expected to fail, now go out and show them otherwise." And they did. My cell phone was superglued to my ear as I relayed scores to Jasmine back at school.

"We have drawn with the Americans!"

"We have beaten the Brits three-nil!"

"We are in the semi-finals."

"You are never going to believe this, but we have won the tournament!"

"Our B team have even won third place!"

We drove back on the school bus, singing and cheering and carrying two large gold colored trophies! I received a phone call from British International School congratulating us on our win. I thanked the sports master for his sportsmanship and although it was a tad naughty I added, "Who did you say your school was again?"

Three Christian colleagues from our school guided us to City Community Church. The church met in a large community building about two and half miles from our compound. The worship music was heavenly and talent abounded. The list of highly skilled musicians was long. Therefore the elders prayerfully selected the best out of the best to minister on Sunday with the praise bands alternating weekly. The worship leaders were sensitive to the Holy Spirit and played as the Spirit led; softly at times as we quietly worshipped God with repentant and humble (often broken) hearts, and loud and joyful at other times as the congregation joined to praise the God of creation.

Jasmine and I were hungry to attend every Sunday. The uplifting praise music, the inspired preaching and nourishing company of other believers sated something deep within us. As we gathered to worship Jesus together, we were fed the best "spiritual bread" –

sustenance that gave the deepest satisfaction to our souls. It came from worshipping Jesus, who referred to Himself as "the bread of life". The church had no class or race barriers, just a few hundred believers who loved Jesus. The likeable American pastor, a former Golf profession, preached mostly using illustrations and personal anecdotes and this was exactly how I loved to be taught and ministered to. Jasmine and I felt a sense of heart-warming joy and spiritually fulfilment after attending each Sunday.

I'd loved football my whole life, but I didn't just love playing it. I loved the communal experience of sitting with other fans at a stadium and cheering our team on together. In some ways, church was like this, except dialed up a million times. We were part of one community with a shared identity, and worshipping Jesus together was a taste of heaven.

The pastor's wife said something one Sunday that blessed me. She stood at the front to welcome everyone and said, "Welcome to CCC, we are a family church where everyone is welcome. Some of us are very rich and some of us are not, but we are the family of God, and in His sight we are all equal." That summed up the highly inclusive City Community Church; it was a welcoming place to be.

After a few months, I began to feel a faint stirring to become involved in ministry again. I arranged to have coffee with the pastor and shared my testimony with the hope that I could be involved in church in some small way. As we shared coffee and stories, I felt a strong bond with him. And then he dropped a bomb. "I am leaving to return to the States," he said. "I have been called back by my old church to pastor there." It was a massive disappointment, but unbeknownst to me at the time, I was not far behind him.

I continued to enjoy the principal's position in Beijing. We designed a new school uniform, created the new school badge and recruited good staff, many of who are still there. Pollution was the biggest factor in our decision to eventually move on. According to the World Health Organization, anything over 200 on the Air Quality Index was dangerous. Most days in Shunyi were over 400! I was still on the road from cancer recovery and I didn't want lung problems on top of this. Towards Christmas time, the principal's supervisor from Singapore International School in Vietnam contacted us. He asked if I would be interested in a deputy principal's position in Hanoi? We prayed over it. I contacted the Senior Pastor at Hanoi International Fellowship, who put me in touch with teachers who attended the church. We decided to go in the New Year so we could enjoy the celebrations and our final Christmas at City Communication Church. We arrived in Hanoi on 10 January 2013. Possibly the biggest adventure to date was about to happen!

CHAPTER 34

We landed in Hanoi at night. The view from our school minibus window reminded me a lot of Thailand with its massive illuminated signs on roadside selling things like "Brass pipe connectors". We were taken to a comfortable three star hotel.

After dropping off our bags off at a small but seemingly clean and friendly looking hotel, we headed to the Sofitel to meet the principal of the Singapore International School. Sue was a gentle, friendly lady in her late 50s and we both enjoyed a "tired" evening meal together. After dinner, she took us up to the Rooftop Bar where we had a wonderful view over Lake Tây Hồ. The panorama almost resembled that of Shanghai... well, almost.

We stayed at the hotel for a week before securing a well decorated fifth floor apartment on the edge of Tây Hồ Lake. We didn't mind the five flights of stairs or the tiny kitchen and windowless bedrooms because the unobstructed vista was gorgeous. Our balcony was massive and the floor to ceiling lounge window gave us a breathtaking view over the lake so that watching TV at night just never entered our heads! The next thing we did was hire a scooter. Riding in Hanoi is one of the most dangerous places I have ever driven, second only to Jakarta in Indonesia for craziness, traffic volume and noise! The traffic rules were simple... there were none! Expats told me that the motorbikes were like schools of fish; you just moved and weaved with the flow. The traffic lights had illuminated red numbers counting to zero before turning green, and learning the new "road rules" were an education. At the start, I dutifully sat at the red lights waiting for zero but soon I discovered that as soon as the numbers hit six... Voooom! The motorbikes would accelerate and remaining still was dangerous!

When we acquired our second motorbike a few months later, I taught Jasmine to ride. I had taught her to drive a car in Borneo so I thought this would be a breeze. After a few days of driving with her on the near empty streets surrounding Lake Tây Ho, it was time to take her onto Hanoi's busy, crazy roads. On our first evening out, I said "Stay behind me and I will give two beeps every few seconds. You respond with two beeps and that will let me know that you are safe following behind." Off we went, and every few moments as agreed, I would press my horn twice and immediately receive the reciprocal "beep." This continued for an hour during this busy wet evening, as I rode around the lake and towards the city. Whenever I turned a corner or sped up, I beeped my horn and there was always the double beep response. My cell phone rang. I indicated and pulled over.

"Charlie, where are you?" Jasmine asked.

"You know where I am, I am just in front of you," I said, confused.

"Don't think so, I got bored and rode home half an hour ago," she said.

"Then who…?"

I realized then, that Hanoians just like to beep their horns… often!

One of the first tourist attractions we visited was Hoa Lò Prison. French colonists in Vietnam held political prisoners at Hoa Lò. During the Vietnam War, North Vietnam forces jailed U.S. Prisoners of War at this prison, and these captives sarcastically nicknamed it the "Hanoi Hilton". We toured this prison museum and witnessed rooms where Americans were tortured and beaten, dormitories where French colonialists were shackled to beds and we even saw the guillotine room that still had a working guillotine. We watched an old propaganda movie showing American prisoners eating turkey legs and drinking wine at their Christmas dinner. I had no doubt at all that as soon as the commander said "Cut," that the turkey and wine would have been quickly replaced with rice soup and stale water.

Thankfully, modern Hanoi is now refreshingly different, compared to its turbulent state during the American War (as it's called in Vietnam). Nowadays, many tourists know it as a city built around about 100 lakes. All of these lakes have unusual names but the most intriguing one I encountered is now called B52 Lake (also known as Hồ Hữu Tiệp). It takes some searching along narrow alleys to find it, but it is worth it. In the middle of the lake, surrounded by tall old houses all knit together, there is the rusty tail wing of an American B52 Bomber jutting out! It is a wonder that such a large piece of debris landed in the small lake, avoiding the houses and alleyways. In 1972, the North Vietnam forces shot the plane out of the sky and that's how part of the wreckage ended up in the tiny neighborhood lake.

The best attraction in Hanoi however, is by far their people. Despite invasions, occupations and attacks from hostile nations throughout her history, Vietnam remains a welcoming, friendly and peaceful country to visit and to dwell in.

Singapore International School was located in the diplomatic sector of Vạn Phúc. The teachers were from a variety of countries, with a different range of ages and experience. The students were loving and easy to teach. Well-mannered and willing to learn, many were the children of embassy staff or from business managers and came from the upper middle classes. From early on I threw myself into building football teams. We purchased sets of fashionable football kits - maroon for the boys (Spain wore this style in the 2012 World Cup) and blue and yellow for the girls (Brazil). As Shakespeare wrote in Hamlet, "Clothes maketh the man", or rather, the kids. The football matches against the American school, St Paul, the British Vietnamese International School, and Singapore International School Ciputra were great occasions with other schools bringing their own supporters to add to the noise and fun. We won about 50 per cent of the games, which was fine by me.

I'll never forget a lovable "huge" 10-year-old Libyan who struggled academically but sparkled like a diamond when I put him in the school football team. He looked about 15 and his mere presence was like a two-nil advantage! On one occasion, we were the invited guests of the Concordia Christian School. We arrived at the sports venue in Cầu Giấy and my lads waited politely at the side while I shook hands with a few of the teachers and chatted about church. It felt good to be in the presence of believers at a football game. Our Libyan friend looked at his watch and in full view of everyone, walked onto the center circle of the pitch, knelt down and began loudly praying to Allah!

On another outing to Singapore International School Ciputra, one of his goals was disallowed (wrongly in my judgment). He swore at the referee, for which he was rightly red carded and sent off. I spoke to him afterwards. "I agree it was a bad call, but I have to ban you from the next game. So next time a call goes against you, do not swear. And if you do, don't do it in English!"

Jasmine was now teaching Mandarin at three schools in Hanoi and enjoying teaching again. She found the staff at the high school that she taught at to be insular and unwelcoming, but she loved teaching at the two kindergartens. Teaching the littlest ones was where Jasmine was at her best.

She often still pined for the child that she could not have in Borneo. Out of the blue, we stumbled upon a fertility clinic run by a wonderful Czech doctor called Dr Ivan. After consultations, interviews, tests and treatment that went on for months, Jasmine visited me at school a week after her fertilized eggs were implanted in her womb. We both looked on with heavy hearts as the home pregnancy test proved negative. We hugged and sighed and Jasmine went home with a heavy heart. I wanted to go home with Jasmine and comfort her, but was already committed to a home football match with my boys .

My phone rang just as the opposing team scored their third goal. Jasmine was crying. The doctor had contacted her with the results of a routine blood test that had come in.

"Don't worry," I said. "We can try again in a few months."
"Charlie..." she sobbed. "I am pregnant, the home kit got it

wrong!" I began to jump up and down, cheer and sing, all at once. My kids looked at me and were asking each other why Mr Charlie was celebrating while his team was being hammered three-nil?

Jasmine's pregnancy was a difficult one, at least in the early stages. After only a few weeks, she was hospitalized in a Vietnamese hospital which seemed only a tad better than Bombo in Tanzania. Rats ran around the corridors at night time and nurses either slept on the job or played with their phones. The overstretched doctors did their best. It was hard for me to watch Jasmine in such a place. She was suffering from over exposure to hormone drugs. Her stomach was so swollen, it looked as though she was nine months pregnant even though it had only been few weeks. After two weeks, a young doctor visited Jasmine and carried out an ultrasound test. He asked to talk to me outside the ward.

"Really by now, we should be seeing signs of life on the ultrasound screen but there is none," he said solemnly. "I think this could be an ectopic pregnancy, which means to save your wife, we may need to perform an abortion."

My heart went deathly cold. An icy chill ran through my entire being as I returned to see Jasmine and kiss her goodnight.

"What did the doctor say?" Jasmine asked sleepily.

"He said everything is fine," I said, trying with all my might to keep my voice steady.

"Ok, see you tomorrow," she said and turned over to sleep.

Once outside the hospital I phoned every Christian I could think of: my friend, Dr Brian, Bettina our friend and a midwife, elders, pastors, and posted an urgent prayer request on the church prayer line. I rode home with a breaking heart to an empty apartment, feeling wretched and alone.

CHAPTER 35

The messages I received were strangely positive. Nearly all of them carried the same message: "Don't give up hope, God is in this, there's still plenty of time for your baby to show up on the screen." Truth was, there wasn't. The doctors planned to do one more ultrasound in 48 hours and if there was still no sign of the baby, they would perform an abortion. Still I said nothing to Jasmine, but my prayer life increased 100 per cent!

On the morning of the planned ultrasound, I had to work as usual. Around 10am, I was on my knees praying in the washroom located near the school gym. I'd only started praying when my phone rung. It was Jasmine. Sweating, I tried to sound nonchalant. "Hi baby, how are you? Have the doctors been?" Jasmine chirped back, "They have just been, they said my blood pressure is good, oh, and I saw our baby, and I am getting another dose of IV, and…" But anything after that was lost on me, as all I heard was, "I saw our baby." I told Jasmine that I loved her but had to go. I ran out into the playground praising the Lord, jumping up and down and praising God in tongues and English with my hands raised to the sky! I ran inside and told Sue who hugged me and celebrated with me, as the tears wet my face. Against all odds again, God had shown that He is sovereign.

The swelling slowly subsided and Jasmine was allowed home days later. WE REALLY WERE HAVING A BABY! After a few more anxious incidents involving ultrasound scans, Jasmine began to enjoy her pregnancy. We had planned to name the child "J.J" after Dr Peng Jun Jie in Shanghai, and I even went as far as to tell him this when I visited Fudan University Shanghai Cancer Center for a check up. Dr Peng said he was honored to have his friend's son named after him.

A few days later, I woke early in the morning with the word, "Holly", in my head. I woke Jasmine and said, "I think we are having a girl, and her name is to be Holly." Jasmine looked up and smiled sleepily. "I love that name," she said. "So do I," I said, smiling. Weeks later, Bettina, a church friend, advised us to book a maternity and delivery package at Vinmec, Hanoi's newest hospital. Bettina was a midwife there and recommended the wonderful Dr Aksana from Belarus, who we met. Dr Aksana explained the package, prices and procedure, all of which impressed us and put our mind at ease. She did a medical check up of Jasmine, listened to the baby's heartbeat, and sent us down the corridor to have a routine ultrasound. We waited our turn outside the ultrasound room until a nurse welcomed us in. The young Vietnamese doctor greeted us and asked, "Ah, Mr and Mrs Mackenzie, so this will be your second pregnancy?" We looked at each other puzzled. "No, it's our first," I said. The doctor looked painfully confused. He said, "It can't be, don't you recognize me?" The realization fell on us and we gasped. It was the same doctor who had examined Jasmine months earlier and said the pregnancy was ectopic! I hugged the doctor, and Jasmine and I praised God.

He carried out the ultrasound and after 10 minutes looked up and announced, "It's a girl."

"We know," I said. "And her name is Holly."

Shopping trips became thoroughly enjoyable "baby trips", as we chose baby girl's clothes, shoes and accessories and in the process, discovered baby markets that we never knew existed! Jasmine ordered online items from Shanghai, and when those huge parcels arrived it was almost like Christmas for us! Picking Holly's pram and crib were especially exciting times. Jasmine's bump grew and grew and Holly began to wriggle and "kick". We had an evening ritual where we would play music to her and I would sing. If she didn't like the song, she would be still, but if she liked it, she would kick hard. I imagined she was dancing in Jasmine's womb! Her favorite orchestral piece was Mozart's *Turkish March* and her favorite song was, *The Northern Lights of Aberdeen*. As Jasmine approached the delivery date, we went out into the Hanoi sunshine and took some "baby bump" photos. These were to be the last ones we would take of Jasmine's pregnancy bump.

The following afternoon while I was at school, my phone rang. It was Bettina.

"Hi Charlie, would you like to see your baby today?"

"You bet!" I said, my heart racing.

"Well, I think Jasmine is in labor, we are going to get a taxi to hospital, can you meet us there?" Bettina laughed, full of joy.

I walked into Sue's office and said, "Eh, I think, I mean, em, Jasmine is going to have her baby today!" Sue looked up and smiled. "You better go then," she said. I grabbed my coat, jumped on my scooter and sped all the way to Vinmec. Upon arriving, I changed into hospital garb and was allowed into the birthing suite, where I found Jasmine sitting on a birthing stool with Dr Aksana crouched below. Bettina was standing next to Dr Aksana, stroking and soothing Jasmine and praying with her. I sat behind and did my best to encourage her. Jasmine was in the last hour of labour, which began a few hours earlier.

Bettina exclaimed, "I have just touched your baby's head! She is going to come soon." I sat awestruck as Jasmine let out a deep painful scream and Holly appeared eyes wide open and arms outstretched. She was truly incredibly awesome in every way conceivable. Jasmine sobbed in relief and joy as she held her miracle from God. Holly began to cry, it sounded like an angel singing. I lifted her up and sung *The Northern Lights of Aberdeen*. She looked at me and stopped crying. She had heard that song in the womb for several months before this day, she knew it, and on hearing it, she listened calmly.

That night, I rode home alone again to an empty home. But oh, how different this was to that cruel night only eight months before. During the 45 minute journey, I was rejoicing and praising God for His kindness, faithfulness and love! Holly had arrived. Praise Jesus.

Jasmine's mum had come to stay for "two weeks" when she was in Bach Mai because sometimes you just need your mother to be there!

On many nights, including the one which the doctor said Jasmine might have an ectopic pregnancy, her mum stayed in the hospital to be with her daughter. I often tell the joke about "the mother in law who came for a fortnight and stayed for a year!" Well that's exactly what happened here. Jasmine's mum coming to stay that long was not really a problem staying (we always had hot Chinese food to eat!), but having a third adult in our small apartment was at times overcrowded. She left a few months after Holly arrived, but returned again a few months later.

Our life at Hanoi International Fellowship was going from strength to strength. Jasmine decided she wanted to be baptized. With a group of around 20, she was baptized in a Roman style sunken pool at the home of an American diplomat who attended our church. At church the following Sunday, she testified to God's saving grace. She told the story about how she had been brought up as a Buddhist and a communist in China. God had directed her path towards her friend Siong Siong in Borneo, who told her about Jesus. Now through the preaching and testimony of the church members in Hanoi, Jasmine had repented and received the living Jesus into her life. Her friends in China were confused when she sent them her baptismal photos. "Why are these people trying to drown you?" they asked.

Jasmine joined the Thursday night Chinese Bible study group and the Tuesday night ladies' Bible study, which were mainly made up of women from Taiwan and the Philippines. It blessed me to see her growing. I also had begun to hunger and thirst after God again. I had been in the desert since leaving Scotland. God found me in Thailand and ministered to me through a 10-year-old kid, he began drawing me back to him through the church in Tanzania, through cancer in Shanghai, the church in Beijing and now here I was taking a backseat in Hanoi. After a few months of simply sitting in the back of the church, I felt prompted to ask if I could share my testimony at West Lake. Pastor Jacob gave me a date and I shared as God had prompted me to. I rose, a tad nervous to begin my testimony, but I should not have worried, for as soon as I opened my moth to speak the words flowed freely. People laughed at my funny recollections and listened intently as I shared the moment I believed in Jesus. I sat down feeling blessed. The next milestone was at the 2015 men's retreat where I was asked to talk for a few minutes. I felt the power of God that I missed so much return briefly, as I shared the Word of God with my brethren.

I returned to Hanoi after the men's weekend away, wondering whether I could preach my first sermon in almost 10 years. (The last was in Tanzania). I emailed Pastor Jacob and asked to preach, saying I was happy to cover any time he was either busy or absent. Not too long afterwards, I was asked to preach on Noah. The series was called "Character counts" and was about how different Bible characters impacted our lives today.

After 10 years of pent up preaching just waiting to burst out, I had a lot to share. I preached my heart out at West Lake that Sunday. I felt the fire return and the supernatural presence of God fall upon me. Not only was I back with Jesus, but also I was back doing what I did best … doing the work of an evangelist and preaching the word of God. The door was open for me to walk back through and I was ready to run through it!

CHAPTER 36

Back at school, I was convinced that predictable waters lay ahead. I had stepped into a comfortable rhythm at Singapore International School. After I'd left Barnsley years earlier, I went through a period of living only for myself. It felt good to find windows of opportunity to serve God, and to this end, squeezing preaching commitments around full-time work. But before long, this wasn't enough. A series of significant events over the next few months soon reminded me it was one thing to merely include God in my life, and another thing to live a brave, passionate, expansive life sold out to God.

It started with Holly's impending baby dedication at Hanoi International Fellowship. I excitedly told my network of Vietnamese and foreign teachers how important this ceremony was to me, as it was returning praise to God for the miraculous gift of our daughter. The event was also a celebration with the church, who had faithfully prayed for Holly when the future looked uncertain. I sent an internal memo to my staff inviting them to the event. Even though it was sent as a courtesy, I hoped that at least a few would make it. To my joy and surprise, 21 teachers turned up, both foreign and Vietnamese. Some were school principals. Most slipped out before the message was preached, but a few stayed. One or two returned. God was up to something good. This whet my appetite to become more of a positive Christian influence to the network of teachers around me.

At this stage, I still saw my future as continuing to do more of the same. Not long after Holly's dedication, I was having a Monday morning meeting with Sue in the principal's office at Singapore International School's Vạn Phúc campus.

I found myself saying, "Y'know, Sue, I am happy here in Hanoi. I like the school and Jasmine is content. I think I will sign another contract at this school and stay on until I retire. Then maybe I'll go teach part-time in Thailand or Cambodia and live out my days there."

"Sounds like a great plan," Sue said, and we left it at that.

That night God spoke clearly through a dream. In this dream, He called me back into full-time Christian service as a pastor. He told me I would need to refresh my calling by attending Bible college again and that this calling would materialize over the next two years. The calling was as clear and powerful as the first call to service in Yorkshire, shortly after I was saved. I woke trembling with my heart on fire. It felt like I had just eaten a hot mouthful of my mother's thick porridge and it got stuck halfway down, burning and warming me!

I shared it with Jasmine but she was skeptical. "Do pastors get paid?" she asked. "Will we have to leave Hanoi? Are you SURE this was God talking to you?" Of course I was sure; there is no mistaking the call of God on a person's life. I had walked away from the call of God almost 30 years earlier; He had been with me as I fell headfirst onto a railway track and as I fell headfirst into drinking and a life without Him. He had whispered to me through a child's prophecy in Bangkok, and now he was loudly and directly speaking to me. The Prodigal Son had returned home, Jonah had been delivered from the belly of the whale; Peter had been given another chance… Charlie had been recommissioned.

I sought confirmation on this, mainly for Jasmine's sake rather than mine, as I had no doubt whatsoever. I wrote to Pastor Irwin Rutherford in Kuala Lumpur, who had ministered at West Lake during a recent visit and was respected by the pastor and elders there. I explained my situation and asked for his heart on this. Pastor Irwin wrote back clearly, confirming this call to be of God. Jasmine said little but quietly noted all of this. The Elim Bible College in New York State gave enough confirmation. I had been communicating with them about beginning a course there, when the registrar wrote to me prophesying over my future ministry without knowing what God had said to me in the dream. Her words conveyed the truth that regardless of the past, the end would be more fruitful than the beginning. The third conformation took 90 per cent of the doubt from Jasmine.

The following Sunday, Jasmine and I attended the West Lake church service and had just stood up for the benediction after Pastor Jacob had spoken. A lady who I knew from the pre-service prayer meeting came over and knelt next to us. Turning to Jasmine, she asked, "Can I speak to Charlie?" Jasmine nodded. The woman closed her eyes and prophesied, "Charlie, whatever God has told you, you must do it, and this means He is going to bless you and use you in a mighty way and He will also bless your wife and your future children." She prayed for us. The service ended and Jasmine and I went to have lunch in a local Vietnamese café.

"Child-REN?" Jasmine said. "We are going to have more than one?"

"What about the other stuff?" I said.

"It's pretty clear, Charlie," Jasmine said. "You are going to be a pastor and I will follow you no matter what or where, even although I don't fully understand all this." She was smiling.

Having now received the confirmation that I had prayed for, I began to contact Bible colleges. The first was my old alma mater, The Faith Mission in Edinburgh. The new principal was helpful and said although he could not offer me a residential place, he could offer an ongoing in-class day course in Scotland. He put me in touch with a college in Belfast that I followed up closely. After thumbing through several enrolment booklets, a few grabbed my attention. Ellel Grange in southern England was the favorite because they had a strong teaching and healing focus. I was also drawn to the Irish Bible Institute in Belfast, not just because of the recommendation from The Faith Mission Edinburgh, but because they had a clear, strong, Bible-focused curriculum. Both were very interested in me attending and the Irish college even sent me some sample modules to study.

Pastor Jacob mentioned a university run by Elim Pentecostal Church in New York State. I had already contacted them to enquire about a residential place, so it was a sensible move to ask about long distance learning as well. When I saw their package I was delighted! I decided to apply immediately and take a degree in Christian Leadership. The Nation-2-Nation Christian University was better than any other I had heard about and so I began to throw myself into the world of online study!

Meanwhile, I still worked as the Deputy Principal at Singapore International School and preached whenever I could at Hanoi International Fellowship. When a vacancy arose for an elder's position at the church's service at the Mỹ Đình campus, I put my name forward and was accepted into the eldership. What an honor! Jasmine and Holly blossomed at home and in church, but eventually the day I was nervously anticipating was almost upon me. I had to fly to Shanghai alone for my five-year post-cancer check up, as getting a passport for Holly was proving difficult. In the lead up, I suffered gripping abdomen pains that kept me awake at night and restricted my study and often my work too.

Still in pain, I arrived at my hotel near the Hongkou football stadium in Shanghai in the early evening. After phoning home to let Jasmine know I had arrived safely, I laid in the fetal position on my bed and tried to ride the storm. I had no sleeping tablets or painkillers left. I felt afraid, lonely and worried the cancer was back. The Devil taunted me, filling me with doubts and anxiety. "You will never see your family again, you will die in pain, tomorrow you will see the cancer is back again. You are doomed." I asked God if this was true and prayed in the weakest of voices for Him to help me. Seconds later, I heard the words of Psalm 118:17: "I will not die but live, and will proclaim what the LORD has done". It was enough for me. I rested on that word with frail strength until the morning came.

I was booked in for the battery of usual tests: tumor blood count, MRI, X-ray, CT scan and colonoscopy. Dr Peng was pleased to see me and I, him. He was his usual optimistic self.

"I think, all will be clear," he said, in a cheerful and confident tone. I smiled at him in response, but behind it lay more nerves than hope. I went through the next three days in a trance. A robotic ritual of catching subways, queuing at Fudan cancer center and then returning to my hotel alone, often late at night after a grueling day at hospital. I was set to receive the results of my test from Dr Peng on the Friday morning, after which I would leave for Hanoi. I waited all morning and then decided to text. The bleep on my phone told me Dr Peng had replied. I took a deep breath and read it. "Tests normal" was all it said. I wrote back, "Am I cancer free?" His reply was like music played by Vivaldi. "Yes, all clear, have a great life." My pain had gone and I was deliriously lightheaded. I texted Jasmine and my school in Hanoi. Sue wrote on the noticeboard: "Charlie. All clear." The messages came fast and were much welcome. I was not a cancer patient any more.

I returned to work at Singapore International School and was hit by a vicious chest flu that knocked me for six and had me on IV for days. I think my staff expected Superman to return but instead, only I came back. Things at school took a turn for the worse. I became aware that Sue, the principal, was spending a lot of time with Trang, the office manager. Trang was a Buddhist like many, but I discerned more than this. The more time Sue spent with her, the more agitated and stressed she appeared to become. I felt the atmosphere at the school becoming spiritually heavy. I asked both my pastors to pray with me because I felt my heart was dark and sore and that just being there was "wadding through deep water". Trang treated me politely in Sue's presence but in her absence, with dire contempt. Of course it was spiritual. I prayed more earnestly for Trang, in Jesus' name binding the demons that often manifested themselves in anger whenever she had to visit my office.

The expected explosion occurred just before Christmas 2015. We had teachers off sick with the flu and Sue was working extra hours on a report for the Western Association of Schools and Colleges (WASC) that was visiting in three months. I was covering two teachers' classes and preparing for the school Christmas concert. I had agreed to cover a playtime duty in the canteen for a sick colleague (something that we often did) but was distracted at the last minute thereby missing most of the duty. Sue was furious and avoided me all day. This kind, gentle lady was fuming with anger and almost in tears. Towards the end of the day, I spoke with her. "What's up

Sue?" I asked. She erupted and chastised me with uncharacteristic coldness. She issued me with a formal warning for being too busy to supervise a colleague's playtime duty and told me if it happened again within the next three months, I would be dismissed. The next day, while I was chatting with Sue about something WASC related, our Head of Studies walked in and said, "One of our teachers has missed her lunchtime canteen duty, what shall we do?" I looked at Sue and asked, "Written warning? Dismissal? Decapitation?" Sue did not meet my gaze, instead gave a half smile and continued talking about WASC.

My Christmas holidays were filled with uncertainty about the future. Jasmine decided to sell everything that we were not using, from kitchenware to children's clothes because she thought we would be losing our income soon. I applied to several places and within days was offered teaching positions in Egypt, Cuba and China. But this was not what God had told me in the dream. He was calling me back into service for Him. So I contacted the schools and said I was not interested anymore!

At a church elders meeting, an elder called David asked if he could talk with me about a position I might be interested in. We met a week later. What he shared was like a lightening bolt from heaven! He was the director of a new school that would be opening up in Hanoi, and it needed a principal. The school was sponsored by a Christian organization called Teach Beyond and all the foreign staff were Christians. They needed someone as soon as possible and David's wife had told David to ask me. The salary was not quite as high as Singapore International School but Holly would be given a free place at the school's kindergarten and Jasmine could receive free Montessori training and then be employed as a kindergarten teacher. I shared it with Jasmine and we decided we would start with the school in August if no churches had called me to be their pastor before then.

CHAPTER 37

I returned to school after the Christmas holidays with a fresh sense of God's presence and His authority. I had been taking analgesics for bowel pain and a sedative for almost five years following my cancer. I decided to go "cold turkey" and stop both. It was tough, tiring and traumatizing at times but I did it. I arrived at school a different person. I saw things I never saw before and had them fixed. Take, for instance the main staff room. It had been shoddy for years and no one noticed, and now I noticed. Within a week it was painted, new chairs installed, new green plants bought and installed and space cleared for teachers to relax and eat lunch. I saw walls that needed painting, noticeboards that needed refurbishing and updating and staid staff meetings that needed fresh inspiration.

Sue was eager to know where this "new" Charlie had come from? I explained that from now on, I was who I was for God. I would lead, work and serve as Deputy Principal not for Singapore International School or with respect, even Sue herself, but for Him. There were not enough hours in the day to do all I wanted to do, but yet there was also the deep quiet knowledge that I would leave soon. I told Sue that I planned to leave at the end of June... but it may be sooner.

The office manager also noted my sense of new authority and intensity that was now eclipsing her own drive. Again, a clash was inevitable from a spiritual perspective. It came in the lead up to Tet, also known as the Lunar New Year. I was commissioned to decorate the main noticeboard in the school corridor. Using black card, colored paper and a pale yellow paper background, I painted a delicate dark brown blossom branch and added multi-colored paper flowers in full bloom. There were tags inscribed with the Chinese characters for "happiness" hanging off the branch of a small potted orange tree in reception. I carefully copied these characters onto yellow card, cut them out and set them onto red card, before placing them onto the colorful collage of the Tet branch. It looked strikingly authentic and teachers were happy to see it on display. I thanked Jesus for giving me the gift of art to please others for Him.

The next day, I was walking past the noticeboard and saw the Chinese characters had been taken off. Confused, I went to Trang's office and enquired, "Do you know who took the Chinese characters from my display?" Trang rose to her feet, her face red with anger and answered uncomfortably, "We need to talk with Ms Sue now!" She stormed off in the direction of the principal's office. Slightly bemused, I walked slowly behind her until I reached Sue's office. What happened next came straight from the bowels of hell.

"I took these 'things' off the noticeboard!" she said. "Tet is Vietnamese, not Chinese... I do not want to see Chinese writing at this time of year."

Sue was shocked, and stared at Trang. I waited for my opportunity, knowing that God was fully in control of this outburst.

"Who ordered the small orange tree to be put in reception?" I asked Trang.

"I did," she answered, "But what's that to do with..?"

"And who is responsible for decorating it?" I continued. "Me, I did it, I do it every year but what... Come here!" I pointed to the tags with the Chinese characters hanging proudly from the tree and said slowly and deliberately, "I only copied the characters that you already decided to display on the tree!"

She looked embarrassed and confused.

"These characters are all over Hanoi!" I said. "And by your own confession, you have also hung them up in reception for the whole school to see! Is that not rather hypocritical?"

Now totally humiliated, Trang screamed, "WE HATE THE CHINESE!"

"Really?" I said. I felt myself calming down. "May I quote you on this?" "Yes you can," she hissed.

"So when you say 'We... hate the Chinese, is that *we* the Singapore International School of whom you are an employee? Is it Vạn Phúc Primary of whom you are office manager? Or is it the Vietnamese people, whose spokesperson you have elected yourself to be?"

Trang opened her mouth to retaliate, but I continued. "And by Chinese, do you mean you hate my wife and daughter, who are Chinese, or is it the owner of this organization who is also Chinese? Or is it the people of China as a whole of whom you know nothing about? You are a racist. Shame on you."

She began to protest, "Ask the Chinese teachers, I don't hate them, they like me..." But it was the feeble response of someone who had been caught out.

I considered writing a letter of complaint to Mr Tan, the Chinese owner of KinderWorld. But instead, I left her to the mercy of God who says clearly, "Judgment is mine." (Romans 12:19). I contacted David and asked if I could commence work as the new principal of Gateway School once I had completed the required 30 days' notice, and the answer was yes. During that time, I met with the owners of Gateway and began recruiting new staff. For the next month at Singapore International School, I got the International Day committees up and running, decorated the school boards and public areas for this event, and led the initial team for the annual school concert. Trang ignored any emails I sent her, although they were usually delegated from Sue. But once news broke out about my imminent departure, she quickly became civil again.

However, I still had a clear calling from God to be a pastor. I was now being called upon to preach at Mỹ Đình and West Lake services on an average of once every one to two months, which I was thrilled about. But the more I preached, the stronger the calling became and the more I longed to be in a pastoral position. The analogy I gave Pastor John was as follows:

Say you were a squad player for Barcelona FC. You rarely played - only once every two months, but it was Barcelona! A great club!

271

You scored the odd goal but not often, as there were many great goal scorers in the first team. A small second division team subsequently offered you a position as their main striker. It was nowhere as glamorous as Barcelona, the stadium was basic, the crowds a fraction the size, but… you were playing and scoring every week. What would you choose?

John thought for only a few seconds and said he'd choose to be a regular player for a smaller club.

My point was simple. At present, I was preaching like a squad player at Barcelona. Hanoi International Fellowship was a great church and I was happy there. But if I was offered a pastorate at a small church with a home and living income anywhere in the world – I would say yes.

At a board meeting, the members discussed whether I should be allowed to preach more regularly at Hanoi International Fellowship. The board eventually decided I would preach at least every month at the West Lake service and after summer, I would become the pastor of our All Nations campus in Hanoi's tourist quarter. The commission that God had given me was coming to fruition. I would be the principal of a Christian school and pastor a church where I could preach weekly in a city that I loved. Only one thing remained a point of concern. That was Holly's passport.

Three months after her birth, I had applied for her British passport, which was an expensive process and included sending numerous notarized documents to England. Trying to get a British passport is a bit like trying to get a Scotsman to support the English football team in the World Cup! They even asked for prenatal proof that Holly existed. (That meant photos of her in the womb!) Months rolled by, I got to know the wonderfully helpful girls at the Hanoi Visa Agency very well. But whenever I phoned England I was told, "Yours is a difficult case. A Chinese mother, a British father and a daughter born in Vietnam. We need to conduct rigorous security checks." I guess it did sound unusual. We prayed hard as we reached three months, four months, six months, with still no news.

One day I was in a class at Singapore International School Vạn Phúc when I received an email. The sender was the "UK Passport Authority". I froze as I opened it, and then dropped to my knees. It read, "We have pleasure in informing you that the passport for Holly Mackenzie is available for collection at the Hanoi agency office, please make arrangements to visit and collect." I sunk to my knees and worshipped Jesus! My grade two kids wondered what Mr Charlie was doing on his knees with his eyes closed! The teacher (Julia) who was a Christian at my church explained, "Mr Charlie is happy."

CHAPTER 38

Gateway International Bilingual School opened its freshly built, dazzling state-of-the-art campus in October 2016. On the same date, their incredible new principal began the role of Christian leader of this new international school where the Christian expat teachers were all actively involved in an evangelical church. In typical Vietnamese style, all teachers had to carry desks, chairs and office equipment from the old rented building to our new one, two hundred yards down the street. Most of our expat teachers were new to teaching; the others had been with us less than a year. Stress levels were high as our exhausted team moved to a new campus with thrice as many students and parents.

But we plodded through it, and the stress lasted another three months before the team of staff began to jell again and I got back to doing what I do best… communicating.

I began a "parents coffee morning" once a week where the rules were "no rules". Parents could come and drink coffee, eat cake and be totally honest with me about anything! These proved (and still do) invaluable. Problems were dealt with before they got out of hand and parents went away with a renewed sense of empowerment and involvement in their children's education. I also continued my habit of greeting parents and children at the school gate at 7-8am and bidding them farewell at the end of the day. Some parents often commented that I was the only principal they knew who did this.

Another regular event was the "Principal's Pals' Lunch". Once a month, students from each class who were identified as being top role models, were rewarded by a free lunch with me. This group of role models would go to KFC, Burger King, Domino's Pizza or another outlet. We all got to ride in the minibus and have fun in a restaurant. It was a great incentive and of course, parents loved this too.

Gateway International School Hanoi

The newly implemented structure and governance of the school was proving to be highly successful. Having the right people in the right positions was critical to this success. Chicago born and educated Jen Cepko shone brightly as Primary School Team Leader and the addition of local girl and former VTV organizational expert Minh as Administration Director added to the structural soundness. The weekly Principal's Advisory Board meetings helped us to take proactive steps towards improving the school and troubleshoot any emerging issues. Our growing school was gaining in reputation. Within one year we had grown from 50 to 250 students and had become one of the top 10 schools in Hanoi.

Meanwhile, at All Nations, things were taking off in a similar way. The church started its life with eight or nine believers from Hanoi International Fellowship West Lake, meeting on a Sunday afternoon for a prayer reading and a short message in the atmospheric 100-year-old downtown church building. The numbers grew to about 20 and stayed that way for months. And then for some inexplicable reason, the size multiplied overnight. Many attendees were overseas holidaymakers, but many were locals too. Expats, Vietnamese professionals, students, and teachers began to walk through its gates. People became believers in the services or directly after the message. The church grew to around 80 and now even in a "quiet week", it is rare to see us drop below 50.

Young adults began to flock to us. All Nations had become a gospel preaching church right there in the heart of Hanoi's bustling tourist area, and it seemed that God was pleased indeed!

Preaching at All Nations English service Hanoi

In October 2016, it came time for my annual post cancer tests in Shanghai. Things had again taken a turn for the worse. I was suffering from agonizing abdominal pains, and the French hospital in Hanoi prescribed morphine to dull the edge. I flew to Shanghai and booked into a small, gloomy tourist class hotel about six miles from the cancer hospital. I resumed the daily commute of three subway trains to and from Fudan cancer hospital. The first big test was the colonoscopy, where the anesthetist administered a general anesthetic. (Again, I played the game where I tried to stay awake as long as I could before succumbing. Doctors often panicked when it got to the nine-second mark and was still smiling at them.) I was informed the result of the procedure seemed fairly normal.

Blood tests, CT scans and an X-ray followed. I'd gotten used to the annual routine, but the week still dragged by. I missed Jasmine and Holly and occupied my time in the hotel by worrying over my results and nursing the pain in my stomach. On the last day, I decided to dress up in my suit and tie to receive my results and then go and enjoy my last day in Shanghai dressed as a tourist!

I arrived upbeat at Dr Peng's office and he invited me to sit. "Colonoscopy normal, CT normal, X-ray fine... but this not fine," he said, pointing to the screen. He explained that my level of cancer tumor markers was higher than normal, indicating a possible recurrence of cancer. I sat stunned, before firing questions at him. "How long do I have?" "Is it operable?" "Will it spread?" I sobbed and mumbled, "But I have a little girl..."

Dr Peng waited until my sobs subsided. "Look, it may not be cancer, but it is likely that it is. Go home and wait a few months and then get tested again. If it is still high, then you need to come back. If it *is* cancer, you will have about 18 months to live, maximum." I continued to weep. "Ok," he eventually said. "There is a scan called a PET scan, if I can fit you in today, it will show up any cancer in your body. This means we could begin treatment now." He wrote up a test appointment slip and passed it to me. "Here. Go register downstairs and then come see me again." Dr Peng booked me in for a PET scan at 4pm.

Shaken, but relieved that my follow up test was being fast tracked, I went downstairs and queued to pay for my scan. I waited for 50 minutes in one of six long queues. My thoughts dwelled on Jasmine and Holly, and drifted to the new opportunities I'd been blessed with these past months. I felt waves of anguish, followed by numbness. While I stood in the queue, I was faintly aware of the annoyed women ahead of me who stared at me as if I was a pervert and shouted at me in Chinese. I was so upset, I just gazed at the floor and said nothing. Eventually, I paid my fee and registered.

Back in Dr Peng's office, he looked at the booking screen in front of him.

"Charlie, why have you just registered for breast cancer treatment?"

I returned at 4pm and waited three hours for the PET scan. Towards the end of the wait, I was instructed to lie down on an operating table. Wearing a thick protective suit, a nurse injected me with radioactive dye from behind a screen. A technician carried out the

20 minute procedure, and then I got dressed and left for my hotel. I was just leaving the second subway exit when I heard the sound of a text message. It was Dr Peng. I took a deep breath and read it, trembling. "No sign of malignancy, no tumor." And that was it! I walked into a McDonalds and sat and wept. The young girl eating the chicken nugget meal next to me stared. I mouthed, "Got a cold." She smiled back as if to say, "No way, your girlfriend has dumped you, mate, it's obvious!" I called Jasmine and told her the news. "Come home, Charlie," was all she could say through her tears.

The pain worsened upon my return to Hanoi. On a scale of one being low and ten being excruciating, I was on about eight most evenings. Only a sleeping tablet brought temporary relief. During the day I went through one to three doses of pain relievers. Two months later, I caught the flu. The abdominal pain stopped. There were still a few flutters, a few sharp moments, but it stopped. I texted Dr Peng and told him. "Ok, no rush to get re-test," he said. "No pain is good sign." I felt ever so slightly encouraged. I would rather have the flu than cancer any time!

After I returned to Hanoi, one of the young men attending All Nations told me that his dad was a CEO at VTV, Vietnam's equivalent of the BBC. I told him I used to have a radio show in Scotland and would be interested in doing some work at VTV. Two weeks later, I had tea with the producer and director of VTV4 International and was invited to train the station's news presenters, reporters, producers and film editors in communication and presentation techniques. The team at VTV4 was a great bunch and the training was fun and productive. (I even got to meet His Royal Highness Prince William when he visited the VTV studios and joked with him about football). This led to a gig narrating a fortnightly culture documentary and hosting a TV series for expats!

CHAPTER 39

Some of the greatest highpoints of my life have been at church. As an uncertain new believer and convicted felon, I was embraced by the warm acceptance of the fellowship at Bridge Street. At City Community Church, I was nurtured by a fellowship that took delight in ministering to the weary and broken-hearted and loving others, just like Jesus did.

At the same time, some of my most crushing disappointments have been at church ranging from my burn out in Hartlepool to the stealthy "vote of no confidence" at Barnsley.

Around mid 2016, Pastor John and I were chatting in his office at Mỹ Đình when he asked me to sit in his chair. "Get used to it, how does it feel?" he asked. And then he added, a little mysteriously, "You could be sitting in it for real this time next year."

I leaned forward to Pastor John and asked slowly, "You thinking of leaving, brother?" John looked serious and lowered his voice. "Well you know I have parents back in the States who aren't getting any younger," he said, before going on to discuss my role at All Nations.

I discovered a few months later that he was leaving the following June. When this became official, I put in my application to be the Mỹ Đình pastor of more than 200 believers. I thought that my hard work at All Nations, in which I helped plant a church and saw it grow from practically zero to a healthy fellowship of regular worshippers was good preparation.

I was wrong.

The week that I lodged my application, I had a meeting with Pastor John. He had changed his tune. "You will *never* be pastor of Mỹ Đình, Charlie, I feel that you are better suited to All Nations." I felt condemned for my exuberance and excessive happiness. Gutted, I promptly withdrew my application. It took weeks for my relationship with Pastor John to fully heal.

I felt that I would have been an enthusiastic pastor at Mỹ Đình and that I would have given it everything I had. At first, I felt robbed and deflated. And then, the waves of grief over what might have been, swept in. Were it not for the grace of God and my strong sense of calling to be a pastor, I would have been tempted to walk back into living for myself again.

For a time, some of the drive and fire inside me sadly died. Yet still I preached (though not as regularly any more) at All Nations and still God blessed His work there.

Around this period, a Baptist church in East Sussex called me to be their pastor, Skyping me several times. Jasmine would likely become a nursery teacher at the church. We would live in a four bedroom semi-detached house with a huge garden for Holly to play in. The village was small and compact and yet only 20 minutes from all the main shops in Brighton. I would be appreciated, loved and wanted.

But, it was just too convenient. It was a massive temptation and beautiful distraction, but God wanted me in South-East Asia, and despite the hurt and disappointment, this was where I was meant to be. I reluctantly emailed the church and told them my reasons for not coming and pledged to stay in touch regardless. They were and still are one of the most gracious body of Christian leaders that I have ever had the pleasure of meeting.

I decided life was too short to sit around feeling disappointed. I threw myself back into the work at All Nations, preaching my heart out on Sundays and following up newcomers. Famous recording artists such as gospel singer Dominique Jones, and singer-songwriters Greg and Glenda Bostock from the States came and ministered to us. People from all parts of the globe wanted to visit Hanoi to preach, worship and sing at All Nations. It seemed God was set on encouraging me, and I would feel my heart soar at times when I thought about the fellowship at All Nations.

The congregation at All Nations was a lively, raw cross-section of class, culture and color. We had a young woman from Nepal, families from India, Filipinos, Scandinavians, Africans and Vietnamese. There was a pilot, doctor, several missionaries, teachers, housewives, TV executives and personalities and business people. It was like a little heaven on earth.

Actually, when I thought about it, many members at All Nations had their "quirks" like the hospitable, highly inclusive congregations at Beijing's City Community Church and Bridge Street Pentecostal. And not just the new believers who were diamonds in the rough, but also some of the larger-than-life mature believers. Given we were such a diverse community, our closeness was special indeed. Like a jigsaw puzzle, every member had a unique role to play and belonged there. Yet I knew that many members counted themselves as "outsiders" in their schools, workplaces, social groups and families.

Maybe this was why All Nations was so special to me. I'd felt like an outsider my whole life. The Bible stories that resonated most deeply with me were about outsiders and underdogs. For example, the story of the Prodigal Son who asked for his inheritance early, squandered it, and contrite and impoverished, planned to beg his father for a menial job as a mere hired hand. Instead his father welcomed him back with open arms giving him all the rights and status as a treasured son. I loved the story of the faith-filled girl who was crippled and ostracized because of a bleeding issue and yet pushed her way through the crowd and touched Jesus' cloak, and was healed. There were the stories of lepers, who Jesus healed, or the parable of a king inviting beggars to his banquet.

The Easter service was a highpoint for All Nations in 2017. Nancy, a multi-talented musician and music teacher, contacted me weeks earlier and asked, "Can I bring a choir to perform on Easter morning at All Nations?" Nancy led a choir called Nova Voce (Italian for "new voice") and was the wife of my school director. I let out an enthusiastic, "Yes!" On Easter Sunday, we had the second largest gathering we had ever had at All Nations (with Christmas being the fullest to date). Accompanied by their musicians playing cello and French horn, Nova Voce performed a moving and professional arrangement of Easter and worship songs with passion and fervor! Three Finnish believers approached me afterwards and said it was the best sermon they had ever heard and the most spiritually uplifting music! I nodded, groggy from a cold. What a day!

The wonderful day was capped off when our friends Brian and Hazel treated Jasmine, Holly and I to a delicious evening meal. Afterwards, I biked off to watch a televised match of Chelsea at the supporters' club on Hoàn Kiếm. Despite seeing my favorite football team lose, I felt invigorated and renewed.

The next day I was attacked spiritually. As I said to my friends, "Something amazing must have happened at church on Sunday as I am feeling the battle now."

I woke up with a cloud of gloom over me, which hung low like a thundercloud all day. At around midday, I was about to ride my motorbike to the bank and reversed hard into my new car. I bashed in the front right side door. I struggled through my school day and cheered myself up with the thought that I would be booking hotels for our trip to Europe in two months! Although I had used this particular website on numerous occasions, I made a non-refundable booking on a hotel in Greece on the wrong date!

Jasmine went bonkers. "You idiot. Do you know how long it takes us to save money?" The dark cloud burst over me and I wept inside. Jasmine made frantic phone calls trying to change the date but it would be another two days until she succeeded. Before I went to bed that night, I cut my right forefinger peeling an apple and infected it. Even though my right hand felt stabs of pain for a week after, the cloud of depression lifted the next day.

The apostle Paul wrote that just as the human body is made up of many parts, so it is with the body of believers. If one part of the body suffers, the whole body suffers, and if one part rejoices, so does the rest of the body. God has placed apostles, prophets and teachers and people with all sorts of spiritual gifts in the church, and we need each other. In Paul's letter to the Corinthian church, he wrote:

"Now if the foot should say, 'Because I am not a hand, I do not belong to the body,' it would not for that reason stop being part of the body. And if the ear should say, 'Because I am not an eye, I do not belong to the body,' it would not for that reason stop being part of the body. If the whole body were an eye, where would the sense of hearing be? If the whole body were an ear, where would the sense of smell be?" As believers, we *all* belong to Christ and His church.

On Sunday, I sat having lunch listening to Pastor Jacob sharing funny stories in his endearing Dutch accent. It was good to be there, enjoying the food and the fellowship. Knowing there is indeed strength in numbers and realizing that no matter how different we all are as individual believers, we need each other as part of the body of Christ.

CHAPTER 40

The text message hit me between the eyes as I lazily played with my phone on a Monday evening at home. "Hi, I am Ms Thu Ha from VTV4. I am the producer of historical programs and have been researching for many months to make a movie about Indochina. I have noticed that you look like the Governor-General of Indochina Albert Sarraut. Would you consider playing him in our film?"

I was surprised and thrilled at the prospect. Thu Ha began to explain there that I would have dialogue in two scenes and no lines in the third. "Of course the whole script for you will be in French," she added. "And you will be paid for it." I thanked Thu Ha and turned to Jasmine. " I am going to be paid to act in a movie," I said, "And it's going to be on TV in a month!" Jasmine looked over from the sofa and smiled indulgently. "Sure you are, Charlie," she said. "So really, who was on the phone just now?"

I met with Thu Ha and her team for lunch the following week and found her to be one of the sweetest, most affable producers that I had ever met. A young looking 30 something, she had an infectious smile and a manner that endeared everyone to her including her team. The following two meetings were at the studio reading through the script, practising French and being taught how to say French words with a convincing accent. The last time I had French lessons was at Langlees Primary School in Falkirk when I was 10!

I told the teachers at my school that I was going to be in a telemovie, but no one seemed to believe me. But why would I lie?

I practised the script at home in my bedroom out loud for days and hours on end (much to the amusement of Holly who often came in and stared at me and then decided to dance and clap her hands to the "funny words" I was saying). In a matter of no time at all, it was time to shoot the film. Thu Ha had kindly invited Jasmine and Holly to come as guests and watch me being filmed. Both VIPs on set, the girls got dressed up like movie stars themselves. "You will be spotted by a famous Hollywood agent," I joked as we arrived at

Studio 15 on a hot sticky Saturday afternoon. Studio 15 was very much as I imagined it to be – huge, dark and full of equipment. Camera operators and stagehands waited around as grips moved the lights into place and the props master set props into place. I was sent off to "makeup" with the rest of the cast and Jas and Holly sat laughing as I was given "the treatment" by the makeup artist (even some subtle lipstick was applied!)

In scene one, I sat opposite the main character (a Vietnamese spy) and was speaking to him in French, acting amenable at first before taking on a sterner tone. Thu Ha stood behind the chair near the camera with script cards in case I forgot my lines. It went surprisingly well and I was buzzing with the thrill of being on a film set and acting a role.

Thu Ha seemed pleased as the scene concluded and we moved aside for the next shoot. Jasmine and Holly decided to go to the nearby shopping mall as I waited an hour or two for my next two scenes. I drank in the atmosphere and marveled at the technology and expertise of those around me. As a child I always wished that one day I could be on TV and here I was 50 years later. Wasn't God good!

I acted my second scene (a non-speaking one) with gusto and feeling. And then it was time for my last scene. I was dreaded this one the most. I hadn't memorized all the text and there were some pretty lengthy French words in it. It was a serious scene with high emotional stakes. After getting into position and doing a quick read through, the director shouted, "Action," and we were off. Thu Ha stood at the back with the script cards but two things happened that threw us into hysterics. Firstly, I was given a pair of round, thick, 1920s glasses to wear and I could hardly see a thing out of them. The second was that Thu Ha kept changing the cards too quickly so that I couldn't keep up!

Afterwards, Thu Ha gathered the fallen cards up from the floor and we began again. But she had gathered them in the wrong order and halfway through my *serious* speech, I realized this. Again we

288

all found this hilarious. I realized although acting in a movie is not nearly as glamorous as one would think, there are still moments of pure unadulterated fun!

After about 11 takes, the director yelled, "It's a wrap." Thu Ha told me that I was free to go home. Jasmine, Holly and I went to KFC. We sat there, watching Holly tuck into rice and chicken and smiled at each other. I turned to the young girl serving us and said "I have just been acting in a movie you know, and it was all in French." She looked at me, shrugged and pointed to the large menu above the counter behind her and said in broken English, "French fries not ready yet."

CHAPTER 41

Sprinting like a victor one moment and limping the next, I made my way through May 2017 in a haze of agony and occasional euphoria. My crippling abdominal pains had returned and the crushing spasms seemed to peak at the most inopportune times. As I flicked through my over-full calendar, I was reminded that there was no slowing down this month.

Maybe it was the pain talking, but I found myself reflecting upon all the searching I'd done until I'd finally found God. I remembered cobbling spare bricks together and climbing into a washroom as a young boy, just so I could listen to the sermons at the Dawson Mission Hall and experience the inexplicable warmth of that community. As a young man, my wanderlust, the drinking, clubbing and living the high life, were all symptoms of a deep-rooted need for purpose and significance that only God could give.

I needed to be closer to God and His Word and this required some changes. I spent the next week fasting and praying whenever I was able. My abdominal pain abated a little and both Jasmine and I took a little encouragement from this. I found that skipping breakfast and lunch not only reduced my weight and pain, it made me more grateful for the food that I ate at night. And my mind became sharper too.

When the strong pain I'd wrestled with two months earlier returned, my heart dropped and the pangs of anxiety set in. By now, I needed Oxycodone every day to cope with the intense pain. I was about to have an in-depth spiritual check up with a Christian pastor from Singapore who had a ministry in deliverance and healing, so I was fervently praying I could be cured. Jasmine asked daily, "How's the pain level? I am worried." I would reply, "I am ok, maybe my pain level is about two out of three," knowing it was at least double that.

Pastor Bernard from Singapore came for his annual visit to run marriage seminars and conduct deliverance ministry. He was a kind-hearted, holy and perceptive man of God with decades of ministry experience. I was invited (as I had been the year before) to meet with him for prayer on 6 May along with another Bernard, his associate and my friend.

For four hours we dug deep into my past and cut "soul ties". Pastor Bernard explained how ancestral involvement in the occult, alcoholism, abuse, adultery and other sins often resulted in "soul ties" which could give the devil a foothold in my own life and even that of my children and their children.

We talked and prayed and renounced and surrendered and wept and committed our lives. I opened up to a God who delivers, purifies, and heals. Pastor Bernard concluded by praying against cancer in my body. I felt uneasy talking about cancer as if it was actually there, but was confident that God had heard these prayerful men and would certainly answer. I rode home tired but feeling cleansed and hopeful.

In the midst of all of this, we were moving house. Our new home was a beautiful spacious apartment in a brand new complex with a swimming pool and play park. It took us three days of car trips and furniture removals to completely shift. When we were able to unpack on 12 May, I sat down to admire the balcony, so very grateful for all of my blessings.

The more appreciative I felt about the good things God had given me, the more I remembered the stark moments of desolation in my past. Since Pastor Bernard had prayed for me, I'd felt a lightness; the slow closing of many painful chapters. At the same time, I found myself wondering about the children and young adults in my midst. How many of them had been bullied and beaten like me? How many had felt the hopelessness I'd felt that night at Bridewell? How many had made mistakes with drugs, bad relationships and crime and were paying the price? I felt a renewed determination to play my part in turning around the situations of those who were struggling or had hit rock bottom.

I felt deeply encouraged whenever I unexpectedly received reports of ministry bearing fruit. I cherished an email I received from Candy McCarron, who was saved during my time at Gorgie Mission's Monday Club. Candy wrote of all the people that her family had pointed to Christ over the years. There were hundreds of them! She wrote, "We are all involved in Christian ministry, Charlie, and it's all down to you. You have hundreds of spiritual children down here that you have never met and I bet, never even knew about!"

But no matter how many reports I received about people like Candy McCarron, who were going from strength to strength, I could not help but be gutted by the losses. I had been in Edinburgh on business, when I ran into a former member of the Niddrie youth group and found out some tragic news. Now in her 20s, Diane, a pretty, dark-haired woman raced up to hug me, and asked why I was *there*. "You haven't heard, then," she said, lowering her gaze. "… Izzy's dead, Pastor Charlie, she took her own life after a bout of depression. The funeral is taking place in less than an hour. I thought you would be taking it." I struggled to comprehend. Isobel Peacock? Suicide? My tears flowed hot and freely down my flushed red cheeks, and I struggled for words that would not come. Finally, I wandered into a side office that was used for storing packs of copy paper and spare desks, closed the door behind me and wept. Poor, beautiful Izzy. "What a waste," I said to God. "Lord, thank you for saving her, but why did you let her go like this?" I never expected an audible answer. But what did come was the reassuring thought deep inside that said, "She's struggled enough with this dark pit of depression and her Savior has taken her home."

As my spiritual life began to quicken, so did my awareness. I spoke with four different young adults in a week and discovered that all were crying out for deliverance from past connections to drugs, the occult, abuse and promiscuity. I emailed Bernard to see if he could fly back from Singapore and meet with us. I had a feeling that this was just the tip of the iceberg and that once I looked deeper into this, there would be many dear, struggling, hurting lambs all needing Jesus, the Good Shepherd to pull out hurting spiritual thorns from them. With my increased sense of awareness, came spiritual attack.

I awoke on 13 May feeling achy, feverish and with an inflamed stomach. My leg muscles hurt and my voice was hoarse. I got dressed and rode my motorbike to speak at a school seminar aimed at recruiting students for our newly opened middle school. I smiled and tried to stay focused for three hours but as soon as it was over I dashed home. Jasmine was with her Chinese friend, Ming Li. "I told Ming Li we would take her for lunch and then shopping in our car," Jasmine said cheerily. I took a deep breath and agreed.

In the restaurant, the heat, the noise and the pain crashed into me like tidal waves. I fought the urge to faint. Looking for a way to keep my mind and body distracted, I stood up and walked about with Holly until Jasmine and Ming Li finished their meal.

In the supermarket, I went off on my own, ready to go find a seat at short notice. Within another hour we were back home in our new apartment. I took another painkiller and fell asleep. The next morning I awoke at noon to prepare for preaching a sermon in church. The pain was spiralling and I felt weaker than ever. In fact, immediately prior to preaching, I felt very frail indeed. And then I remembered how God loves to use the "weak things of this world". I began to look forward to preaching, frail physique and all! And preach, I certainly did! With power, anointing, fluency and authority!

There were several non-believers who had been brought to church by their friends. There were also young and middle-aged adults who I personally knew were struggling with past sins that were affecting their present. Some had ties to witchcraft and were receiving deliverance counselling, some were struggling with drugs and abuse from their parents.

I passionately preached the cross of Jesus. As soon as I stepped down, the abdominal pain returned and my exhausted muscles burned and ached. When I returned home I fell straight asleep. But God had done something powerful, of that I was aware.

I woke up around 8:30pm and wandered into my office. I looked at all of my Chelsea FC paraphernalia including two baseball caps, my jacket and scarf. We had just won the English premiership after a great season and I was proud that everyone on Facebook knew that I was a Chelsea fan. A small loving voice then spoke. "Does everyone on Facebook know that you love me, Charlie?" I knew this voice. And knew that my support of Chelsea FC was almost becoming a subtle form of idolatry. "Tone it down," the still, quiet voice said. And so I did, giving away the Chelsea calendar on my school desk, the Chelsea coffee mug I used at school and playing down the fact that I was a Chelsea FC fan. I took the drastic step of changing my profile photo on Facebook. It's so easy for us to wander subtly from God's presence and start putting other things in place of Him.

If May was a month where my pain was near its peak, it was also a time when I was continually reminded of my blessings and the unexpected opportunities I'd been given. A few days after we moved into our new apartment, Jasmine and I sat back and watched the film documentary featuring my debut performance. A puzzled Holly looked on. Only a few minutes into the film, there I was. "Baba," Holly exclaimed, pointing to the TV. It was great fun to watch and something we will keep forever – me, a pastor, acting the role of the Governor-General of Indochina on national TV. The film lasted about 50 minutes and we all enjoyed the fun. My French was, well - passable. But it didn't matter, I had done something I had always dreamt of - "acting in a movie".

The next day we were celebrating our fifth anniversary and I'd hatched a cunning plan.

We had been to the luxurious Crown Plaza Hotel a few months earlier with Dr Brian and his wife Hazel, and loved the food and the ambience. I'd phoned and booked the meal and a nice sized room a few days before. Early in the morning while Jasmine slept, I packed some of Jasmine's clothes, along with Holly's clothes and diapers, and then left for work.

At lunchtime, I rode to the hotel and after signing in, put all the clothes in the room along with the presentation box of Korean

295

cosmetics on the pillow and returned to work. I had told Jasmine that morning to "Put on something nice, we may go somewhere tonight."

After work, I walked into our apartment to see my stunning bride of five years in a sleek black off-the-shoulder dress that could have graced Buckingham Palace! I beamed with pride as we drove to the restaurant. Holly was her usual cute self and hugged her mum all the way there. Jasmine and I relished the top-class meal - cheese oysters in their shells, and lots of fresh meats, vegetables and sweets.

About an hour into our meal, I said casually, "I wonder what the breakfasts are like here?"

"I suppose they are amazing," she replied, cutting into a slice of honey roast ham.

"You can tell me how food it is after tomorrow," I said smiling at her.

The whole night was wonderful and even the gift on her pillow was well accepted (even if it *was* all in Korean and no English translation to tell us if a bottle was face lotion or foot cream!) We ate a huge breakfast the next day and drove home smiling from ear to ear. It wasn't until early evening that my pain kicked in again with a vengeance. But what a beautiful anniversary it had been.

CHAPTER 42

The following day marked the first baptism at All Nations. We arrived at 1pm on 21 May knowing that many believers had been praying. As I entered the church the atmosphere enveloped me like a glorious cloud… God was there!

The seven candidates were all robed in traditional black gowns and I wore a burgundy gown to add to the visual occasion. The four piece band (all of whom had joined All Nations in the last few months) played and sung with enthusiasm and overflowing joy. All Nations, our little church in the tourist quarter of old Hanoi that had begun just over a year ago with a dozen of us from Hanoi International Fellowship West Lake and a few faithful members of Hanoi Evangelical Church, was now packed with more than 110 people in the century old church building. We sung the old gospel song, *Oh, Happy Day* several times as the Holy Spirit moved among us, lifting the volume and the praise.

The candidates were all trophies of grace. Ming Li was a lovely dear Chinese teacher who Jasmine had helped lead to Christ a year earlier. Lucelia was a once professional dancer with two small children (who we dedicated that day). Kim Chi and My were two graceful and attractive Vietnamese ladies who had only recently been saved. Chi, who was a busy professional, a Vietnamese mum and member of Hanoi Evangelical Church, Sylvester, who had joined us from Hanoi International Fellowship Mỹ Đình, and Jack from one of our local Chinese house churches, made up the total of seven.

When each of them arose from the waters of baptism, the band struck up the song, "Oh Happy Day… when Jesus washed my sins away… *I will never be the same.*" This was the theme for the day. The Billy Graham team were with us and testified to God's greatness in Vietnam and spoke about the upcoming national crusade. Then Senior Pastor Jacob gave his vision for the future of All Nations, Hanoi International Fellowship and indeed Hanoi.

We floated home in the car… it had been a good day, a great day and a glorious day all rolled into one. God had indeed answered the prayers of many. My pain resumed later that night, but I refused to let it steal my joy.

The next day, I looked at my "to do" list with all the many items to cross off in a short space of time. The next on the list was to be Holly's birthday, and Jasmine and I began to excitedly plan something special for her. I was in a lighthearted mood at Tuesday's Hanoi International Fellowship staff meeting when my phone rang. It was my former employer, Singapore International School. Brad Robinson, a former teacher of mine at that school, was fighting for his life. He was in a coma in ICU after having multiple surgeries to remove gangrene and infections from his lungs, legs and abdomen. Could I please come urgently?

Excusing myself from the staff meeting, I rode out to the hospital to be greeted by Brad's mother and sister. After explaining who I was, I was allowed to put on the surgical gown and shoe coverings and see Brad. What I saw was not Brad. I saw a body covered with tubes and drains and monitors and censors and more tubes. Brad's face and arms and legs were so swollen, it did not look like him. With no assurance that Brad was saved, I prayed over him. Next, I prayed with his Christian family. Heavy hearted, I rode home.

I went to see Brad every second day at 4pm. I prayed with him and asked God to save him and redeem him. Sometimes I shouted at him, "Get better Brad, you have a life God wants to bless you with!" but often I just stood by him, silently praying and not always knowing what to pray. I think just being there regularly gave his mum and sister encouragement.

Two weeks after Brad was admitted, and two days after he was taken out of the medical coma, I arrived to see Margaret his mum sitting on a chair in the waiting room. "Charlie, I gotta tell you something," she said seriously.

"Go on," I said, fearing the worst.

"Well, I went into see Brad today and he was awake and I said to him, 'Well, Brad, what's new?' Brad thought about it and told me, 'I'll tell you what's new. Jesus is my Saviour and He is in charge of my life now and God has saved me and will heal me."

A huge smile spread onto my lips. We praised God together, then, as Brad began to get stronger, he asked his mother to pray with him every day. As I write this, Brad is now back in the United States at home with his family and contemplating his next overseas post as a teacher. He's almost fully recovered and is "itching" to do what he loves most… teach!

Straight after Brad went back to America to recuperate, I had to tie up loose ends and pack for our family's holiday to Greece, Switzerland, Austria then France. It was a revitalizing, whirlwind trip filled with gorgeous scenery and magnificent food. Upon my return, I oversaw two summer camps at school and ran three days of training for filmmakers and presenters at VTV.

Holiday of a lifetime, with jasmine and Holly in Greece.

When the school semester started, I was faced with a situation where I had to sternly caution a staff member at the school over a particular matter. Her name was My (pronounced "Me"). I'd gotten to know My about two years ago, after Jasmine posted a sales ad for Holly's outgrown baby clothes in the local expat classified site. The next evening, a young couple came to our apartment to buy the clothes. The young woman, My, told me in near-perfect English that she was a teacher but had not worked since giving birth and now she couldn't find a job. Two weeks later, My came in for an interview as an assistant teacher. She cruised confidently through the interview and was offered a job.

My was a conscientious teacher and friendly with everyone but on this particular day, I needed to speak to her as a principal.

Halfway through the conversation, My said, "I am jealous of you."

This caught me completely off guard. "Jealous, who?" I said, slightly confused.

"You Christians," My said. "I am jealous of the peace you all have. I go through each day always worried about one thing or another, but you people don't seem to worry at all, I wish I had this peace."

On my lap, I had a notebook with all the things I still had to discuss with her, but I closed it. The Holy Spirit whispered into my heart, "Drop everything, Charlie, she is ready to know Jesus." I sent a prayer silently to God and then explained to My, "You can have this peace too, right now, here in this room."

My looked directly at me. "Yes, I am trying and I know once I learn more about Jesus and read the Bible more, that maybe one day I will be good enough to have what you have."

"Good enough?" I thought. "When are *any* of us ever *good enough?"*

I spoke as gently as possible. "All you need to know right now, My, is that all of us have sinned and are unworthy of God's love, yet *He loves us anyway*. In fact He loves us so much that He sent His only son Jesus to die on the cross and pay the price for our sin. All we need to do is come to Him and admit the fact that we are sinners and turn away from trying to do things our way and do things God's way instead. If we will humbly hand over our lives to Him and

300

accept Jesus as our Savior and Lord of our life, He will make you a child of God right this very minute. The growing comes later. KNOWING comes first."

I paused for a moment to catch my breath, and then asked her quietly, "My, do you want to know Jesus and own Him as your own?"

"If it's possible, then yes, I want to know him," My said.

And there, in a school office on an ordinary weekday, I led My to Jesus. She prayed "The Sinners' Prayer", much like the one I had said with Paddy Flynn 32 years earlier in Leeds. She closed her eyes as a sinner and opened them as a child of God. The peace she was jealous of only a few moments before was now flooding every part of her being. I walked with My to the staff room on the fifth floor and called all the Christian teachers to join me. "Meet your new sister," I said joyfully, "My has just given her life to Jesus."

Hugs and praises followed as we all gave thanks to God and welcomed My into her new family. I was all too familiar with the expression of jubilant awe and disbelief in her eyes. I had seen it in my own eyes decades ago, in Bridewell, and in the expressions of many since then. It was like the face of a prisoner rescued from jail, given royal robes in exchange for their dirty prison uniform, and being invited to forever live in the king's palace. But it's much much more than that. It's as though that desperate, wretched outsider has also been adopted into the king's family and been given a share of the titles and royal inheritance. As believers, that's our true status, but it seems too good to be true.

My began attending church and started bringing her husband too. Her face now shines with peace. But I would never forget the moment of her salvation. That stunned disbelief. Like a beggar suddenly invited to a king's banquet and being given a place of high honor.

Epilogue

We all come to God from different paths and from a million different backgrounds. All I know is I am richer for the path God has brought me through. I love being married to Jasmine, my beautiful young wife and being a dad to Holly.

Being a pastor is the most rewarding calling ever. It's not God's choice for everyone, but to those He calls to this noble profession... the very gates of Hell shall not prevail against them nor the churches they will lead!

I hope this book has given you hope, made you smile but most of all, revealed what an amazing person God is. If reading this story has moved you to find out who He really is, then can I encourage you to seek Him. It really is as simple as A B C.

A   **A**ccept that He died to pay the price of your sin and **A**sk Him to forgive you.

B   **B**elieve on Him with your whole life, **B**egin to follow Him with all your being today.

C   **C**onfess Him to others, let people know that you have **C**laimed him as your own Savior.

Pray this simple prayer with me now…

Dear Lord Jesus, I know that my sin has separated me from you and stopped me from knowing your peace and joy in my life. Thank you that on the cross you paid the price for my sin with your own blood so that I could be forgiven and know a life that is free from bondage and even death. I now by faith receive that forgiveness and cleansing as I turn my back and renounce all sin in my life and follow you with all my being forever. In Jesus name, Amen.

If you prayed that prayer and meant it from your heart, then the Bible, God's Word, says you are saved. You are a believer and a member of God's family. No one and nothing can ever pluck you from God's hand. And even if you slip and fall away, He will find you. Trust me on this, for He found me too.

Charlie Mackenzie
Hanoi. September 2017
Charliemac69@hotmail.co.uk

Charlie with MY the first Vietnamese teacher to become a Christian at Gateway.